Study Textbook Copyright Agreement

Copyright

Disclaimers

While every effort and special care has been taken to ensure that information contained in The IAB's publication is accurate and correct at the time of publication, changes in circumstances after the date of publication may impact on the accuracy of this information. Laws and regulations are complex and are liable to change; readers should check the current positions with the relevant authorities in the country of use. The IAB gives no warranty to the reliability of any information in the documentation.

In order to demonstrate realistic scenarios, fictitious names, business names, email addresses, business addresses and phone numbers etc, have been used in the publication. Any resemblance to any real persons or business is purely coincidence and unintentional.

IAB Level 2 Certificate in Computerised Accounting for Business

By

Barry Curran

IAB Level 2
Certificate in Computerised Accounting for Business (RQF)

Contents

Lesson Number	Lesson Title	Pages
-	**Introduction to the qualification**	**10**
	Section 1	
1	**Financial Services and Payment Methods**	**15**
	- Introduction	17
	- Deposit accounts	17
	- Current accounts	18
	- Personal and business loans	20
	- Mortgages	21
	- Overdrafts	21
	- The customer and bank relationship	23
	- Telephone and internet banking	23
	- Retaining banking documents	25
	- Payment methods	26
	- Cash (notes and coins)	26
	- Cheques	28
	- Words and crossings	29
	- The cheque clearing system	30
	- The 2-4-6 rules	31
	- Dishonoured cheques	32
	- The 'life' of a cheque	32
	- Postdated cheques	32
	- Stopping a cheque	32
	- Receipt of a cheque	33
	- The use of plastic cards	33
	- Debit cards	34
	- Prepayment cards	34
	- Credit cards	35
	- Company credit cards	36
	- Processing card transactions	36
	- The BACS system	38
	- BACS direct credit	38
	- BACS direct debit	39
	- Faster Payments Service	40
	- Standing order	41
	- Payment by CHAPS	41
	- New technology	41

- PayPal 42
- Banking money received 43
- The physical security of money 45
- Lesson 1 practice questions 47

Section 2
2 Business Organisations 57

- Introduction 59
- Sole traders 59
- Partnerships 61
- Limited companies 63
- Not for profit organisations 65
- Lesson 2 practice questions 67

3 Ethics and Business Legislation 69

- Introduction 71
- Ethics 71
- Accounting ethics 72
- Integrity 72
- Objectivity 72
- Professional competence and due care 72
- Confidentiality 73
- Professional behaviour 73
- Membership of the IAB 74
- Data protection 74
- Office health and safety 76
- Risk assessment 76
- The employer's duty of care 77
- Maintaining a safe and healthy workplace 77
- Fire safety 78
- Lighting 78
- Air quality 79
- Adequate workspace 79
- Office machinery 79
- Noise 79
- Manual handling 80
- First aid and workplace injuries 80
- General office safety 80
- Welfare facilities 81
- The use of computers 81
- Employee's health and safety responsibilities 82
- Money laundering 83
- Requirements of the Money Laundering Regulations 84
- Risk assessment 84
- Due diligence measures 86
- Appointing a nominated officer 87
- Reporting suspicious activity 88
- Lesson 3 practice questions 89

4	**Bookkeeping and Accounting**	**95**
	- Introduction	97
	- Bookkeeping and accounting	97
	- Bookkeeping	97
	- Accounting	98
	- The profit and loss account	99
	- The balance sheet	100
	- Lesson 4 practice questions	103
5	**Bookkeeping Systems**	**105**
	- Introduction	107
	- Double entry bookkeeping	107
	- Advantages of using a computerised bookkeeping system	108
	- The need for training	108
	- Safety, security and confidentiality	109
	- Backing up data	111
	- Lesson 5 practice questions	112
6	**Source Documents**	**115**
	- Introduction	117
	- Source documents	117
	- Purchase order	117
	- Delivery note	118
	- Invoices issued	119
	- Credit notes issued	121
	- Invoices received	122
	- Credit notes received	123
	- Cash register (till) receipt	123
	- Other documents	123
	- Petty cash vouchers	123
	- Cheque book counterfoils	126
	- Paying-in slips	126
	- Supplier statement of account	127
	- Remittance advice	128
	- Bank statement	130
	- Payroll records	132
	- Wages	132
	- Salaries	132
	- Gross pay	132
	- Net pay	133
	- Deductions from pay	133
	- Statutory deductions	133
	- Voluntary deductions	133
	- Employer costs	133
	- Internally generated note	133
	- Customer and supplier files	134
	- Catalogues and price lists	134

- Goods received note 135
- Goods returned note 136
- HMRC rules for retaining source data 136
- The journal 136
- Bookkeeping errors 137
- Error of omission 137
- Error of commission 137
- Error of principle 137
- Error of original entry 138
- Lesson 6 practice questions 139

7 Principles of Value Added Tax 143

- Introduction 145
- Value Added Tax (VAT) 145
- The VAT system 145
- Rates of VAT 146
- Standard rate 146
- Reduced rate 146
- Zero rate 147
- Exempt and outside the scope 148
- Registering for VAT 149
- Compulsory registration 149
- Voluntary registration 150
- Deregistration 151
- The use of coding 151
- VAT accounting schemes 152
- Standard scheme 152
- Annual accounting scheme 152
- Cash accounting scheme 153
- Flat rate scheme 153
- VAT schemes for retailers 154
- Making VAT calculations 155
- VAT and discounts 157
- Trade discount 157
- Prompt payment discount 157
- Making a VAT adjustment 159
- The VAT invoice 162
- Less detailed VAT invoices 164
- Modified invoices 164
- Proforma invoices 164
- The VAT date and tax point 165
- The taking of deposits 167
- Accounting for imports and exports 168
- VAT bad debt relief 168
- Keeping VAT records 169
- Control visits 171
- VAT penalties for mistakes and delays 171
- The late registration penalty 172
- The default surcharge 172

	- Misdeclaration penalties	172
	- Changes in VAT rules and rates	173
	- Lesson 7 practice questions	174
8	**Classification and Coding**	**183**
	- Introduction	185
	- Classifying transactions	185
	- Capital income	185
	- Revenue income	185
	- Capital expenditure	185
	- Revenue expenditure	185
	- Coding transactions	187
	- The chart of accounts	188
	- Lesson 8 practice questions	190
9	**Introduction to Double Entry Processing**	**195**
	- Introduction	197
	- Basic accounting concepts	197
	- Business entity concept	198
	- Dual aspect concept	198
	- Money measurement concept	199
	- Historic cost concept	199
	- Accounting terms – assets, capital and liabilities	199
	- Assets	200
	- Fixed assets	200
	- Current assets	201
	- Capital	201
	- Liabilities	201
	- Long-term liabilities	201
	- Current liabilities	201
	- The effect of transactions on the accounting equation	202
	- Double entry bookkeeping	207
	- Real time and batch processing	210
	- Double entry processing	211
	- The use of control accounts	213
	- Double entry processing – worked example	217
	- Lesson 9 practice questions	251

Section 3

10	**Cost and Cost Classification**	**265**
	- Introduction	267
	- Financial accounting	267
	- Management accounting	268
	- Cost and cost classification	269
	- Material costs	269
	- Labour costs	269
	- Expenses	269
	- Cost nature and classification	270
	- Direct costs	270
	- Indirect costs	270
	- Direct materials	271
	- Direct labour	271
	- Indirect labour	271
	- Indirect expenses	271
	- Cost per unit	271
	- Cost classification by function	274
	- Production costs	274
	- Selling and distribution costs	274
	- Administration costs	274
	- Finance costs	274
	- Specialist costs	274
	- Cost centres and profit centres	275
	- Cost centres	275
	- Profit centres	275
	- Lesson 10 practice questions	276
11	**Cost Behaviour Patterns**	**279**
	- Introduction	281
	- Variable costs	281
	- Fixed costs	282
	- Stepped fixed costs	283
	- Semi-variable costs	284
	- Cost per unit using cost behaviour patterns	285
	- Budgets	286
	- Planning	286
	- Communication	286
	- Authorisation	286
	- Monitoring and control	286
	- Motivation	287
	- Lesson 11 practice questions	288

12	**Cost Coding**	**289**
	- Introduction	291
	- Numeric codes	291
	- Alphabetic codes	292
	- Alpha numeric codes	293
	- Coding manual	294
	- Lesson 12 practice questions	296
13	**Valuing stock**	**299**
	- Introduction	301
	- Types of stock	301
	- Raw materials	301
	- Work-in-progress	302
	- Finished goods	302
	- Stock valuation	302
	- Stock valuation methods	303
	- FIFO (first in, first out)	303
	- LIFO (last in, first out)	303
	- AVCO (average cost out – weighted average cost)	303
	- Stock records	303
	- Stock valuation using the FIFO method	304
	- Stock valuation using the LIFO method	305
	- Stock valuation using the AVCO method	306
	- Advantages and disadvantages of the three stock valuation methods	307
	- Lesson 13 practice questions	309
14	**Labour costing**	**313**
	Introduction	315
	Basic rate of pay	315
	Direct labour	316
	Clock cards	316
	Time sheets	316
	Electronic swipe cards	316
	Job cards or job sheets	316
	Calculation of gross pay	317
	Time rate	319
	Piecework rate	321
	Bonus payments	321
	Advantages and disadvantages of methods of calculating gross pay	323
	Lesson 14 practice questions	325

IAB Level 2
Certificate in Computerised Accounting for Business (RQF)

The IAB Level 2 Certificate in Computerised Accounting for Business (RQF) qualification is regulated by Ofqual (Office of Qualifications and Examinations Regulation). Ofqual is the official body responsible for regulating qualifications, examinations and assessments in England. The qualification at Level 2 is made up of the following units:

- Financial services and payment methods (knowledge unit)
- Introduction to computerised accounting for business (knowledge unit)
- Basic principles of costing (knowledge unit)
- Use a computerised accounting system (skills unit)

Learning outcomes and assessment criteria

Each of the units within the IAB Level 2 Certificate in Computerised Accounting for Business (RQF) qualification is made up of a range of learning outcomes and assessment criteria. Learners can access the qualification specifications, which give precise details of the content of each unit, via the IAB website at www.iab.org.uk.

Assessment of competence

Several types of assessment are used by the IAB as the basis of measuring the competence of learners in the learning outcomes and assessment criteria within each of the units that make up a qualification. These assessments may be in the form of Knowledge Tests, Assignments or Examinations. Competence is achieved by learners displaying a high level of accuracy when completing assessments. The units which make up the IAB Level 2 Certificate in Computerised Accounting for Business (RQF) qualification are assessed as follows:

Unit	Method of Assessment
Financial services and payment methods	Knowledge test
Introduction to computerised accounting for business	Knowledge test
Basic principles of costing	Knowledge test
Use a computerised accounting system	Assignment

Learners must successfully complete each of the unit assessments in order to gain the qualification.

Knowledge tests

The three knowledge tests are open book tests which are completed online using the IABOnline platform. The knowledge tests are time constrained and can be completed under controlled or non-controlled conditions, for example in the workplace or at home, as well as in a classroom environment.

Knowledge tests comprise a number of questions in the form of:

- Multiple choice questions – learners are required to select an answer from several options

- Picklist questions – leaners are required to select an answer from several drop-down options

- Gap-fill questions – leaners are required to complete a sentence by selecting appropriate words from several drop-down options

Assignment

The assignment used by the IAB to assess competence in the skills unit is time constrained and can be completed under controlled or non-controlled conditions. The assignment is made up of two parts and must be completed online using the IABOnline platform.

Part one of the assignment requires learners to complete a number of tasks. These include:

- Setting-up a computerised accounting system
- Generating and using source documents to account for credit sales, purchases and returns
- Accounting for cash sales and sundry income
- Processing customer receipts and refunds
- Processing supplier payments and refunds
- Processing payments through the bank current account
- Processing payments from petty cash
- Reconciling the balance on the bank current account
- The preparation and recording of journal entries
- Generating reports

Part two of the assignment is made up of several practical exercises and short answer questions. Some of the tasks that learners are required to complete in Part two are based on the reports they have generated in Part one of the assignment. The short answer questions within part two of the assignment are designed to test the learner's knowledge of the use of computerised accounting systems.

It is recommended that in completing the assignment, you take a hard copy of the data and tasks given in part 1. As you may find it easier to work from a paper-based copy, then you would from onscreen data. Having worked through the part 1 tasks using your accounting software, you then go to part 2 of the assignment and complete the questions in this section of the assignment. One of the tasks in part 2 will be to submit the reports generated in part 1 to the IAB. Instructions as to how this is done are given at the end of the part 2.

The study text

This study text has been prepared for use by learners studying the knowledge and skills units within the IAB Level 2 Certificate in Computerised Accounting for Business (RQF) qualification.

Each of the lessons within the study text is supplemented with practice questions and exercises designed to test the learner's knowledge, understanding and skill.

The model answers to the practice questions are not published in the study text, but learners can access them by going to http://iabonline.org.uk and then using the following login details:
Username: RQFmodelanswers@iabonline.org.uk
Password: Answers01

Learners will then have the choice of selecting the model answers they require by clicking on one of the following buttons:

Model Answers Level 1 Award in Computerised Accounting for Business (RQF)

Model Answers Level 2 Certificate in Computerised Accounting for Business (RQF)

Model Answers Level 3 Certificate in Computerised Accounting for Business (RQF)

Learners must select the button relevant to their level of study and they will be provided with a list of downloadable PDF's containing the model answers for the practice questions and exercises at that level.

The lessons within the study text have been arranged in sections which enables learners to work through the lessons in each of the sections and then at the end of each section complete the assessment relevant to that section as they progress through the course. The following study plan is recommended:

Unit	Study Plan
Financial services and payment methods	Work through Lesson 1 in the study text and complete the Knowledge Test for this unit
Introduction to computerised accounting for business	Work through Lessons 2 to 9 in the study text and complete the Knowledge Test for this unit
Basic principles of costing	Work through Lessons 10 to 14 in the study text and complete the Knowledge Test for this unit

Pilot and live assessments

Pilot and live assessments (Knowledge Tests and Assignment) are to be found on the IABOnline platform for each of the units making up the Level 2 in Computerised Accounting for Business (RQF) qualification.

The pilot assessments are designed to be used as practice assessments. Learners can practice by sitting the unit pilot assessments as many times as they wish before they move on to sit live assessments.

Learners are only able to access 'live' assessments when they have successfully completed the relevant unit pilot assessment.

Section 1
(Lesson 1)

Financial Services and Payment Methods

Method of Assessment – Knowledge Test

Lesson 1

Financial Services and Payment Methods

Financial Services and Payment Methods

Objectives:

By the end of this lesson you should be able to:

- *Understand the role of banks and building societies as financial intermediaries*
- *Understand the relationship between banks, building societies and their customers*
- *Understand the features of the following financial services offered by banks and building societies – deposit and current accounts, term loans, overdrafts, mortgages, telephone and internet banking*
- *Recognise the features of each of the following payment methods and understand when they are appropriate as methods of payment – cash (notes and coins), cheque, plastic card (debit and credit card), BACS, direct debit, standing order, CHAPS, Faster Payments Service, PayPal*
- *Understand how payments received reach the bank account of a business*
- *Understand the purpose and use of banking documents including – cheque book counterfoils, paying-in books/paying-in slips, bank statements and loan agreements*
- *Understand the need for appropriate security measures for the safekeeping of cash on the business premises, and in transit from the business premises to the bank*

Introduction

Bookkeepers are required to carry out a number of routine tasks associated with keeping financial records for a business. These tasks include recording a business's receipts and payments. Therefore, it is essential that bookkeepers have a knowledge and understanding of the main services offered by banks and building societies, and of the methods by which business's and members of the general public make and receive payment.

Banks and building societies are financial intermediaries; in the main the profit they make comes from taking in money from some customers (depositors) and lending it to other customers (borrowers). Their profit is made by charging a higher rate of interest to borrowers than they give to depositors.

Banks are large companies owned by shareholders to which they distribute profits in the form of dividends, whereas building societies are mutual societies owned by members who join the society by opening a share account on which they receive interest rather than a dividend.

Banks provide services to both businesses and members of the general public, whilst building societies deal mainly with members of the general public. Although, in the main, the profit banks and building societies generate is earned from lending, they also make a profit by offering a wide range of other financial services to their customers. For example:

- Deposit and current accounts
- Loans, mortgages and overdraft facilities
- Telephone and internet banking facilities
- Foreign exchange and foreign currency services
- Safety deposit facilities
- A range of payment methods

Deposit accounts

Deposit accounts are a form of 'savings account' where funds can be invested without risk. Banks and building societies pay account holders interest on the balance on their account. Different types of deposit account are offered to attract different types of saver.

Some deposit accounts give savers easy access to their savings i.e. account holders are able to make unlimited withdrawals from the account giving little or no notice, but easy access accounts tend to offer very low rates of interest.

Regular saver accounts provided by banks and building societies offer higher rates of interest to savers than easy access accounts. These types of account have been introduced to attract those who can afford to save regularly e.g. by saving say a fixed amount from their wages or salary. The regular savings account restricts the number of withdrawals that the account holder can make from the account – in some cases funds can only be withdrawn on closure of the account.

The deposit accounts which carry the highest rates of interest are the 'fixed term deposit accounts'. These accounts require savers to tie-up their savings for a minimum period of time, usually twelve months or more.

Current accounts

Current accounts are offered by both banks and building societies. Those who hold a current account are able to use the account to make regular and unlimited deposits and withdrawals. Many current accounts offer account holders internet access and telephone banking facilities.

Many individuals have their wages or salary paid directly into a current account, they are then able to transfer monies from the account to other accounts, say a deposit account, and also make payments from the account using a variety of payment methods.

A bank current account is used by businesses as a form of 'working capital' account. Many businesses pay monies over the counter into their current account on a daily basis, and may also receive monies directly into the account from their customers. Businesses then make regular payments from the current account, for example, to suppliers of goods and services, for business running costs, or wages and salaries to employees.

When a current account is opened the account holder is provided with a paying-in book and cheque book, and are also periodically sent a statement of account by the bank. Debit cards i.e. plastic cards which allow account holders to make payment by automatically transferring monies from their account are also a feature of current accounts. A debit card also allows the account holder to withdraw cash from their current account using an ATM (automated teller machine).

To businesses paying-in books, cheque books and bank statements are important banking documents and sources of information that a business is legally required to keep on file.

A paying-in slip is completed each time an individual or business pays money over the counter of the bank into their current account. Businesses use the counterfoils (stubs) within the paying-in book as the source document for the purpose of recording transfers of monies from the business cash account into the business bank current account.

Paying-in books should be kept under secure conditions when not in use. Many businesses choose to keep the paying-in book in a safe, or the lockable drawer of a filing cabinet or office desk.

The banking procedures of a business should also include tight control over the issue of cheques and the safe keeping of cheque books. Cheques should only be issued with appropriate authorisation; usually a cheque requisition form is completed to support the issue of each cheque.

It is recommended that a business only has one cheque book in use at any one point in time. Cheque books should be stored under secure conditions, say in a lockable drawer or safe. Used cheque books - where all the cheques are issued, should also be stored in a safe location.

The cheque book stubs are often used as the source of recording payments in the books of the business, and are also likely to be used in the bank reconciliation process. As the cheque book stubs are evidence of payments made from the business current account they are likely to be required by the accountant of the business, its auditors or HMRC.

Bank statements are provided by the bank periodically to each current account holder. Businesses will use the bank statement to prepare a bank reconciliation statement i.e. agree the balance on the bank account in their own books with the balance per the statement of account provided by the bank. The business will, therefore, request its bank to provide a bank statement say at the end of each week, two weeks, or at the end of each month.

The bank statement is also a source document to the business as, more often than not, businesses post bank charges and their standing order and direct debit payments directly from the bank statement. Businesses using a manual accounting system, rather than a computerised accounting system, will also most probably post internet or telephone banking transactions into their accounting system from the bank statement.

Bank statements should be treated as confidential documents and, as with paying-in books and cheque books, kept under secure conditions. Bank statements are usually filed chronologically (in date order) and should be kept in files or binders in a lockable drawer or cupboard. These too may be required by the accountant, the auditors of a company, or HMRC.

Where a business or individuals use internet banking they are able to view their bank statement online and will most likely keep their statements on file on their computer. It is important that such confidential information is kept safe and secure so that unauthorised persons are unable to get access to it.

Personal and business loans

Banks and building societies offer a variety of loan facilities to their customers. Loans extended to private individuals by banks and building societies are commonly referred to as 'personal loans'. Most banks and building societies provide personal loans that are repayable over a period ranging from one to seven years. Personal loans are commonly used for the purpose of financing home extensions, buying a car, or home makeovers.

Business loans tend to be offered by banks rather than building societies. Banks tend to offer a range of loan facilities for the specific purpose of funding the expansion of the business, the buying of business premises and the purchase of high cost items (assets) acquired for use in a business, such as items of plant, machinery, equipment and vehicles.

Business loans are for a fixed amount for a predetermined period of time. The rate of interest is fixed at the time the loan is arranged and repayments are fixed over the lifetime of the loan. Such loans are often referred to as 'term loans' and are usually arranged over the term of the lifetime of the asset they are used to finance. A loan for the purpose of financing the purchase of business property for example (usually referred to as a mortgage), is likely to be over a period of from fifteen to twenty-five years.

Banks often require security from businesses against loans given for the purpose of financing the purchase of business premises and assets. Where security is required the loan is usually secured on the assets purchased. This means that should the business fail to meet the loan repayments the bank will have first claim on the assets financed by the loan.

On arranging a loan with a bank or building society the customer will be provided with a loan agreement, the agreement will give full details of the amount borrowed the rate of interest applicable, the term of the loan and the repayment instalments.

For a business, the loan agreement is a source document which verifies the amount to be repaid in terms of capital and interest; it is also a highly confidential document and, therefore, needs to be filed in a safe and secure location. The payment of interest on a loan is a business expense and will be offset by a business against the income it earns each year when calculating its profit or loss.

Mortgages

The word 'mortgage' is used to describe a loan given for the purpose of acquiring residential or commercial (business) premises. Under a mortgage agreement the lender keeps the deeds to the property purchased as security against the loan until the mortgage is repaid. Mortgages tend to be repayable over an extensive period of time, a mortgage term of from fifteen to twenty-five years is quite common.

Although building societies now actively compete with banks by offering a range of banking and financial services they were originally established for the purpose of making loans secured on residential property. The giving of mortgages to private individuals to fund the purchase of residential property remains their prime objective.

Banks extend mortgages both to private individuals, for the purpose of buying residential property, and to businesses for the purpose of buying commercial premises.

Overdrafts

Banks and building societies will often agree to give their current account holders a loan in the form of an overdraft. An overdraft is a facility whereby the account holder is allowed to make payments from their current account in excess of the amount paid into the account.

Technically an overdraft is a short term borrowing facility which is repayable on demand.

Overdraft facilities need to be authorised by a bank or building society, often current account holders are allowed an overdraft facility, up to a predetermined limit, interest free when they open a current account.

Should a current account holder overdraw on their account without permission or in excess of an agreed overdraft limit, this is known as an 'unauthorised overdraft'. Where overdraft authorisation has not been given a bank, or building society, can refuse to meet any withdrawals from the account in excess of the account balance or agreed overdraft limit. In such circumstances, any cheques drawn on the account will be 'bounced' (dishonoured) and the bank will return the cheques, usually making a charge for doing so.

Individuals tend to use overdrafts to smooth out their cash flow when, for a short period of time, their regular income does not match their outgoings. They can overdraw on their account in the knowledge that funds will shortly reach the account which will bring the overdrawn balance on their account into a positive funds balance.

Many businesses, particularly those that experience seasonal trading patterns, make use of overdraft facilities, as do many businesses that carry out contract work. For example, a business with seasonal trends may use an overdraft as a source of funds to buy in stock in readiness for a busy season. As the stock is sold the receipts from sales are then paid into the current account to pay off the overdraft. Where a business carries out contract work it may use an overdraft for the purpose of funding the purchase of materials, the payment of expenses and wages until the contract is completed (or they are paid in stages), they can then pay any receipts from their contractor into their current account to pay off the overdraft.

In practice overdrafts can be an expensive method of short term borrowing if used in the wrong way. The bank will charge interest on the overdrawn balance on a current account on a daily basis, however, if an individual, or a business, is given an overdraft facility of say £2,500 by its bank, but only overdraws on its account balance by £1,500 it will only pay interest on the amount actually overdrawn. Where a business has an overdraft on its current account it should bank receipts regularly in an attempt to reduce the balance and, therefore, pay less interest.

For a business, any interest paid on an overdraft is treated as a business expense which can be charged against income earned by the business each year in calculating profit or loss. The interest payable on an overdraft is usually posted into the books of account directly from the bank statement.

The customer and bank relationship

The relationship between the customer and the bank or building society, in respect of its deposit and current account, is that of a debtor or creditor.

A debtor is someone who owes money to the business; a creditor is someone the business owes money to.

A customer, whether it be an individual or a business, can only ever have positive funds in a deposit account (there is no facility to overdraw on a deposit account); therefore, to the customer the bank or building society represents a debtor i.e. the bank or building society owes money to the customer.

The balance on a customer current account could carry a positive balance or a negative balance (be overdrawn). If a current account carries a positive balance, then the bank or building society is a debtor to the business (the bank or building society owes the customer money). If, however, the customer current account balance is overdrawn the bank or building society represents a creditor to the customer (the customer owes money to the bank or building society).
Where a customer (individual or business) receives funds from a bank or a building society in the form of a loan then the customer obviously owes money to the lender until the loan is repaid. The bank or building society is, therefore, a creditor of the business.

Telephone and internet banking

Advances in technology and the increased use of computers has enabled banks and building societies to offer customers telephone and internet banking facilities in addition to their traditional over-the-counter service. Such services enable customers to access their account 24 hours a day 365 days a year. Telephone banking is often described by banks and building societies as a 'push button fast-track service', that is secure and confidential.

Users of a telephone banking service are given a membership number and pass code for the purpose of accessing their account, they are able to:

- Request a statement of account
- Check their account balance
- Make payments
- Transfer money between accounts
- Speak to an advisor

Online (internet) banking is a service which allows bank and building society customers to perform some banking activities using a computer. Users access their account using a combination of passwords and PINs (personal identification numbers) and can use the service to:

- View their statement of account and check their transaction history
- Pay bills
- Transfer money between accounts
- Request cheque books and paying-in books
- Make credit card and loan applications

Individuals and businesses have been quick to recognise the advantages of both telephone and internet banking, however, of the two facilities internet banking is seen by many as the most useful facility. Being able to view their account online, make online payments, transfer monies between accounts and view a history of their transactions, enables bank and building society customers to control their finances to a far greater extent than was possible in the past.

It is important that those who use telephone and internet banking recognise the need for strict security procedures and take steps to restrict access to accounts by protecting information relating to membership numbers, pass codes/passwords and personal identification numbers (PIN's).

On advice from the banks, businesses which use telephone and internet banking facilities take a number of simple precautions in the interests of security. Many of the precautions recommended also apply to private individuals using telephone and internet banking facilities, and include:

- Keeping passwords and PIN's information safe. Never writing down passwords and PIN's or storing them on a phone or computer
- Only giving information relating to passwords and PIN's to those within the organisation who will need to use them and are in a position of trust
- Ensuring that staff are aware of the organisations security procedures relating to telephone and internet banking
- Changing passwords regularly
- Keeping software up to date, especially operating systems and browsers
- Using firewall software such as McAfee, Symantec and Zone Alarm, and anti-virus software such as McAfee, Norton and Sophos
- Not opening unexpected email attachments which could contain viruses. Banks will never communicate information or request information relating to telephone or internet banking details using email
- Never downloading software where they aren't sure of the source — this includes websites which prompt the user to click "yes" or "OK" to run a program or install a browser plug-in
- Using a private computer for internet banking whenever possible as they recognise that publicly accessible computers, in places such as internet cafes, are not always secure
- Never choosing or changing a password if they use a computer in a public place
- Regularly checking bank accounts for suspicious transactions, and contacting the bank immediately should they notice anything out of the ordinary

Retaining banking documents

The importance of recognising that banking documents are confidential and should be held under safe and secure conditions has already been emphasised a number of times in this lesson. Whether records are paper based, or held on a computer, there must be appropriate measures in place to ensure they cannot be accessed by unauthorised individuals.

There is a legal requirement that banking documents such as paying-in books, cheque book stubs, bank statements and loan agreements are kept on file for a minimum period of six years. When the six-year period has elapsed banking records can be destroyed. Paper based records are usually shredded, whereas records held electronically (computer based) are 'wiped' clean.

Payment methods

The services offered by banks and building societies include a number of methods by which payment is made. The following is a list of some of the common methods of payment used by individuals and businesses to pay for goods and services, followed by an overview of how the payment methods are used and operate:

- Cash (notes and coins)
- Cheque
- Plastic card (debit cards, credit cards and prepayment cards)
- BACS (direct credit and direct debit)
- Faster payments
- Standing order
- CHAPS
- PayPal

Cash (notes and coins)

Although most businesses tend to keep the payments they make in cash (notes and coins) to a minimum, those that operate within the retail, catering and leisure sectors, find that a good number of their customers still see payment in cash as one of the simplest methods of making payment, particularly for small value transactions and, therefore, find that some or most of their daily takings are in the form of cash sales.

For those businesses where the taking of cash, in the form of notes and coins, is still an important aspect of their business, then banks provide them with services that, enables them to pay cash into their account over the counter of the bank, or pay cash into their account outside normal banking hours. As well as taking cash from them, banks will also issue cash to businesses should they want to top-up their cash float for the purpose of giving change to customers, paying minor expenses from petty cash, or paying cash wages.

In general, businesses process their cash sale transactions through a cash register, more commonly known as a 'till'. The till issues each customer with a receipt to support the transaction, and also provides the trader with a record of each transaction, together with a summary of each day's total takings.

A typical till receipt issued to a customer will show:

- The name of the trader
- The trader's VAT registration number (where VAT registered)
- The date of the transaction
- The value of each sale item
- The VAT element of the transaction
- The total value of the transaction

Modern tills may also provide a receipt that gives additional information to that listed above. This may include:

- Change to be given
- An analysis of transactions - goods value and VAT content

Some businesses may verify their sales by issuing customers with a written receipt. Such traders often use a carbonised receipt book, they write out a receipt on taking payment from the customer, issue a copy of the receipt to the customer and keep a carbon copy for themselves. The carbon copies within the receipt book are used as the source of sales and VAT postings to the books of account. The receipt issued to the customer should contain details as follows:

- The name of the trader
- The trader's VAT registration number (where VAT registered)
- The date of the transaction
- A description of the sale transaction
- The total value of the goods / services provided
- The VAT element of the transaction
- The total value of the transaction

On the occasions where businesses themselves pay for goods / services in cash then a receipt must be collected from the supplier as evidence of the expenditure. HMRC will generally disallow claims for items of expenditure not supported by a receipt. The receipt is used not only as evidence of expenditure, but also as the source document from which the payment transaction is posted into the books of account. As source documents receipts issued or received by a business must be kept 'on file'.

Cheques

A cheque was once the most common form of making payment from a bank current account. However, in recent years, with the emergence of automated payment methods, the use of cheques has declined rapidly.

A cheque is an order in writing to the bank, signed by the account holder or designated signatory, instructing them to pay a specified sum to a 'person' nominated on the cheque. The following is an example of a cheque:

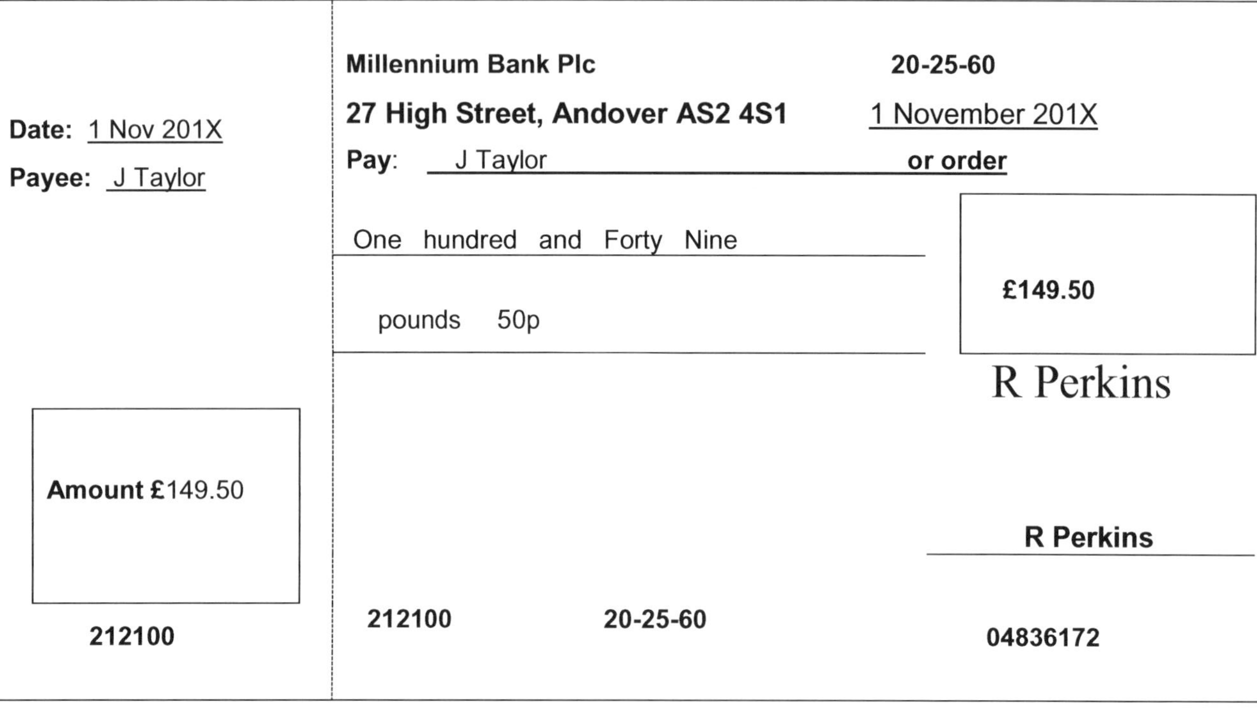

The face of the cheque provides 'spaces' where the name of the person to whom the cheque is payable can be entered, the sum to be paid can also be entered – this is written in both words and figures. The cheque must then be signed and space is provided on the cheque for doing so. It is important that in making-out a cheque care is taken to ensure that all the details which have to be entered on the cheque are entered correctly, otherwise the bank will most probably refuse to process the cheque when it is presented for payment.

The cheque also includes a counterfoil on which details from the face of the cheque must be copied. The cheque can be detached (being perforated) from the counterfoil leaving a 'stub' within the cheque book giving details of the payment made. In some circumstances the counterfoil is used as the source document from which a payment transaction is posted into the books of account, with evidence of the payment also appearing on the Bank Statement.

As can be seen from the example cheque provided above the face of the cheque bears the name of the bank on which the cheque is drawn and carries a series of numbers. These are:

- The unique code number of the bank and branch on which the cheque is drawn – **20-25-60**, this is known as the sort code.
- The number of the cheque. Each cheque within a cheque book is numbered in sequence – **212100**.
- The account number, each account holder being given a different account number – **04836172**

Payment by cheque is an arrangement between various parties. In banking terms these are known as:

- **The drawee** - The bank on whom the cheque is drawn.
- **The drawer** - The account holder ordering the bank to make payment.
- **The payee** - The person to whom the bank is ordered to make payment.

With regard to the cheque in the example the parties to the cheque are:

The drawee	-	Millennium Bank Plc
The drawer	-	R Perkins
The payee	-	J Taylor

Words and crossings

The adding of a crossing (two parallel lines across the face of the cheque) and the printing or writing of 'wording' within the crossing has vastly improved the security aspect of payment by cheque. The most common form of crossing is the **'A/C Payee'** crossing.

Adding the words 'account payee' to the crossing is an instruction to the bank that the cheque should only be paid into a bank account held in the name of the payee. Nowadays, banks and building societies tend to issue cheque books containing cheques with 'account payee' pre-printed in the crossing and have replaced the 'or order' instruction with the word 'only'.

Example – account payee crossing

Millennium Bank Plc 20-25-60

Date: ______

27 High Street, Andover AS2 4S1 ______ 20 ______

Payee: ______

Pay: ______ only

A/C Payee

£

Amount £

212102

212102 20-25-60 04836172

The cheque clearing system

Once presented to a bank for payment a cheque must pass through the banks 'clearing system'. A cheque takes three working days to pass through the bank's central clearing system; the clearing system works as follows:

- Day 1 – when a cheque is paid into an account at a bank (the collecting bank) it is sent at the end of the working day to the bank's clearing centre
- Day 2 – all cheques received by the clearing centre are sorted and details of the cheque sort code, account number on which the cheque is drawn, serial number, and amount payable are sent electronically by the clearing centre to the banks on which the cheques are drawn (the paying bank)

- Day 3 – the paying bank receives any cheques made out by its own customers and has to check that a cheque is valid before it can be paid. Cheques that are not valid and cannot be paid must be returned, by first class post on the same day, to the original collecting bank (the bank to which the cheque was presented for payment on day 1 of the cycle)

On the same day all banks calculate how much they owe each other and the net balances are settled through an account which each clearing bank maintains with the Bank of England.

The 2-4-6 rules

There is often confusion about how the clearing system works and the time it takes for a cheque to be treated by banks and building societies as cleared funds. The central clearing cycle (the time it takes for a cheque to pass through the banks clearing system) is 3 working days as explained above, however, there are rules known as the '2-4-6 rules' that set maximum timescales for when bank and building society customers will start earning interest on a cheque paid into their account (where they deposit cheques in an account which pays interest), and when they will be able to draw on cheques they deposit in the knowledge that the money is in their account and guaranteed safe and cannot be dishonoured (bounced).

The 2-4-6 clearance rules work in the following way (note that the days referred to in the 2-4-6 cycle are working days and exclude Saturdays, Sundays and bank holidays):

Assume that Kate has a current account, on which interest is paid, with her bank and she pays a cheque for £1,000 into her account at the bank on Monday 1 May 201X. Kate would start receiving interest on the cheque on Wednesday 3 May 201X (day 2), on day 4 (Friday 5 May 201X) Kate can withdraw the £1,000 although there is still a risk that the cheque can be bounced, on day 6 (Tuesday 9 May 201X) Kate can withdraw the £1,000 from her account and be guaranteed that the money is hers and the cheque she paid in cannot now be bounced.

2-4-6 cycle summary

Monday 1 May 201X – Kate pays the cheque into her account (day 0, the day on which a cheque is paid in is not counted as a day within the cycle).

Tuesday 2 May 201X – day 1 within the cycle,

Wednesday 3 May 201X – day 2 within the cycle, Kate will receive interest on the cheque from day 2.

Thursday 4 May 201X – day 3 within the cycle

Friday 5 May 201X – day 4 within the cycle, Kate can withdraw the £1,000 but there is still the risk that the cheque may bounce.

Saturday 6 May and Sunday 7 May 201X – non-working days, so not counted within the cycle,

Monday 8 May 201X – day 5 within the cycle.

Tuesday 9 May 201X – day 6 within the cycle, the money is now safe and Kate can withdraw the £1,000 from day 6 onwards in the knowledge that the cheque can no longer be bounced.

Dishonoured cheques

A dishonoured cheque can be described as a cheque on which the bank refuses to make payment as the amount written on the cheque exceeds the amount that is available in the account on which it is drawn.

Cheques dishonoured by the bank are commonly referred to as 'bounced cheques' and are usually returned by the bank, to the person who has presented the cheque for payment, marked 'refer to drawer'.

The 'life' of a cheque

It is generally accepted that a cheque is valid for a period of six months from the date of issue. After six months a cheque becomes out of date (stale) and will not be processed by the bank on which it is drawn.

Postdated cheques

It is possible that a drawer may post date a cheque i.e. enter a date on the cheque which is later than the date on which the cheque is actually made out. In such circumstances the cheque does not become valid, and should not be banked, until the payment date is reached.

Stopping a cheque

The drawer of a cheque has the right, at any time prior to payment being made by the bank, to put a 'stop' on a cheque. To do so the drawer must contact the bank in writing and the instructions to stop the cheque must include:

- The cheque number
- The name of the payee on the cheque
- The amount payable on the cheque

Receipt of a cheque

All cheques received have to be examined prior to paying them into the bank to confirm that they have been completed correctly by the drawer. The details to be confirmed are:

- The **date** (which must include the year) is entered.
- The name of the **payee** is entered and is correct
- The **amount** is written in both **words** and **figures** and the amounts (words and figures) correspond.
- The cheque is **signed** by the drawer.

The details above, other than the signature of the drawer, may be added to the cheque by the payee. This is acceptable provided it is done to the satisfaction of the drawer (as the drawer would have wished).

Whilst certain details can be added to a cheque by the payee it is not permissible for anyone but the drawer to alter any of the details they have entered on a cheque. The drawer may amend details but must initial any alterations made.

The use of plastic cards

For those traders who receive payment for goods and services from customers paying by plastic card the sale is regarded as being a 'cash sale' as the 'monies' resulting from card transaction are received immediately, or almost immediately by the trader.

For customers, payment by plastic card is seen as convenient, easier than writing out a cheque and safer than carrying cash.

Those customers who take advantage of credit card facilities receive the benefit of goods / services immediately whilst having the opportunity to spread the cost of their purchases over a period of time.

For businesses, accepting payment by plastic card increases turnover opportunities and enhances profits. Sales channels can be extended so that in addition to payment via traditional face-to-face transactions payment can now be accepted by telephone, mail, or via the internet.

Automation of the system means less paperwork for businesses, funds are credited to the bank account of the trader instantly, or within days of the transaction taking place, and immediately become cleared funds. Automation also means that full reconciliation of all transactions is available to the trader from which postings can be made into accounting system.

Debit cards

Debit cards are extensively used by individual and businesses for face-to-face transactions, and to make payment by telephone or over the internet.

Debit cards can also be used to make cash withdrawals from an ATM (automatic teller machine). Some traders also allow cardholders a 'cash back' facility when making payment by debit card i.e. the cardholder can withdraw cash from their current account as they pay for their purchases.

When payment is made using a debit card funds are transferred automatically from the account of the card holder to the account of the trader and the funds immediately become cleared funds.

The use of new technology by banks and building societies means that more and more debit cards are being upgraded with new contactless technology making it even simpler to pay by card. The 'Tap and Go' facility is an example of the use of new technology.

Tap and Go allows the cardholder to make everyday purchases, for items with a transaction spend of less than £30, without having to swipe their card. Instead, a simple tap of the card on a terminal usually sited at a checkout (in a shop or a store for example) or entry point (for example when boarding a bus, or passing through the barriers at a tube station) is all that is required to complete the transaction.

Prepayment cards

Prepayment cards are plastic cards that are pre-loaded with credit (spending money) before buying goods or services, they are sometimes referred to as 'stored-value cards'. They are an alternative to cash or cheques and make it possible for someone to benefit from the use of a plastic card without having to open a current account or take out a credit card. Prepaid cards can be reloadable or only used once (non-reloadable). The balance on the card is reduced as the cardholder uses the card to make payments.

There are several situations in which prepaid cards are useful, for example:

- They may be an attractive option if you are travelling abroad as you can pre-load the card with currency before you go away. Used in this way they can help you budget as, unlike a debit or credit card, they don't allow you to go into debt.
- Reloadable cards can be topped up online, a facility that may be useful to parents wanting to send money to a child overseas or travelling.
- Students find prepaid cards attractive as they are usually faced with the problem of having only limited funds. The prepaid card gives them the opportunity to budget their spending, offers them the convenience of a traditional plastic card in terms of where they are accepted, but there is no option to use the card to run up debts.
- Younger children may benefit from being given prepaid cards instead of cash by parents. They are a safer alternative to cash, can help children budget their spending, and allow parents to monitor their children's spending.

Credit cards

As with a debit card, a credit card can be used by the card holder to purchase goods or services in a face-to-face transaction, over the telephone or online, credit cards issued more recently may also offer the 'Tap and Go' facility. Credit cards can also be used to obtain cash (known as a 'cash advance') from an ATM.

Under the credit card system, however, the cardholder is taking credit from a credit card company and not the trader from which they are buying goods or services. The credit card company pays the trader supplying the goods or services, usually within a few days of the sale transaction taking place, and the cardholder then makes payment to the credit card company.

When a credit card is issued the cardholder is set a credit limit i.e. the total amount they are allowed to spend using their credit card The credit card company periodically issues the cardholder with a statement of account which gives details of all transactions, the balance to be paid, and the date by which payment, if made in full, can be made without the cardholder incurring interest charges. Alternatively, the cardholder is given the option of making a minimum payment or paying-off only part of the balance, thereby spreading the cost of purchases over a period of time. Where the cardholder elects for payment by instalments interest is charged on the balance unpaid.

Some credit card companies charge cardholders a fixed annual membership fee in addition to charging interest. The trader offering the service to customers is also charged a fee by the card merchant who provides the card service to them. Usually the charge by the card merchant to the trader is a percentage of sales value, which is likely to vary depending on the volume of credit card transactions processed by the trader.

Company credit cards

Whilst credit cards are used predominately by private individuals, some business organisations too are registered as credit cardholders. They have corporate credit cards which they issue to staff to pay business expenses such as fuel (petrol / diesel), accommodation, fares, meals etc. In such circumstances the credit card company provides a Statement of Account to the business organisation for payment.

Processing card transactions

Several years ago, the majority of card transactions for 'over the counter' face-to-face sales were processed using a manual system, which required a sales voucher to be written out for each transaction. However, nowadays, card transactions tend to be processed using an automated system known as EFTPOS (Electronic Funds Transfer at Point of Sale). The system allows cardholders to benefit from what is known as 'smartcard technology'.

Each plastic card contains an embedded microchip (CHIP) and cardholders are given a personal identification number (PIN), the CHIP and PIN technology allows transactions to be authenticated automatically.

A 'customer present' card transaction requires the cardholder to place their card in a terminal (Pin-pad), which accesses the chip on the card. Once the card has been verified as being authentic the customer enters their 4-digit PIN into the terminal, this number is then submitted to the chip on the card, usually by pressing an 'Enter' key on the terminal. If the PIN matches the information stored on the chip the chip tells the terminal that the PIN was correct and the transaction is completed. The terminal prints out a slip to be retained by the cardholder which verifies details of the transaction. A more detailed VAT receipt will be issued by the trader if requested by the cardholder.

At the end of each day's trading the trader is able to print out a summary of card transactions. This summary provides a breakdown by 'card type' of the day's plastic card transactions, and is usually used by the bookkeeper as the source document from which receipts from card sales are posted into the books of account. As source documents the end of day reports need to be kept on file.

Some credit transactions are processed when the cardholder is not present, for example, where payment is to be made over the telephone or the internet by debit card or credit card. A set procedure is followed by those processing 'customer not present' card transactions.

Obviously the 'chip and PIN' system cannot be used when the customer is not present, therefore, most businesses use a special 'customer not present' terminal when processing such transactions.

A person accepting a card payment over the telephone will ask the cardholder to confirm the following details:

- The name of the cardholder, as printed on the card
- The card number
- The card expiry date
- The card issue number (usually debit card)
- The card security code (a three-digit code printed on the back of each card)

Businesses selling goods online from a website carry out sales transactions on a 'remote control' basis and there is no direct contact with the customer. When a 'customer not present' card payment is made over the internet information, almost identical to that required for a telephone card transaction, is required. However, internet transactions require the cardholder to 'key in' details from their card, they will also have to provide delivery details/email address to the seller, so that (where goods are being purchased) details of the transaction can be confirmed and the goods can be despatched by the business to the delivery address stipulated.

Where services are being purchased, for example a flight or hotel booking, the seller will normally confirm details of the transaction by email, usually giving the customer a unique code by which to identify the transaction.

Where businesses sell goods online from a website they receive payment directly into their bank account and receive a schedule of the payments from the card merchant providing them with the card service, they need to check the schedule details against their bank statement.

The BACS system

BACS (Bankers' Automated Clearing Services) is a central electronic payments system owned and operated by the leading banks and building societies. The majority of BACS payments are direct credits or direct debits.

The BACS system is regarded as being cheap and efficient as the transfer of monies is set up on a computer file and transferred between the bank's computers, with payments going directly from one account to another.

BACS direct credit

The use of direct credit as a method of payment has grown rapidly in recent years. It is used for the purpose of making regular bulk payments of varying amounts, for example:

- To make wages and salary payments to employees (the vast majority of UK wages and salary payments are made using the BACS direct credit system)
- To make payments to suppliers, say at a month end

To make payment using BACS direct credit the payer needs to collect details of the payees (recipients) bank or building society account number and sort code. The payment process operates on a three-day cycle as follows:

Day 1 (Input) - payment file submitted to BACS.

Day 2 (Processing) - the payment is processed.

Day 3 (Entry) - the payers bank account is debited with a single entry covering the value of all the payments made. Simultaneously the accounts of all individual payees are credited.

If a business is paying its employees, or suppliers, using BACS direct credit and wants the payments credited to the payee bank accounts on a Friday of a particular week it must submit its payment file by the Wednesday of that week.

BACS direct debit

BACS direct debit is a system used for the purpose of making payment electronically of fixed or variable amounts, where the time interval between payments may vary. Direct debits are typically used to make payments to meet regular financial commitments, such as mortgage payments, utility bills and telephone bills.

To make a payment by direct debit the payer authorises their bank or building society to allow the receiver (company being paid) to **collect varying amounts** from their account at regular intervals. Advance notice of the first collection must be given by the receiver to the payer and the receiver must advise the payer of any future changes.

The authorisation given by the payer to allow payments to be collected from their account is known as a 'direct debit instruction'. To set-up the instruction the payer must complete a form generated by the receiver, the form will require the payer to give details such as the name of their bank, the bank sort code and their account number.

The receiver can collect the information from the payer over the telephone, online or using a paper based form which the payer is required to complete, sign and send back. The direct debit mandate will set out the terms of agreement between the payer and the receiver, including the date the instruction is given and the frequency of the payments to be made (annually, quarterly, monthly etc.). The receiver sends the information to the payer's bank and the bank sets up the direct debit.

The receiver, who draws the funds from the payers account, instructs their own bank to collect directly from the payer's bank account (debit) and pay the amount they collect directly into their account (credit). They process amounts received from collection details they give their bank and a report they receive from their bank giving notice of any bounced payments and cancellations.

Where a business makes payments to other companies by direct debit from its bank account it will usually process the payments from the bank statement it receives from its bank.

Faster Payments Service

The Faster Payments Service (FPS) is a UK banking initiative introduced to reduce payment times between different banks' customer accounts from three working days using the BACS system, to a few hours. The Faster Payments Service is used by the banks to process the vast majority of internet and telephone payments and is also used to process most Standing Order payments.

The service enables bank customers to send same-day payments from their account to another account at a bank or building society (which participates in the scheme). Funds transferred using the service should reach the receiving customers account within two hours, but generally the monies are available within minutes of the transaction being processed. Each bank or building society has a limit on the amount of money which can be sent using the Faster Payments Service, and those using the service need to check the limits if they intend to use the service.

Businesses tend to use Faster Payments to make single one-off payments to other traders, for example to make payment to a trader with whom they don't have a credit account, or to a trader who requests 'cash with order'.

Bank customers using the Faster Payments Service can initiate the payment instruction over the telephone, online, or in a branch of the bank where they hold their account. To make payment the customer must give their bank the name of the business/person they want to pay, the receivers bank account number and bank sort code and, where payment is being made by phone or online, an identifying reference. It is vital that the information provided is correct as once a payment is made using the service it cannot be cancelled and it could prove difficult to get money back should it end up in a wrong account.

Standing order

A standing order is an instruction by a customer to their bank to pay a **fixed amount** at regular intervals to a nominated payee (receiver), say monthly, quarterly or annually. **The amount payable can only be changed by the payer (bank customer).** Once the standing order is set up the bank automatically makes payment by computer link. The vast majority of standing order payments are processed by banks using the Faster Payments Service.

Standing orders are typically used to – make rent payments, pay annual subscriptions to a club, society or trade association, pay magazine/trade journal subscriptions, make monthly charity donations, make loan repayments, or to make payments from a current account into a savings account.

Any person or business with a current account can set up a standing order by completing a paper based form (mandate), or by giving instructions to their bank online, over the phone or in the bank branch.

Businesses which make payments by standing order from their bank account usually process the payments from the statement of account they receive from their bank.

Payment by CHAPS

CHAPS (Clearing House Automated Payment Service) is a same-day automated payments system used primarily by banks for the purpose of processing one-off very high value payments. CHAPS payments can be sent to most UK bank accounts and funds transferred can be drawn on the same day providing the funds are released before 3pm.

CHAPS is mainly used by solicitors for the purpose of transferring funds between the bank accounts of those involved when property is bought and sold.

New technology

The emergence of wireless and mobile networks and the use of the internet has revolutionised traditional business practices and in doing so has significantly increased the exchange of goods, services and information.

Future developments in banking services are centred around the use of mobile handheld devices such as smartphones and tablets (handheld computers), giving customers easy access their bank account and flexible safe and secure methods of making payment for goods and services The use of new technology is giving customers the options of paying for goods and services directly from their bank or building society account how they want, when they want and where they want.

PayPal

PayPal is not a bank; it doesn't pay interest or give loans. However, the receipts and payments system it provides to individuals and businesses is worthy of a mention in this topic area of the textbook.

PayPal is a financial transaction broker providing a payment service that allows businesses and individuals to make and receive online payments between accounts without the need to exchange bank account or credit card details. PayPal can be used for making purchases from businesses or for personal payments between individuals, and also for making payments abroad.

To open a PayPal account applicants must have a valid and reliable email address, a valid bank account and a valid credit card. Accounts are free to open and the service is free to use when the account holder is buying something and making a payment in the UK. Transferring money, for example sending money to friends and family in the UK, is free for those sending and receiving money when the sender funds the transfer from their bank account or PayPal balance. Account holders can also use a debit or credit card or make an international transfer for a small fee.

PayPal accounts can be linked to the account holders bank account and debit and credit cards, so users don't necessarily have to keep money in their PayPal account, instead they can choose to make payment from one of their linked accounts. However, a PayPal account is often regarded as a 'wallet' by account holders, into which they can pay monies whenever they wish to do so from a linked account, keep a balance of funds in their wallet at a level which enables them to effectively manage their PayPal account transactions, and withdraw monies from their wallet whenever they want.

As a middleman PayPal makes its money by charging a fee to sellers/receivers of money. PayPal charges sellers a transaction fee on the total sale amount plus a fixed fee per transaction. The fee depends on the volume of business conducted by sellers, the higher their level of sales the lower the percentage fee.

Users of PayPal are able to view and download their PayPal account history which will give them details of transaction dates, types and, if they are sellers, transaction fees. Sellers who are trading as businesses will need to access and use this information for the purpose of posting sales transactions and transaction fees into their accounting records. Sellers can withdraw funds from their PayPal account at any time. Businesses with a PayPal account will need to record details of transfers from their bank account into a PayPal account in their accounting records, likewise receipts into the account and withdrawals from the account will have to be recorded.

Banking money received

Some business receipts may reach the bank account of the business automatically. Funds banked in this manner include money received via:

- Plastic card (where transactions are processed using EFTPOS)
- BACS
- Faster Payments Service
- Standing order
- CHAPS

It is necessary to confirm that money due to be received from any of the sources listed above has been credited to the business bank account on the Bank Statement.

Where funds are to be paid over the counter of the bank into the business bank account then 'monies' have to be prepared for banking and suitable arrangements made for the transporting of the money from the premises of the business to the bank.

The document used in business for paying money into a bank account is a **Paying-in Slip**. It is a pre-printed form on which funds banked can be listed and summarised. A business will use the paying- in slip to bank cash (notes and coins) and cheques.

You should note that any debit card or credit receipts which are processed by a business using the manual sales voucher system would also have to be banked and entered from a summary voucher onto the paying-in slip. However, as the processing of card transactions manually is, nowadays, a very rare occurrence then this will not be assessed in any of the assessments conducted by the IAB.

The following is an example of a paying-in slip:

Paying-in slip: front

Counterfoil:

Date: 19/1/1X

Credit: 37970995

	£	p
£50 notes	50	00
£20 notes	360	00
£10 notes	120	00
£5 notes	45	00
£2/£1	14	00
50p	4	00
20p	3	00
10p, 5p	2	00
Bronze	1	50
Total Cash	599	50
Total cheques etc	211	45
£	810	95

bank giro credit

Date: 19/1/1X

Cashier's stamp and initials

Code No 81-60-32

Bank: **Millennium Bank Plc**

Branch: **Anytown**

Credit: Glamour Boutique

Account No: 37970995

Number of Cheques 6

Paid in by: ____________________

	£	p
£50 notes	50	00
£20 notes	360	00
£10 notes	120	00
£5 notes	45	00
£2/£1	14	00
50p	4	00
20p	3	00
10p, 5p	2	00
Bronze	1	50
Total Cash	599	50
Total cheques etc	211	45
£	810	95

Paying-in slip: reverse

Cheques etc

	£	p		£	p
			Brought forward		
			T Prince	12	99
			R Binns	24	99
			S Tate	19	99
			K Lyle	49	99
			J West	87	50
			P Robb	15	99
Carried forward			Carried over	211	45

counterfoil carried over

	£	p
	12	99
	24	99
	19	99
	49	99
	87	50
	15	99
Carried over	211	45

The physical security of money

The physical security of monies is a problem which faces many businesses.

Retail businesses for example are exposed to problems related to the forgery of notes and coins, and stolen cheque books and credit cards. It is advisable where a business accepts notes and coins in payment that staff are encouraged to examine notes (particularly larger denomination notes) carefully on receipt.

The theft of cash is also a common business risk which can be reduced by adequate systems and precautions. The trustworthiness of staff who are employed to handle cash should be verified before they take up employment, and their activities in the workplace should be closely monitored. Procedures should also be in place that ensure monies are kept safe and secure whilst on the business premises.

Where a business operates a cash register staff should undergo adequate training on the use of a cash register, security keys and systems. Staff should be warned against the risk of leaving the cash register unattended or open. Furthermore, they must be aware of the need to keep cash register security keys (which should only be issued to authorised staff) safe. It is good practice to organise the regular collection of monies from a cash register to a strong box or 'in-house' safe.

There are several types of safe available for use by businesses. These include:

- Stand-alone safes
- Wall safes
- Floor safes

Keys to the safe will normally only be issued to senior staff.

Monies should be transferred on a regular basis (preferably daily) from the business premises to the bank. Some businesses use their own staff to do so, or have 'in-house' security staff. The larger organisation which regularly transfers large sums of money to and from the bank is more likely to use an external security service such as Securicor or Group 4.

Where a business uses its own staff to take monies to the bank the following precautions are recommended:

- Send more than one person to the bank
- Vary the person(s) taking monies to the bank i.e. use different individuals
- Suggest that the individuals taking monies to the bank vary the time they depart and vary their route

Banking out of hours is often preferable to leaving large amounts of cash on the business premises overnight. Banks provide a night-safe facility whereby monies can be banked outside normal banking hours.

Lesson 1 Practice Questions

Question 1.1

Which **one** of the following financial services is **not** usually offered by a building society?

	✓
Savings account	
Mortgage on commercial property	
Mortgage on domestic property	

Question 1.2

A firm of solicitors needs to send £250,000 to another solicitor today on behalf of a client to finalise a deal to buy business premises.

Which **one** of the following payment methods is the most suitable for the purpose of making the payment through the banking system?

	✓
Standing order	
Direct debit	
CHAPS	

Question 1.3

An overdraft facility may be offered on which **one** of the following types of bank or building society account?

	✓
Mortgage account	
Current account	
Deposit account	

Question 1.4

A business has credit accounts with over 300 suppliers. It sends payments of varying amounts to suppliers on the 15th of each month and on the last Friday of each month.

Which **one** of the following payment methods would be most suitable to the business for the purpose of transferring funds directly from its bank current account directly to the bank accounts of its suppliers?

	✓
BACS direct credit	
Standing order	
CHAPS	

Question 1.5

James is a farmer. On 1 April each year he makes a payment of a fixed amount of £60.00 from his bank current account to Farmers Monthly magazine.

Which **one** of the following payment methods would be most suitable to James for the purpose of making the fixed annual payment of £60.00?

	✓
BACS direct credit	
CHAPS	
Standing order	

Question 1.6

Indicate below the number of days it takes a cheque to pass through the bank's central clearing system?

	✓
3 days	
4 days	
8 days	

Question 1.7

A builder wants to buy a new dumper truck at a cost of £10,000 for use in his business, but doesn't have sufficient funds available to buy the truck.

Which **one** of the following facilities would be most suitable to the builder for the purpose of borrowing money from the bank for the purpose of financing the purchase of the dumper truck?

	✓
Mortgage	
Overdraft	
Business loan (term loan)	

Question 1.8

Which **one** of the following payment methods is designed for use by someone who regularly makes payments of less than £30 in cash (notes and coins), but is finding the need to carry cash an inconvenience?

	✓
Contactless payment (Tap and Go)	
Credit card	
Cheque	

Question 1.9

Amir is at university and finds he needs to budget his spending as he doesn't want to get into debt.

Which **one** of the following would be most suitable to Amir considering his circumstances?

	✓
Credit card	
Overdraft facility	
Prepayment card	

Question 1.10

Anya has a current account with a building society. The building society is open for business from Monday to Friday each week. She pays a cheque of £250.00 into her current account on Monday 1 September 201X.

On which **one** of the following dates would Anya be safe to draw on the cheque and be guaranteed that the cheque will not bounce?

	✓
2 working days later - Wednesday 3 September 201X	
4 working days later- Friday 5 September 201X	
6 working days later – Tuesday 9 September 201X	

Question 1.11

Which **one** of the following payment methods would be most suitable to a business wanting to collect varying amounts at regular intervals from its customers?

	✓
Direct debit	
Standing order	
Faster payments	

Question 1.12

Today's date is 5 December 201X. Your name is Tina Murray and you are the proprietor of a hairdressing salon trading in the name of Hairport. You work in and manage the salon and also act as bookkeeper. You have sole responsibility for issuing and signing business cheques.

Complete the cheque below to be issued to a supplier Hairflair Ltd. The amount payable is £1,430.60. You are also required to complete the cheque counterfoil:

Date: ______	Millennium Bank Plc	20-25-60
Payee: ______	27 High Street, Ambleside AB 6SD ______	
	Pay: ______	only
Amount £		
176108	176108 20-25-60 39590763	

Question 1.13

Catering Equipment Ltd supplied goods on 2 October 201X to the value of £1,125.50, allowing them 30 day's credit.

On 31 October 201X Catering Equipment Ltd sent a statement of account to Continental Catering, requesting payment of the invoice for the goods supplied.

The following cheque was received by Catering Equipment Ltd on 6 November 201X:

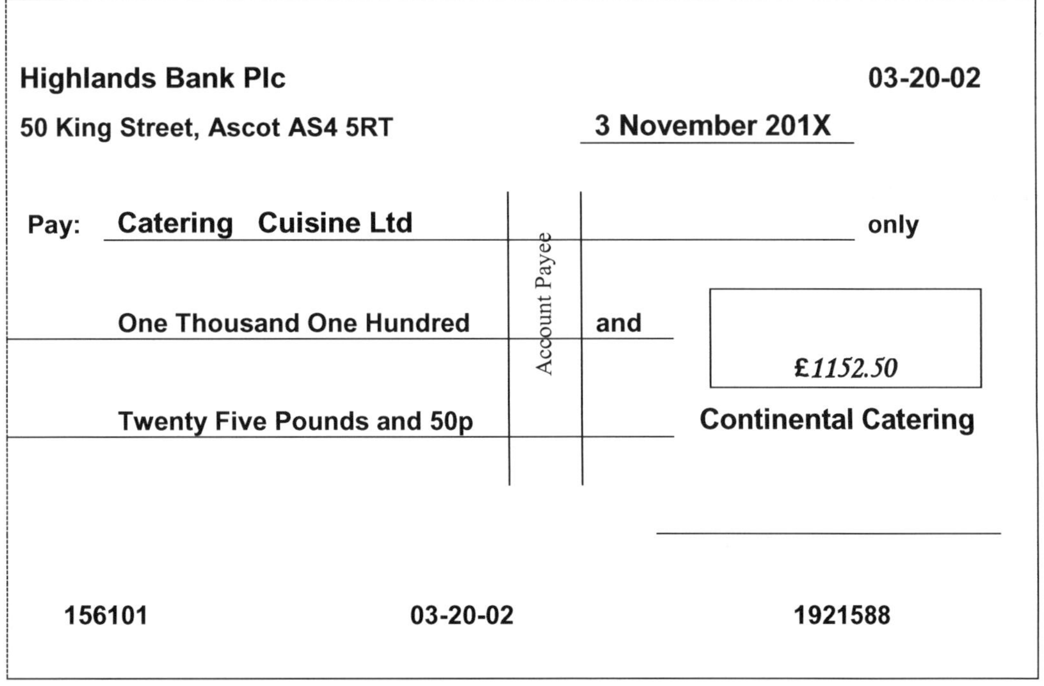

Highlands Bank Plc 03-20-02

50 King Street, Ascot AS4 5RT 3 November 201X

Pay: Catering Cuisine Ltd only

Account Payee

One Thousand One Hundred and

Twenty Five Pounds and 50p

£1152.50

Continental Catering

156101 03-20-02 1921588

REQUIRED:

Examine the above cheque, review each of the questions below and for each question place tick in either the 'yes' or 'no' box?

Statement	Yes ✓	No ✓
Is the cheque in date?		
Has the correct payee name been entered on the cheque?		
Is the amount written in words on the cheque correct?		
Do the amounts written in words and figures on the cheque correspond?		
Has the cheque been signed?		

Question 1.14

A business has an overdrawn balance on its bank current account. Based on the balance on the current account, which one of the following statements describes the relationship of the bank to the business?

	✓
The bank is a debtor to the business as the bank owes the business money	
The bank is a creditor to the business as the business owes the bank money	

Question 1.15

Which **one** of the following plastic card payment methods would allow the cardholder to spread the cost of goods or services they purchase over several months by paying the card balance in instalments?

	✓
Debit card	
Credit card	
Prepayment card	

Question 1.16

Sam is the owner of a fashion boutique. She allows customers to pay for the goods they buy in the boutique in cash (notes and coins), or by plastic card (debit card and credit card).

Which **one** of the following banking services allows Sam to pay the cash (notes and coins) received from customers into the business bank current account outside the bank's normal opening hours?

	✓
Telephone banking service	
Internet banking service	
Night-safe facility	

Question 1.17

Which **one** of the following payment methods allows businesses and individuals to make and receive online payments without the need to exchange bank account or credit card details?

	✓
BACS	
Direct debit	
PayPal	

Question 1.18

For which **one** of the following periods of time, from the issue date entered on a cheque, is a cheque treated by a bank as being valid?

	✓
3 months	
6 months	
12 months	

Question 1.19

Francis owns a small building firm. He has recently taken on some work for a main contractor. Francis needs to buy materials to use on the contract, but has insufficient funds in the business bank current account to pay for the materials. Once the contract is underway Francis will be paid in stages by the main contractor and the monies he lays out in materials will soon flow back into the business bank account.

Which **one** of the following services offered by his bank would be most suitable to Francis for the purpose of financing his short-term cash flow problem?

	✓
Bank loan (term loan)	
Bank overdraft	
Mortgage	

Question 1.20

In the table below you are presented with payments to be made by three businesses. You are also provided with a list of payment methods commonly used by businesses. You are required to match the payment method from the list given against the payments to be made, thereby selecting what you consider to be the most suitable payment method for each of the payments.

This task is to be completed by entering a payment method from the list into the appropriate box headed up **'Most Suitable Payment Method'** in the table beneath the list:

Payment methods:

- Faster Payments Service
- Business debit card
- Cash (notes and coins)

Payments	Most Suitable Payment Method
Payment of £75.00 to a local garage for fuel for the delivery van	
Payment of £3.84 to the local post office for a book of six first class postage stamps	
A one off payment of £1,200.00 to a company for a supply of goods required urgently, which they will supply immediately provided they receive payment before they dispatch the goods	

Section 2

(Lessons 2 to 9)

Introduction to Computerised Accounting for Business

Method of Assessment – Knowledge Test

Lesson 2

Business Organisations

Business Organisations

By the end of this lesson you should be able to:

- *Identify business organisations operating in the private sector of the UK economy*

- *Understand the characteristics of sole trader, partnership, limited company and not for profit type organisations in terms of ownership, control, and owner's personal financial liability*

Introduction

To meet the demand for goods and services within the UK, the UK operates what is known as a 'mixed economy', comprising of a private sector and a public sector.

The **public sector** is the part of the economy owned, financed and controlled by the state through central government and local authorities. In the public sector the main objectives relate to the provision of services which benefit the whole of society, are affordable or free at the point of use, and which promote and encourage equal opportunity.

The **private sector** is the part of the economy where business activity is organised by private individuals operating on their own or collectively. The main objective of those operating in the private sector is profit. However, there are some organisations operating in the private sector which are non-profit making.

The IAB qualifications concentrate on keeping financial records and preparing financial statements for business organsations operating in the private sector. These include:

- Sole traders
- Partnerships
- Limited companies (private and public)
- Clubs and societies (not for profit organisations)

Sole traders

The term 'sole trader' refers to the type of business entity **owned** by one person, the capital of the business is provided by one person and one person claims any profit made by the business, or is charged with any loss, should the business makes a loss.

Many individuals who want to set up and run their own business choose the sole trader structure. Most sole trader type businesses are easy to establish and run, with few start-up costs (unless initial permits or licences are required).

In most cases, all that is necessary for individuals intending to set up in business as a sole trader, which is often referred to as becoming 'self-employed', is that they register their business with HMRC This may also include registering the business for Value Added Tax (VAT).

Once registered the trader must complete a tax return at the end of each year, and complete VAT returns if the business is VAT registered. Of course, the completion of a tax return by someone who is self-employed, and VAT returns for their business, is dependent on adequate business records and source documents being kept.

A sole trader can employ as many other people in the business as they wish. However, the owner of the business has total control over the activities of the business, as a result most business decisions can be taken quickly as there is no need, necessarily, to consult with others.

Having total responsibility is not without its risks, as the sole trader type entity is regarded as being an unincorporated business. This means that the law makes no distinction between the business and its owner. The owner of the business is personally responsible for all actions or inactions of his/her business. Therefore, as well as benefitting from making good business decisions the trader will personally suffer the consequences of making bad business decisions.

In terms of personal financial liability sole traders have what is known as **'unlimited liability'**. Should their business fail they may well be forced to sell-off private assets to raise funds to meet the debts of the business, as there is no distinction made between their business wealth and their private wealth.

Although sole traders are regarded as being self-employed they are not treated as employees of their business and do not take a salary or wage from their business. Instead they take profit generated by their business in the form of 'drawings'. Most sole traders will take drawings in the form of cash and/or goods which they tend to take at regular intervals throughout each financial year – say on a weekly or monthly basis. However, it should be noted that sole traders are taxed personally on the profit generated by their business and not on the level of their drawings.

More than 60% of businesses operating in the private sector are sole traders. You yourself, with the appropriate bookkeeping qualifications, practice and experience, might consider a career as a self-employed bookkeeper. This would give you the opportunity to put your knowledge and skills to good use by providing bookkeeping and accounting services to those businesses who outsource their bookkeeping and accounting work.

Partnerships

The term 'partnership' is used to describe a business entity **owned** by two or more people (usually to a maximum of twenty), who carry on business collectively with a view to making a profit. Forming a partnership is a relatively simple way for several individuals to set up and run their own business.

A partnership has several advantages and disadvantages when compared to a typical sole trader type entity. These include:

- The potential to raise a large amount of capital as several people, rather than one person, contributes to the finance necessary to set-up and expand the business
- There is a 'pooling' of talents and skills as a number of people from the same, or different, backgrounds are able to work together as joint owners of a business
- The responsibilities of running a business can be shared between the various partners
- Any losses made by the business are shared between the partners

A partnership does of course have several disadvantages compared to a sole trader, for example:

- Control is shared and the decision making process can be slow as there has to be agreement between partners before decisions can be reached and implemented. This can sometimes lead to disputes between partners where partners don't get their own way and have to compromise
- A commitment or contract made by one of the partners on behalf of the business is binding on all of the other partners
- There is a lack of continuity, as the death of a partner, or a partner wanting to withdraw from the partnership brings the business relationship to an end
- Profits are shared between the partners

As with sole traders, partnerships are unincorporated businesses, therefore, the partners are held responsible for any actions or inactions of the business. Individuals within a partnership generally have **unlimited liability** and are equally responsible, along with other partners, for the debts of the business, irrespective of their personal financial investment in the business.

In some form of partnerships, a partner can elect to have limited liability. This would mean that should the business fail the partner concerned would lose only the amount they have contributed as capital to the partnership, and their own private and personal wealth could not be called upon to settle the debts of the business. However, a partner who chooses the protection of limited liability is allowed only to invest capital in the business and cannot take an active part in the running and management of the business.

Those individuals who form a partnership are recommended to think carefully about a business relationship with others and are often advised to draw up a Partnership Agreement.

A Partnership Agreement is usually drawn up with the help of an accountant and a solicitor and is a legally binding agreement designed to set the internal rules by which the partnership is governed. The agreement will be used to help settle any internal disputes between the partners.

In the UK if those in partnership choose not to draw up a Partnership Agreement their business relationship is governed by the Partnership Act 1890. The Act states that profits and losses of the partnership must be shared equally between partners irrespective of the amount of capital they have personally contributed, the hours they work in the business, or the level of their personal responsibility within the business.

Partnerships are quite common forms of business organisation for tradesmen, and are also popular with professionals, for example, many doctors, dentists, solicitors, estate agents and accountants operate as partnerships.

If you are considering operating as a self-employed bookkeeper it may be worth considering forming a partnership with other bookkeepers, as a 'firm' you would be able to take on more clients and probably offer a wider range of services than you could if you operated as a sole trader.

As is the case with sole trader type organisations, those in partnership usually take monies or goods from their business on a regular basis in the form of drawings. However, each partner is taxed personally on their share of the profit of the partnership business and **not** on the level of their drawings.

Limited companies

The limited company is a form of business organisations **owned** by individuals who contribute to the capital of the business by buying shares, as a result they are known as 'shareholders'.

Although limited companies are owned by shareholders they are run by 'directors'. Some shareholders are also directors, but it is not a legal requirement that shareholders also act as directors. Therefore, it is possible for the owners of a company to appoint other people as directors to run the business on their behalf.

Limited companies are incorporated businesses; this means that in law each company is treated as though it were a 'living person'. The company is given its own legal identity which is separate to that of its owners. The company can enter into contracts, employ people and sue and be sued in its own name.

Limited companies are divided into two groups i.e. private limited companies and public limited companies.

A **private limited company** cannot offer its shares for sale to members of the general public which tends to restrict the amount of share capital the company can raise. The share capital is determined by its directors and can be less than £50,000.

The registered name of a private limited company must end with the word 'Limited' or the abbreviation Ltd.

Most private limited companies are small to medium-sized business organisations with relatively few shareholders. Quite often the private limited company is seen as a form of natural progression by many sole traders and partnerships. Private limited companies are in fact relatively cheap to set-up, although the administrative burden of running a private limited company is greater than that associated with running a sole trader or partnership business.

The **public limited company** tends to be a much larger business organisation than the typical sole trader, partnership or private limited company.

It is a legal requirement that the share capital of a public limited company be at least £50,000 and that the registered name of the company end with the words 'public limited company' or the abbreviation 'plc'.

The shares of a public limited company are listed on the Stock Exchange and can be bought and sold by members of the general public. Before it can offer its shares for sale however, a public company must comply with very strict registration criteria which makes them very expensive to set up.

Limited companies both private and public offer their owners (shareholders) **limited liability.** This means that should the company become insolvent the amount a shareholder can lose is limited to the amount they have invested in shares. For example:

A shareholder has invested in a company by buying shares in the company at a cost of £10,000. If the company should fail and go into liquidation, the maximum amount the shareholder can lose is the amount they have invested in shares.

The advantage of limited liability makes share ownership an attractive investment proposition, and public limited companies are generally able to raise vast amounts of capital from a large number of individual investors.

As limited companies are treated as though they were 'living persons' they are taxed personally. Tax is paid on the profits of the company and is known as corporation tax.

Owners (shareholders) of a limited company are not allowed to take drawings from the company. The company can, however, employ them and pay them a remuneration in the form of a wage or salary. It can also distribute profits to them in the form of a dividend.

The limited company is subject to far greater regulation than the sole trader or partnership type organisation. The Companies Act requires limited companies to keep full financial records and stipulates, particularly for public limited companies, the range of financial statements they must prepare and the format in which the financial statements must be presented.

The following table summarises the characteristics of sole trader, partnerships and limited companies in terms of ownership, management, legal status, taxation and the distribution of profits:

	Sole trader	Partnership	Limited Company
Ownership	One owner	Two or more joint owners usually to a maximum of twenty	Multiple owners known as shareholders
Management	Managed by the owner	Managed by the partners	Managed by directors
Legal status	The business is not a separate legal entity, the owner of the business has unlimited liability and is personally liable for all debts of the business	The business is not a separate legal entity. The partners have unlimited liability and are jointly responsible for all debts of the business	The company is a separate legal entity. The debts of the company must be settled using company assets. The liability of shareholders is limited to the amount they have invested in shares
Taxation	The sole trader pays tax on the profits of their business	The partners pay tax on their share of the profits of the partnership	The company pays tax on its profits. The owners and directors only pay tax on income received from the company e.g. from wages, salaries and dividends
Distribution of profit	Profit is taken by the owner in the form of drawings	Profit is taken by the partners in the form of drawings	Profit is distributed to shareholders in the form of dividends

Not for profit organisations

Not for profit organisations generally exist to provide a service, rather than generate profit.

Not for profit organisations include well known charities and voluntary organisations such as Barnardo's, Marie Curie Cancer Care, BBC Children in Need, Royal Society for the Protection of Birds (RSPB), Oxfam and the Prince's Trust. These organisations support a range of worthy causes and mainly rely on donations to finance their charitable work.

Many not for profit organisations are clubs and societies which are organised and owned by groups of individuals who join the club or society as 'members'. The main objective of most clubs and societies is that of providing some form of service or activity to their members, usually at a subsidised cost.

Although most clubs or societies may generate a surplus of income over expenditure (profit) from membership subscriptions, fees charged for the activities they provide, and other fund raising events, they tend to operate as near as possible to cost. Any surplus income they generate is not distributed to members, instead it is used within the club or society to provide better services or activities for club members.

Lesson 2 Practice Questions

Question 2.1

Which one of the following types of business entity is owned by shareholders?

	✓
Partnership	
Not for profit club or society	
Limited company	

Question 2.2

Using appropriate words from the following list complete the gaps in **each** of the sentences below.

- partnership
- limited liability
- unlimited liability
- sole trader
- dividend
- profit
- drawings

1. The term ________________ is used to describe a business owned by one person.

2. Those who have set-up a business and operate as sole traders, or in partnership with others have ____________________________. This means that should their business fail their personal wealth, as well as the amount they have invested in the business as capital, is at risk.

3. The income tax and national contributions paid by sole traders and those in partnership is based on the ____________________their business makes.

4. A limited company distributes the profit it makes to its owners in the form of a ______________.

Question 2.3

In which **two** of the following types of business organisation do the owners of the business take profit from their business in the form of drawings?

	✓
Not for profit club or society	
Sole trader	
Limited company	
Partnership	

Question 2.4

Which **two** of the following statements describes advantages that a partnership generally has when compared to a sole trader?

	✓
The potential to raise more capital to set-up and expand the business	
Profit made by the partnership is shared between the partners	
Responsibilities can be shared between a number of different individuals	
The sharing of management of the business and decision making sometimes leads to disputes between partners	

Question 2.5

Indicate for **each** of the statements below whether the statement is true or false:

Statement	True ✓	False ✓
A not for profit club or society is owned by its members		
The shares in public limited companies are bought and sold on the Stock Exchange		
Those operating in partnership have no option but to share any profit the partnership makes equally between the partners		
A limited company has its own legal identity which is separate to that of its owners. As a 'living person' a company can enter into contracts, employ people, and sue and be sued in its own name		

Lesson 3

Ethics and Business Legislation

Ethics and Business Legislation

Objectives:

By the end of this lesson you should be able to:

- *Understand the term 'ethics'*
- *Understand the need for those working in the accounting profession to comply with a code of conduct and identify the five fundamental principles on which most accounting bodies base their code of conduct*
- *Recognise the need for professional bookkeepers to apply the principles of integrity, objectivity, professional competence and due care, confidentiality and professional behaviour when carrying out their work*
- *Understand the benefits to a professional bookkeeper of operating as a a member of the IAB, and as an IAB 'Registered Bookkeeper'. Recognise grades of membership and understand that IAB members are bound by its framework for regulation and code of practice*
- *Recognise the primary objective of the Data Protection Act 1998*

Introduction

Whether you are employed within the accounts section of a large or medium sized organisation, employed by an independent practice offering accounting services to clients, or are self-employed as a bookkeeper or accountant, you are in a position of **trust**.

Those who employ you, or use your services, will see you as a professional. They will expect you to be competent, reliable and objective and will trust you to do a good job, not only for yourself, but for them. You can gain their trust by acting ethically, with integrity and in a professional manner.

Ethics

Ethics is concerned with the moral principles, values or standards that influence behaviour and are based on what is generally regarded in society as being an acceptable level of behaviour.

Professional ethics are standards, core values, or codes of practice recognised by professional bodies. A **code of ethics** sets out the level of conduct expected from those working within a profession. Society expects a much higher level of moral conduct from professionals than it does from anyone else. Professionals, and those working within a profession, tend to share a number of values which are at the core of establishing an acceptable level of conduct. As a professional bookkeeper you will be expected to:

- Set a good example to others
- Act honourably and with integrity
- Be open and transparent in your dealings
- Be accountable for your actions
- Know your limitations and act within those limitations
- Respect the need for confidentiality
- Always act within the law and comply with regulations

It is worth noting that the code of conduct expected of professionals applies to their personal life as well as their professional life.

Accounting ethics

It is widely recognised that it is in the public interest that those working within the accountancy profession provide services of a consistently high quality, and that as well as having a responsibility to individual clients or employers, they also have a responsibility to act in the public interest.

Most professional accounting bodies have established their own code of conduct which they expect their members to adopt. Such codes of conduct tend to be based on five fundamental principles of professional ethics identified and established by a body known as the International Federation of Accountants (IFAC).

The five fundamental principles established by the IFAC's code of ethics are:

- Integrity
- Objectivity
- Professional competence and due care
- Confidentiality
- Professional behaviour

The principles above can be described as follows:

Integrity – This principle requires those working in the accounting profession to be straightforward and honest in all professional and business relationships. Integrity also requires that bookkeepers and accounting practitioners are fair and truthful in all their dealings either with clients or their employers. They should not be associated with reports, returns or any form of communication that contains false information or omissions and conveys misleading information.

Objectivity – This principle requires those working in the accounting profession not to compromise their professional or business judgement because of personal bias, conflict of interest, or the undue influence of others. Professional accountants are encouraged to avoid relationships that will bias or unduly influence their professional judgement.

Professional competence and due care – Professional competence concerns the requirement that those working in the accounting profession both attain and maintain a level of knowledge and skill that ensures that their clients or employers receive a competent level of service based on current developments in practice. They are expected to keep up to date with changes in legislation, regulations and techniques. Maintaining competence is usually achieved by means of continuing professional development (CPD).

The requirement to act with due care is achieved by acting diligently. Diligence is achieved by acting in accordance with the terms of an assignment, taking care to ensure that tasks are completed carefully, thoroughly and in good time.

Confidentiality – The principle of confidentiality emphasises the need to keep the affairs of clients and employers confidential.

The financial affairs of a business organisation should never be discussed with those outside the organisation, and should never be discussed in a public place where the conversation could be overheard.

Information of a confidential nature should be circulated only to authorised individuals within the organisation and should never be openly discussed. For example, it would be unacceptable for the payroll clerk to discuss the pay of specific employees with other colleagues outside the payroll section. Likewise, it would be a breach of confidentiality if a person responsible for keeping customer and supplier accounts were to openly discuss the account of one particular customer or supplier, with other rival customers and suppliers.

In a private accounting practice it is essential that client confidentiality be respected. A client's business affairs should never be discussed with other clients, or a client's family and friends, without the express permission of the client themselves.

The only circumstances when it is acceptable for any business to provide information to a third-party without the permission of someone in authority to do so, or without the permission of a client to do so, is where there is a legal requirement to pass on information to authorities such as HMRC, or say, information relating to a criminal investigation.

Professional behaviour – This principle imposes an obligation on those working in the accounting profession to comply with relevant laws and regulations. In promoting themselves and carrying out their work they should avoid any action that would discredit the accounting profession or bring it into disrepute.

Professional behaviour also requires those working in the accounting profession to be honest and truthful by not making exaggerated claims for the services they are able to offer, the qualifications they hold, or the experience they have gained.

Membership of the IAB and the framework for regulation

Professional membership of the IAB can enhance your career in accounting financial administration or payroll. The grade of membership awarded is dependent on the level of qualification(s) attained and in some cases the applicants level of practical experience. Membership grades are as follows:

- **AIAB** (Associate Member of the International Association of Bookkeepers)
- **MIAB** (Member of the International Association of Bookkeepers)
- ***FIAB** (Fellow of the International Association of Bookkeepers)

*Fellow members are also entitled to use the title of 'Registered Bookkeeper'

Those applicants who are given IAB membership status are bound by the IAB's 'Framework for Regulation' and its 'Code of Best Practice'. The framework and code is particularly relevant to those individuals who intend to work as self-employed bookkeepers.

Full details of the IAB's Framework for Regulation and its Code of Best Practice are available from the Membership department of the IAB.

Data protection

The Data Protection Act 1998 was introduced to improve the confidentiality of personal data. It establishes principles that must be observed by those business organisations that collect and store personal data which relates to an 'identifiable living person'.

The Act applies to data stored on a computerised system, and to data stored where manual paper based records are kept.

Although the Act relates to all data collection and storage systems it was mainly introduced in response to concerns expressed regarding data stored by businesses and the government about their customers, clients and employees, on a computer database.

The concerns were based on the fact that the computer systems on which personal data is stored are much more accessible than paper based filing systems, computers are often networked which gives organisation-wide access to databases. The use of a computer database also makes it much easier to share information with other organisations

The Act refers to a set of common sense principles that must be followed by those who collect and hold data. These principles, usually referred to as 'The Data Protection Principles', are:

1 Data must be collected and processed fairly and lawfully.

2 Data must only be processed for one or more specified lawful purposes.

3 Data held must be adequate, relevant and not excessive when compared to the specified purpose for which it is required.

4 Data must be accurate and, where necessary, kept up to date.

5 Data must be kept for no longer than is necessary for the purpose for which it is being used.

6 Data must be processed in line with the rights of individuals (data subjects).

7 Data must be kept safe and secure with appropriate technical and organisational measures to protect the information from unauthorised access.

8 Data files may not be transferred outside the European Economic Area, unless the country to which the data is being sent has suitable data protection law.

Whether data is paper based, or computer based, the data must be kept under secure conditions. At the same time, however, there is a need to recognise that information needs to be accessible to those authorised to use it.

A number of simple security measures can be put in place to ensure that information is kept safe and secure, and yet is accessible to authorised persons. For example, measures such as keeping office doors locked when offices are unoccupied, keeping paper based data in lockable cupboards, lockable filings cabinets, lockable desk drawers, or in a safe, should be in place. Paper based materials of a private and confidential nature should be shredded when they are disposed of.

Computer files should be protected by the use of passwords and PIN's to restrict access. Confidential information should be stored on removable files (tapes, discs or CD's) and kept in secure locations. To ensure that personal data is kept under safe and secure conditions requires the use of firewalls to protect the system, and information stored on the system, from contamination or hackers.

Office health and safety

There is no agreed definition as to what constitutes an office, although it is generally accepted that an office is a place where clerical and administrative work is carried out. Although offices are not considered to be high risk places in which to work there are health and safety risks common to office environments that must be identified and controlled.

By law employers have responsibilities for the health and safety of their employees. They are also responsible for the health and safety of customers/clients, suppliers and members of the general public who may visit their premises.

Employees also have health and safety responsibilities. They are responsible for taking steps to ensure their own wellbeing whilst in the workplace, as well as the wellbeing of their colleagues.

The primary piece of legislation covering work-related health and safety in the United Kingdom (UK) is the Health and Safety at Work Act 1974.

The Health and Safety Executive is responsible for enforcing the Act and any other legislation relevant to the working environment.

Risk assessments

The responsibility for health and safety at work should start with the employer carrying out a risk assessment, the purpose of which is to spot health and safety hazards. An employer is legally required to assess risks in the workplace as part of their formal health and safety policy. They are required to:

- Identify hazards
- Decide who could be harmed and how
- Evaluate the risks and decide on precautions
- Record their findings and implement them
- Review their assessment regularly and update their policies and procedures where necessary

The employer's duty of care

All employers have a 'duty of care' in respect of the health, safety and welfare of their employees whilst at work. The main requirements of employers concerning health and safety in an office environment include:

- Making the workplace safe
- Preventing risks to health
- Ensuring that equipment and machinery is safe to use, and that safe working practices are set up and followed
- Making sure that all materials are handled, stored and used safely
- Providing adequate first aid facilities
- Telling employees about any potential hazards from the work they do and giving them information, instructions, training and supervision as needed
- Setting up emergency plans
- Making sure that ventilation, temperature, lighting and toilet, washing and rest facilities all meet health, safety and welfare requirements
- Checking that equipment provided is properly used and regularly maintained
- Preventing or control exposure to substances that may damage their health
- Taking precautions against the risks caused by flammable or explosive hazards, electrical equipment, noise and radiation
- Avoiding potentially dangerous work involving manual handling and, if it can't be avoided, take precautions to reduce the risk of injury
- Ensuring that the right warning signs are provided and looked after
- Reporting certain accidents, injuries, diseases and dangerous occurrences to either the Health and Safety Executive (HSE) or the local authority, depending on the type of business

Maintaining a safe and healthy workplace

Based on their obligation to ensure that the workplace is a safe and healthy environment, and to safeguard employees and visitors to their premises against some of the risks identified above, employers should have a range of general precautions in place. These are likely to include:

Fire safety

- Fitting fire alarm systems in buildings to warn occupants to leave the building in the case of fire. The fitting of smoke and heat detection systems which will automatically trigger the alarm system, giving early warning of a possible fire is a safeguard used by many businesses
- Ensuring that easily combustible materials such as paper, cardboard, or plastics are not left where they clutter-up escape routes, but instead are correctly stored in offices and/or storerooms
- Storing any flammable office materials in appropriate flammables containers and keeping volumes of flammable materials stored on the premises to a minimum
- Implementing a policy of ensuring staff switch off electrical equipment at the end of each day
- Providing a sufficient number of electrical sockets in work areas and limiting the use of three way plug adaptors and multi-way extension leads which could overload circuits
- Providing fire extinguishers which can be easily located, and ensuring that staff know how the fire extinguishers should be used
- Ensuring that fire evacuation procedures and policies are made known to staff and that fire exits are clearly marked
- Holding regular fire drills and regularly testing fire alarms and smoke detectors

Lighting

- Keeping the office and any parts of the building, such as walkways and stairways used by staff and/or visitors, well-lit by providing a mixture of good natural light and artificial light so that people can work and move about safely

- Controlling the direction of natural light and artificial light to ensure an absence of reflections on any display screen equipment (DSE) used by staff

- Reducing problems caused by glare and shadows by fitting adjustable blinds or shades to windows

Air quality

- Making sure that workplaces are properly ventilated with a supply of clean and fresh air and keeping temperatures at a comfortable level

Adequate work space

- Ensuring that workrooms are big enough in which to work and to allow easy movement. There is a legal requirement that at least 11 cubic metres of workspace per person be provided

- Providing workstations which suit employees and the work they carry out

Office machinery

- Keeping office machinery and equipment in good working order

- Ensuring that office machinery is serviced only by authorised service engineers and that staff are aware that they should carry out only basic functions themselves e.g. changing toner cartridges

- Guarding machines such as paper shredders and electric hole punches so that staff cannot come into contact with the moving parts

- Isolating machines which may emit toxic fumes or excessive light, such as photocopiers, by placing them in a well ventilated room away from staff workstations

Noise

- Ensuring that the office layout keeps noise levels to a minimum so that staff are not distracted and can concentrate on their work

- Isolating noisy office machinery, such as printers, by placing them in an enclosed area

- Using noise control methods such as acoustic absorbent room dividers, or even re-siting the office where noise is a problem

Manual handling

- Ensuring that staff are aware of lifting techniques and providing them with the basic skills that will enable them to lift objects without fear of injury from strain

- Providing basic equipment for the purpose of lifting or moving heavy loads e.g. lift trucks, sack barrows, goods lifts etc.

First aid and workplace injuries

- Ensuring that staff are aware of the first aid and accident and emergency procedures in place

- Providing first aid kits

- Appointing a person(s) to take charge of first aid arrangements and accident situations e.g. administering first aid, arranging qualified help and/or calling an ambulance where necessary

- Providing employees with first aid training and providing at least one trained first aider

- Maintaining a system for reporting and recording all work place accidents and/or injuries, however small

General office safety

- Ensuring that floor surfaces are kept clean and are free from clutter – wiping-up any spills immediately, displaying cautionary notices during cleaning and polishing, repairing damaged flooring immediately (loose carpets and damaged floor coverings)
- Fitting handrails to stairways and edge protection to balconies and in elevated walkways
- Ensuring that desks and chairs are regularly inspected for wear and tear and relaying a clear message to staff that desks and chairs are not to be used for the purpose of climbing
- Ensuring that electrical leads or cords do not cross aisles, walkways or workstations and that electrical leads/cords are safe for use

- Ensuring that appropriate storage facilities are in place and that such facilities are used in the correct manner e.g. that shelves and drawers are not overloaded, that storage cabinet doors are not left open, and that materials in filing cabinets are evenly distributed between drawers and that file drawers are closed immediately after use
- Providing bins and/or recycles containers for waste and rubbish and ensuring that the bins/containers are emptied regularly
- Providing stools, steps and ladders for use by staff when storing or retrieving materials from high shelving
- Warning staff against the misuse of office 'tools' such as pens, pencils, paper, letter openers, scissors, and staplers, which can cause cuts, punctures, and related infections if not used correctly

Welfare facilities

- Providing suitable washing facilities with hot and cold water and access to a supply of clean drinking water
- Setting aside areas for rest breaks and to eat meals, including suitable facilities for pregnant women
- Letting employees take appropriate rest breaks and their correct holiday entitlement
- Making sure that employees who work alone, or off-site, can do so safely

The use of computers

Where employers expect their employees to use computers or visual display units (VDU's) as part of their job then the health and safety regulations require them to:

- Look at the VDU workstations in use and assess and reduce any risks
- Ensure that workstations comply with health and safety requirements
- Plan work so that regular breaks are given. The HSE guidance suggests that for every 50-60 minutes continuous screen or keyboard work a break of 5-10 minutes should be allowed. A 'break' can be in the form of a routine that includes different types of work say after every 50-60 minutes VDU/keyboard work

- Arrange for employees using computers and VDU's to have eye tests where necessary
- Give health and safety training and information to employees using a computer and VDU. This will include encouraging employees to sit in a comfortable position, and not to sit in the same position for too long, keep a good posture and sit with their eyes level to the VDU screen

Employees health and safety responsibilities

Whilst the Health and Safety at Work Act gives employees certain rights it also gives them personal responsibilities. Employees have a degree of responsibility for their own wellbeing and that of their colleagues whilst at work.

These responsibilities include:

- Taking reasonable care for their own health and safety
- Where operating equipment or machinery avoiding wearing jewellery or loose clothing
- Taking reasonable care not to put colleagues and members of the public at risk by what they do or don't do in carrying out their work
- Co-operating with employers by undergoing appropriate training and understanding and following the health and safety policy of the employer
- Not interfering with, or misusing, anything provided by an employer for their health, safety and welfare
- Reporting health and safety hazards they identify
- Reporting injuries, strains or illnesses sustained as a result of carrying out their work
- Reporting any injuries or events that might affect their ability to work e.g. becoming pregnant which for example would affect their ability to lift heavy parcels
- Where they operate machinery or drive as part of their job telling their employer if they are taking medication that will make them drowsy. The employer can then make plans to move them to another job or change their duties whilst on medication

Money laundering

Money laundering is the process by which criminally obtained money and other assets (criminal property) are exchanged for 'clean' money or other assets with no obvious link to their criminal origins. Money laundering also includes money, however come by, which is used to fund terrorism.

Money laundering offences include:

- Acquiring, using or possessing criminal property
- Handling the proceeds of crimes such as theft, fraud and tax evasion
- Being knowingly involved in any way with criminal or terrorist property
- Entering into arrangements to facilitate laundering criminal or terrorist property
- Investing the proceeds of crimes in other financial products
- Investing the proceeds of crimes through the acquisition of property/assets
- Transferring criminal property

The Money Laundering Regulations are designed to protect the UK financial system and apply to a number of different types of business. Every business covered by the regulations must be supervised by a supervisory authority. To be fully compliant with the Regulations sole traders and all other firms must implement policies and procedures designed to detect and thereby disrupt activities relating to money laundering and terrorist financing.

Her Majesty's Revenue and Customs (HMRC) supervise the following four business types:

- Money service businesses
- High value dealers
- Trust or company service providers
- Accountancy service providers

The IAB is also one of a number of organisations' which has been granted supervisory authority and can supervise the activities of those IAB members who act as Accountancy Service Providers (this includes those offering bookkeeping and payroll services).

Those practicing members who choose to be supervised by the IAB will be subject to a compliance visit and will need to provide evidence that they are fully conversant with the requirements of the Money Laundering Regulations, are compliant with the principles of 'best practice' set-out in the IAB Code of Conduct for practicing members, and that they have systems and procedures in place that enable them to comply with the Money Laundering Regulations.

Members who are able to demonstrate these requirements must apply for a Certificate of Supervision (associate members), Certificate of Compliance (0-3 years' experience or part-time practice) or Practicing Certificate (4 years + of registration). These certificates can be displayed by members at their office/place of business.

Information on how the IAB discharges its role as a supervisor can be obtained by contacting the IAB Membership Department.

Requirements of the Money Laundering Regulations

Businesses which are registered under the Money Laundering Regulations have certain day-to-day responsibilities, they are required to:

- Assess the risk of their business being used for the purpose of money laundering
- Carry out 'customer/client due diligence measures'
- Put in place internal controls and systems for monitoring suspicious activity
- Appoint a nominated officer who will be responsible for ensuring that the business complies with the Money Laundering Regulations
- Report suspicious activity to the National Crime Agency (NCA)

Risk assessment

Businesses regulated by the Money Laundering Regulations must assess the risk that they may be used for the purpose of money laundering.

The main factors to consider by any business in assessing the risks involved include:

- The types of customers/clients the business has
- Where the business and its customers/clients are based
- The behaviour of its customers/clients

- How customers/clients are introduced to the business
- The products the client business sells and/or the services it offers
- The delivery channels, payment processes (cash over the counter, cheques, electronic transfer etc.) of the business
- Where the funds of the customers/clients of the business come from and go to

The following customer/client 'types' pose the greatest risk to a business:

- Customers/clients who are involved in a business that handles large amounts of cash
- New customers/clients carrying out large 'one-off' transactions
- Customers/clients who aren't local to the business
- Businesses with complicated ownership structures which could conceal underlying beneficiaries
- New customers/clients introduced to the business by others who may not have carried out 'due diligence' thoroughly

Customer/client behaviour patterns that tend to indicate that they pose a potential risk include:

- Not wanting to give identification or providing identification that is unsatisfactory
- Not wanting to reveal the name/identity of a person or persons they represent
- Entering into transactions that don't make commercial sense
- Agreeing to bear very high uncommercial penalties or charges
- Being involved in transactions where it is difficult to check where funds have come from or go to

Having assessed their potential exposure to the risks of money laundering activities, businesses are required to take steps to identify and lessen the risk of money laundering, these include:

- Identifying risks relevant to their business
- Putting in place systems and controls to reduce any risks identified
- Monitoring the business on an ongoing basis to make sure the controls are working
- Identifying and report suspicious transactions or activities to the National Crime Agency (NCA)
- Keeping records of what they did and why

Keeping detailed records shows that a business has made every attempt to comply with the requirements of the Money Laundering Regulations. Types of records that it is good practice to keep include:

- Daily records of transactions with customers/clients
- Receipt books
- Cheque book stubs
- Paying-in books
- Files for correspondence with customers/clients

Due diligence measures

Due diligence involves businesses taking steps to identify their customers/clients and providing evidence that they have a process for monitoring their customer/client business activities.

For an accounting practice, or a self-employed bookkeeper, this means the following information and details must be obtained from clients:

- Their name
- Their photograph on an official document which confirms their identify
- Their residential address or date of birth

The best way of acquiring the above information from clients is by asking them to provide a government-issued document such as a passport or a driving licence. They should also be asked to provide evidence of place of residence which could be established from recent utility bills, bank statements, or other official documents.

Other sources of information about clients include the electoral register and information which may be held by credit reference agencies.

If you have any doubts about a customer's identity and motives for asking you to take on work on their behalf you would be wise not to deal with them.

It is important that a business keeps a record of all client due diligence measures it carries out. An accounting practice or self-employed bookkeeper would need to keep copies of identification documents it obtained from clients. Records kept as part of the due diligence process should be kept for a minimum of five years.

In undertaking due diligence work it is recommended that some detailed research is carried out. Those carrying out due diligence work should not just take information or documentation provided by customers/clients at face value. It is important to recognise that some documents, such as passports and utility bills can be forged, and that identity fraud and identity theft is becoming more and more commonplace.

Simply taking photo-copies of documents provided by clients or noting their responses to questions you ask does not necessarily comply with the requirement of due diligence. Those carrying out due diligence work should undertake at least one independent identity check. There are several Independent organisations which, on payment of an initial registration fee and an additional small fee per enquiry, will help businesses trace, identify and profile their customers.

Appointing a nominated officer

Businesses that are regulated by the Money Laundering Regulations must appoint a 'nominated officer'. The nominated officer must be someone from within the business who will be responsible for ensuring the business complies with the requirements of the Money Laundering Regulations.

For a person acting as a self-employed bookkeeper with no employees, or any other regulated sole trader with no employees, then they themselves would act as the nominated officer of the business.

The role of nominated officer is important, therefore, the person appointed must be someone who:

- Is capable of taking on the responsibility
- Is honest and trustworthy
- Is senior enough to have access to all customer/client files
- Has a sound knowledge of the accounting practices and procedures of the business
- Has the power to make independent decisions regarding the reporting of what is believed to be suspicious customer/client activity

The role of the nominated officer includes liaising with other employees who may report instances of suspicious customer/client activity, and evaluating, and where necessary, reporting suspicions to the National Crime Agency (NCA).

In addition to appointing someone to act as their nominated officer a business must give its staff appropriate training regarding the requirements of the Money Laundering Regulations, their internal policy in respect of complying with the Money Laundering Regulations and the procedure for reporting suspicious activities to the nominated officer.

Reporting suspicious activity

As soon as someone becomes aware of suspicious activity associated with money laundering they should report it to the nominated officer within the business. It is the responsibility of the nominated officer to decide whether or not to send a report or 'disclosure' about the incident to the National Crime Agency (NCA). If the nominated officer believes the incident referred to them could involve a money laundering activity they should suspend transactions associated with the suspicious activity immediately, unless it is unsafe to do so.

If the nominated officer decides to report a suspected money laundering incident they must send details in the form of a Suspicious Activity Report (SAR) to the NCA.

Lesson 3 Practice Questions

Question 3.1

'Those working in the accounting profession must be straightforward and honest in all professional and business relationships. Bookkeepers and accounting practitioners must be fair and truthful in all their dealings with clients or employers, and must not be associated with reports, returns or any form of communication that contains false information or omissions and conveys misleading information'.

Which **one** of the following ethical principles does the statement above refer to?

	✓
Objectivity	
Professional behaviour	
Integrity	

Question 3.2

You work as a self-employed bookkeeper. You are keen to expand the level of your knowledge and skills so that you can offer your clients the best possible service. Having seen several seminars advertised on the HMRC website you recently attended two training days on the subjects of 'Filing VAT Returns' and 'How to Complete an Online Tax Return'.

Your attendance at the two training days is evidence of that you are complying which **one** of the following ethical principles?

	✓
Professional competence and due care	
Objectivity	
Professional behaviour	

Question 3.3

You have recently attended a job interview with a local accounting practice where you had applied for a job as a senior accounts clerk.

At the interview, the manager who interviewed you, made it clear that they were looking for someone who could prepare financial statements for sole traders and partnerships. You told the manager that you had lots of experience in preparing financial statements, although in fact you have no such experience as your only previous experience comes from working for a small company, where your duties were related to bookkeeping rather than accounting.

By giving false information to the manager who interviewed you, and by making exaggerated claims about your experience and competence, which **one** of the following ethical principles have you failed to observe?

	✓
Objectivity	
Professional behaviour	
Confidentiality	

Question 3.4

You work in the payroll section of a local company. Gemma, one of your best friends who works in the sales ledger section of the same company, has asked you if you can let her know what her line manager's salary is.

Which **one** of the following ethical principles would you be failing to comply with if you provided Gemma with the information she has asked for?

	✓
Integrity	
Confidentiality	
Professional behaviour	

Question 3.5

Indicate whether the statement below is true or false:

Statement	True ✓	False ✓
The Data Protection Act 1998 applies only to information and data being stored in a paper-based filing system, and does not cover information and data stored on a computer		
There is no restriction on the period of time for which personal data can be held		
Data must be kept safe and secure with appropriate technical and organisational measures to protect information from unauthorised access		

Question 3.6

Using words that you consider are applicable from the following list complete the gaps in the sentences below:

- Own
- employees
- Offices Shops and Factories Act 1968
- Health and Safety at Work Act 1974
- Local Authority

1 The primary piece of legislation covering work related health and safety legislation in the UK is the ______________________________.

2 Employers are responsible for the health and safety of their ____________________.

3 Employees are responsible for their __________________ health and safety in the workplace as well as the health and safety of their colleagues.

Question 3.7

Which **two** of the following form part of **your** health and safety responsibilities at a place of work?

1 Carrying out repairs to office machinery that you use every day.

2 Complying with your employers health and safety policies.

3 Promptly reporting any work place hazards you identify.

	✓
1 and 2 only	
1 and 3 only	
2 and 3 only	

Question 3.8

Indicate whether **each** of the statements below is true or false:

Statement	True ✓	False ✓
Money laundering is the process by which criminally obtained money and other assets (criminal property) are exchanged for 'clean' money or other assets with no obvious link to their criminal origins. Money laundering also includes money, however come by, which is used to fund terrorism		
The Money Laundering Regulations only apply to large public limited companies. Those operating as sole traders or in partnership are exempt from the requirements of the regulations		

Question 3.9

Indicate whether **each** of the statements below is true or false:

Statement	True ✓	False ✓
You are a self-employed bookkeeper and suspect that one of your clients is laundering money. Your client is important to your business, therefore you would be wise to keep your suspicions to yourself, otherwise the client may take their business elsewhere		
Due diligence involves businesses taking steps to identify their customers/clients and providing evidence that they have a process for monitoring their customer/client business activities		

Question 3.10

Which **two** of the following are essential qualities of someone who is to act as a nominated officer within an accounting practice with a large number of clients?

1 They have been employed by the practice for some time and have proven that they are honest and trustworthy

2 They are senior enough within the organisation to have access to the files of all clients of the practice

3 They are employed at a junior level and, having been with the practice for only a few weeks, have had little or no association with most of the clients of the practice

	✓
1 and 2 only	
1 and 3 only	
2 and 3 only	

Question 3.11

You are employed as an accounts clerk by a local accounting practice. The practice requires its staff to follow correct procedures within the Money Laundering Regulations.

You have a meeting with a prospective new client of the practice and she has been asked to provide proof of her identity so that you can register her as a client with the practice.

Which **one** of the following documents would be suitable as proof of the client's identity:

	✓
A gas bill from 18 months ago	
A letter of reference from a member of the family	
A current full driving licence	

Lesson 4

Bookkeeping and Accounting

Bookkeeping and Accounting

By the end of this lesson you should be able to:

- *Understand the functions of financial accounting and management accounting*
- *Recognise the difference between the activities of bookkeeping and accounting*
- *Recognise the link between the bookkeeping system and the financial statements*
- *Understand the purpose of the trading and profit and loss account, and balance sheet*

Introduction

Accounting is made up of two main functions i.e. financial accounting and management accounting. These functions can be described as follows:

Financial accounting is concerned with financial record keeping and the use of information from within the financial records to prepare financial statements.

Management accounting is specifically associated with the process of providing financial information for use within the business. The purpose of management accounting is to provide financial information at a time and in a format that makes the information suitable for use in the planning and control of a business.

Bookkeeping and accounting

Bookkeeping is the routine by which day-to-day business transactions are systematically processed and recorded in a business's accounting system. The role of the bookkeeper is mainly concerned with the preparation and checking of business documents, the recording of transactions in the accounting system, and the preparation of reconciliations to check the accuracy of their processing.

The system used by a business to record its business transactions usually depends on the volume and nature of the transactions to be processed, and the competence of the individual(s) responsible for keeping the financial records. However, the basic requirement of any accounting system is that it is effective, efficient and secure. Transactions need to be processed with speed and accuracy and the procedures used, and controls in place, must ensure that opportunities to commit acts of fraud by those operating the system are minimised, and that data contained within the system (much of which is confidential) is kept under safe and secure conditions.

Smaller sole trader and partnership organisations often use a bookkeeping system known as the single entry system. This system requires transactions to be recorded only once in the system. The single entry system usually consists of a simple cash book or spread sheet, where receipts and payments of the business are recorded and analysed. Such systems are easy to operate and meet the bookkeeping requirements of most small businesses.

Medium size or large businesses tend to use a system of bookkeeping known as the double entry system.

Whichever system of bookkeeping a business uses the system must be set up so that the financial information provided by the system includes:

- The income earned by the business from trading and/or non-trading activities.

- The costs of buying materials to be used in a manufacturing process, goods for resale, and expenses incurred in the running and administration of the business.

- The nature and value of the assets of the business (what it owns, what it is owed and the amounts it holds as cash in hand or in a bank account)

- The amounts owed by a business to organisations or individuals other than its owner or owners i.e. the liabilities of the business

- The claim of the owner or owners on the assets of the business (the capital invested in their business by sole traders, partners, or shareholders)

Accounting is associated with the classification, summarising, measurement, interpretation and communication of financial information. The accountant uses financial information from within a bookkeeping system to prepare financial statements for a business. Financial statements include the:

- Profit and Loss Account
- Balance Sheet

The profit and loss account is prepared for a specific period of time (normally a financial year), its purpose is to show whether, over the period of time, the business has generated a profit or loss. The account is prepared using the following information from within the bookkeeping system:

- The income earned by the business from trading and/or non-trading activities.

- The costs of buying goods for resale (where a business trades), and the expenses incurred in the running and administration of the business.

If the income a business has earned in an accounting period from its trading and/or non-trading activities exceeds its costs and expenses in the same accounting period then the business has operated at a profit. However, should the costs and expense of a business exceed the income it has earned in the period, then the business has made a loss.

The profit and loss account prepared for a business which trades is often referred to as the 'trading and profit and loss account'.

Having prepared the profit and loss account at the year-end any net profit made by a business belongs to the owner(s) of the business and is added to the capital claim of the business owner(s). Where a business makes a net loss, the loss is deducted from the capital claim of the owner.

An example of a profit and loss account prepared at the financial year-end 31 May 201Y from the financial records kept on behalf of Tots-2-Teens, a business which is owned by Amy Dejak, is provided on the next page.

Tots-2-Teens Profit and Loss Account for the Year Ended 31May 201Y			
	£	**£**	**£**
Sales			375,296
Less Cost of Goods Sold			
Opening stock	58,056		
Add Purchases	249,730		
		307,786	
Less Closing stock		52,180	
Cost of Sales			255,606
Gross Profit			119,690
Less Expenses			
Rent, rates and insurances		15,880	
Heat and light		2,210	
Wages and salaries		50,440	
Vehicle expenses		6,800	
General expenses		6,560	
Depreciation charges		6,620	
			88,510
Net profit			31,180

The balance sheet is prepared for a business using the following financial information within the bookkeeping system:

- The nature and value of the assets of the business (what it owns, what it is owed and the amounts it holds as cash in hand or in a bank account)
- The liabilities of the business (amounts owed by a business to organisations or individuals other than its owner or owners)
- The claim of the owner(s) on the assets of the business (the capital invested in the business by its owner or owners)

The balance sheet is prepared after the preparation of its profit and loss account. It shows the financial position of a business as at a particular point in time (usually the financial year end). The balance sheet is sometimes referred to as a 'financial window' as it provides the reader with information relating to what a business owns (its assets) and what it owes (its capital and liability claims) 'frozen in time'.

The following is an example of a balance sheet which was prepared on behalf of Tots-2-Teens at the financial year-end 31 May 201Y, following the preparation of the business's profit and loss account.

Tots-2-Teens Balance Sheet at 31 May 201Y			
	£	**£**	**£**
Fixed Assets	**Cost**	**Less Depreciation to Date**	**Net Book Value**
Fixtures and fittings	10,000	4,500	5,500
Vehicles	40,000	19,520	20,480
	50,000	24,020	25,980
Current Assets			
Stock	52,180		
Trade debtors	44,250		
Bank	12,600		
Cash	100		
		109,130	
Less Current Liabilities			
Trade creditors	46,980		
Value added tax (VAT)	6,950		
		53,930	
Working capital			55,200
			81,180
Financed By:			
Capital	82,000		
Add Net Profit	31,180		
		113,180	
Less Drawings		32,000	
			81,180

At this level in your studies your ability to prepare financial statements is **not** assessed. Therefore, at this point in time there is no need to concern yourself with the procedures required to prepare financial statements, or their presentation. Your ability to prepare and present financial statements will be developed as you progress through the qualification framework.

The example profit and loss account and balance sheet above are provided only for reference, and to emphasise the importance of the work of the bookkeeper.

The financial statements are prepared using balances on accounts within the bookkeeping system. Therefore, the need for transactions to be correctly classified, coded and accurately recorded in the bookkeeping system is of prime importance. The bookkeeping system links with the financial statements and the information in the financial statements i.e. the profit or loss made by the business and its financial position, is largely dependent on the accuracy of the financial records kept by the bookkeeper.

Lesson 4 Practice Questions

Question 4.1

Which **one** of the following statements best describes the function of accounting?

	✓
The classification, summarising, measurement, interpretation and communication of financial information	
The routine of systematically processing and recording the day-to-day financial transactions of a business in the accounting system	
The provision of financial information at a time and in a format that makes the information suitable for use within the business for the purpose of planning and control	

Question 4.2

Which **one** of the following is prepared for the purpose of showing the financial position of a business as at a particular point in time?

	✓
Trial balance	
Trading and profit and loss account	
Balance sheet	

Lesson 5

Bookkeeping Systems

Bookkeeping Systems

By the end of this lesson you should be able to:

- *Define the term 'business transaction' and recognise the system of recording business transactions known as 'double entry'*
- *Recognise the advantages of using a computerised bookkeeping system*
- *Understand the need for safety, security and confidentiality and recognise measures taken to protect computer hardware, software and restrict access to a computerised accounting system*
- *Understand the need for a back-up policy as a safeguard against the loss of data*
- *Understand the purpose of the Data Protection Act and recognise the principles which apply to the collection and storage of data*

Introduction

In the previous Lesson, you learned that the work of the bookkeeper is at the core of the financial accounting system. The records kept by the bookkeeper are used to prepare the financial statements of the business. It is, therefore, extremely important that the bookkeeper can correctly classify transactions and process them accurately.

Double entry bookkeeping

A business transaction is a business event which results in goods and/or services being provided by a supplier, for which the customer will pay either immediately (cash transaction), or at a later date (credit transaction). In a double entry system a record of the goods or services a business has supplied and received, and payments it has made and received, are entered in accounts which are kept in a ledger.

Each ledger account is given an account title and has a left-hand side - debit (DR) side, and a right-hand side - credit (CR) side. Transaction dates, details and amounts (values) can be entered on each side of a ledger account. Each transaction is recorded in the bookkeeping system with corresponding debit and credit entries.

Nowadays, many businesses use computerised accounting systems which are double entry based. Large businesses tend to use computerised accounting systems that are customised i.e. specifically tailored to their own needs. Unfortunately, such bespoke systems are usually beyond the means of most medium sized or small businesses as they are expensive to develop and operate.

However, this is not to say that medium sized and small business cannot benefit from the advantages of using a computerised accounting system. In fact, there are several 'low cost' off-the-shelf accounting programs which are readily available to such businesses. These accounting programs are suitable for use in preparing business documents, keeping financial records and generating financial statements and reports.

Advantages of using a computerised bookkeeping system

Compared to a manual bookkeeping system a computerised system offers a number of advantages to the user, these include:

Speed and accuracy – the processing of data using a computerised accounting system is much quicker and more accurate than processing data using a manual system. This is mainly due to the fact that a computerised accounting system is integrated. This means that a transaction is entered once in the system and the software has the capability of recording all the entries relating to the transaction in appropriate ledger accounts.

Automation – some of the routine tasks associated with bookkeeping such as the preparation of business documents, bank reconciliation, generating reports on customer and supplier activity, and preparing a trial balance can be generated automatically from the system.

Control and decision making – the system is capable of providing up-to-date information to the owner(s)/managers of a business which allows them to better control the business by being able to make informed decisions quickly.

The need for training

Perhaps the main problem associated with the use of computerised accounting systems is that they are often used by untrained bookkeepers. Such individuals have little or no knowledge of the principles of double entry bookkeeping, nor do they have the appropriate training and experience in bookkeeping to classify and process business transactions correctly. As a result, they often make errors which impact on the value of the information they process, inaccurate information is then used to prepare financial statements for the business, which are then used by owners and managers for the purpose of controlling and managing the business and making business decisions.

It is, therefore, recommended that those who intend to use a computerised accounting system acquire a sound knowledge of the basics of bookkeeping before they start to use such a system to process business transactions and prepare financial statements and reports.

Safety, security and confidentiality

It is important that those who intend to process financial data using a computerised accounting system carry out several basic safety checks before they turn on their computer. Checks include:

Checking that power plugs are connected properly, that power sockets are not overloaded, and that power sockets are switched on.

Checking that power cables are not frayed. Should cables become frayed then live wires could be exposed which may cause an electric shock. It is also necessary to check that cables running from the computer to the power socket are not causing a trip hazard.

Checking that peripherals such as a mouse, keyboard, screen, external hard drives and printer are properly connected. Failure to do so may result in the system not operating correctly and a loss of data.

At the end of each working day the computer needs to be correctly shut down. This procedure includes ensuring that each program which is open on the computer is closed down having first saved the data. The computer itself will then also have to be shut down. Peripheral such as the screen and printer must be switched off and the power can then be switched off and all plugs disconnected at the power socket.

Security measures also need to be in place and the confidentiality of the system needs to be maintained.

Business premises, including offices where computers are kept, need to be made safe and secure. Measures taken to prevent unauthorised access to business premises and the theft of computer hardware include:

- Restricting access to business premises
- Deterring thieves by fitting CCTV systems and alarms
- Keeping office doors locked when offices are unoccupied

Computer viruses can corrupt computer software and lead to the loss of data and in extreme cases failure of the computer system. Measures taken to protect software from viruses include installing virus protection software which will:

- Provide a firewall to act as a barrier to keep destructive elements out of a computer or computer network
- Regularly run checks to detect viruses and destroy any viruses found
- Check for damaged and corrupt files and, if possible, repair damaged files

Computer hackers and predators are also a threat to computer security. Hackers and predators break into computer systems to steal, change or destroy information. Several steps can be taken to protect a computer system from hackers and predators, these include:

- Installing a 2-way firewall (a firewall that's designed to help protect a computer system from hackers getting in and any malicious programs on a computer from sending data out)
- Using protective software to check that storage media (devices that store application and user information) is virus free before opening or downloading any files
- Practicing safe email protocol – by not opening messages from unknown senders and immediately deleting messages suspected to be spam
- Installing antivirus and antispyware protection

Threats to computer hardware and software can come from within, as well as outside, the organisation. There are several measures that will reduce risks faced by a business from its employees. These include:

- Keeping office doors locked when offices are unoccupied
- Using passwords to restrict access to the computer system
- Ensuring that confidential and sensitive data is not left in open-view on the computer screen
- Ensuring paper-based data is filed away in a locked filing cabinet or cupboard and not left out in open view, say on a printer or a desk
- Not allowing employees to borrow software discs which they could copy or give to others to copy, thus creating illegal versions of software

Those who operate as bookkeepers and process data, either for an employer or for a client, must recognise that sensitive information should not be discussed with, or distributed to, individuals within or outside the organisation who are not authorised to receive such information.

The business affairs of customers and suppliers of the organisation should never be disclosed to, or discussed with, other customers and suppliers. Nor should the affairs of a business be openly discussed in a public place, such as a café, restaurant or pub.

If working in an accounting practice, either on an employed or self-employed basis, the need for confidentiality in dealing with the business affairs of clients is important. Information must never be disclosed to third-parties without the permission of the client, even if information is requested by the client's close family or friends.

The only circumstances when it is acceptable to provide information to a third-party is where there is a legal requirement to pass on information to authorities such as Her Majesty's Revenue & Customs (HMRC), or say, information relating to a criminal investigation.

Security within an organisation is also improved by having systems based upon appropriate procedures and controls. For example, those working at a junior/general clerical level will have limited responsibilities and very little or no authorisation within the organisation. They will most probably need to seek authorisation from appropriate people within the organisation to place an order or pay an invoice. Although they may be required to prepare cheques to be issued by the business it is very unlikely they will be authorised to sign cheques – in which case they would need to present cheques for signature to those with the authority to sign cheques (designated signatories).

In their dealings and communications with those outside the organisation, particularly customers, clients and suppliers, those employed in a business at any level need to be courteous and polite. If a promise is made to someone outside the organisation to provide information, resolve an issue or correct an error, then the promise must be acted on in a timely and effective manner.

Backing up data

It is recommended that where computerised accounting systems are in use a business introduce a policy regarding the backup of data.

Copies of data are necessary as a safeguard against unforeseen events such as fire, theft or computer failure, which may result in the loss of data.

Businesses are advised to take backups at regular intervals, some computer systems have in-built programmes which will automatically take backups at regular intervals, or can be programmed to take backups of all or specific files at set times during each working day.

Lesson 5 Practice Questions

Question 5.1

Which **one** of the following is a measure taken as a safeguard against unforeseen events such as fire, theft or computer failure, which may result in the loss of data?

	✓
Making sure office doors are locked when offices are unoccupied	
Taking regular backups of data	
Fitting CCTV systems and alarms	

Question 5.2

Which **one** of the following is an example of a credit transaction?

	✓
A business supplies goods to a customer and gives the customer 30 days in which to pay for the goods supplied	
A business supplies goods to a customer on a cash and carry basis	

Question 5.3

Which **one** of the following is most likely to give credit to its customers?

	✓
A supermarket supplying goods to members of the public	
A large company whose only customers are other traders	

Question 5.4

Which of the following are measures taken by businesses to restrict access to their business documents and records?

1. Keeping documents and records in a lockable drawer, cupboard, filing cabinet or safe.
2. Checking that power plugs are connected properly, that power sockets are not overloaded, and that power sockets are switched on.
3. Restricting access to computer systems by issuing passwords and PIN's to staff.
4. Keeping office doors locked when offices are unoccupied.

	✓
1, 2 and 3 on the list	
1, 3 and 4 on the list	
2, 3 and 4 on the list	

Question 5.5

You are working in the accounts section of a local business. Which of the following are examples of confidentiality that the business would expect you to observe?

1. Not discussing the affairs of the business in a public place.
2. Not discussing the affairs of customers of the business with other customers.
3. Not disclosing business information to third-parties without permission to do so.

	✓
Examples 1 and 2 on the list	
Examples 2 and 3 on the list	
All three examples on the list	

Question 5.6

Which of the following are examples of safety checks that should be carried out before users of a computerised accounting system turn on their computer?

1 Checking the system for damaged and corrupt files

2 Checking that power plugs are connected properly, that power sockets are not overloaded, and that power sockets are switched on.

3 Checking that cables running from the computer to the power socket are not trailing and causing a trip hazard.

	✓
1 and 2 on the list	
1 and 3 on the list	
2 and 3 on the list	
All three examples on the list	

Lesson 6

Source Documents

Source Documents

By the end of this lesson you should be able to:

- *Recognise the purpose of a range of business documents files and supplementary information, and understand how they are used as the source from which transactions are recorded in a bookkeeping system*

- *Recognise the HMRC rules for retaining source documents*

Introduction

The process of recording transactions in a computerised accounting system involves several stages. These include:

- Creating or collecting appropriate source documents to support transactions
- Classifying transactions
- Coding transactions
- Inputting transactions

Each of the above stages is important as it impacts on the reliability and validity of the information within the accounting system, however the purpose of this lesson is to introduce you to some of the source documents used in business.

Source documents

A range of business documents are used as the source from which documents are prepared and/or recorded in a business's accounting system. These include:

Purchase order – when a decision to buy a supply of goods or services has been made the buyer makes out an official purchase order, a copy of which is sent to the supplier. A typical purchase order contains the following information:

- A purchase order number
- the goods that are required (with catalogue number or product code number)
- the place for delivery (this may be different to the address given on the letter head)
- the date delivery is required
- the agreed price
- the quality or specification required

The following is an example of a purchase order sent by the head buyer of CED Limited to Lamex (Office Products) when they ordered new workstations and swivel chairs for their telesales office on 13 March 201Y:

PURCHASE ORDER			**Order No:** 7609	
		CED LIMITED **28 Gathurst Road, Orrell WN6 OXX**		
			VAT Reg No: 987 6543 21	
To:	Lamex (Office Products) 66 Bankes Avenue Pemberton WN2 OPP		**Date:** 13 March 201Y	
Quantity	**Cat No**	**Description**	**Unit Price** **£ p**	**Total Price** **£ p**
6	RP 3682	Beech Workstations	125.00	750.00
2	FS 0938	Swivel Chairs	70.00	140.00
		Sub-total		890.00
		VAT @ 20%		178.00
		Total		1,068.00

Delivery to:

CED Limited, 28 Gathurst Road, Orrell WN6 OXX

Delivery 10 days from date of order. Carriage paid.

P Roberts
P Roberts (Head Buyer)

Delivery note – when goods are received from a supplier a document known as a delivery note is usually packed in with the goods. The customer uses the delivery note to check that the items stated on the delivery note have been received. The delivery note should also be matched against the purchase order to which it applies.

The following is an example delivery note sent by the sales manager of Lamex (Office Products) to the head buyer of CED Limited having delivered to them the goods they ordered on 13 March 201Y:

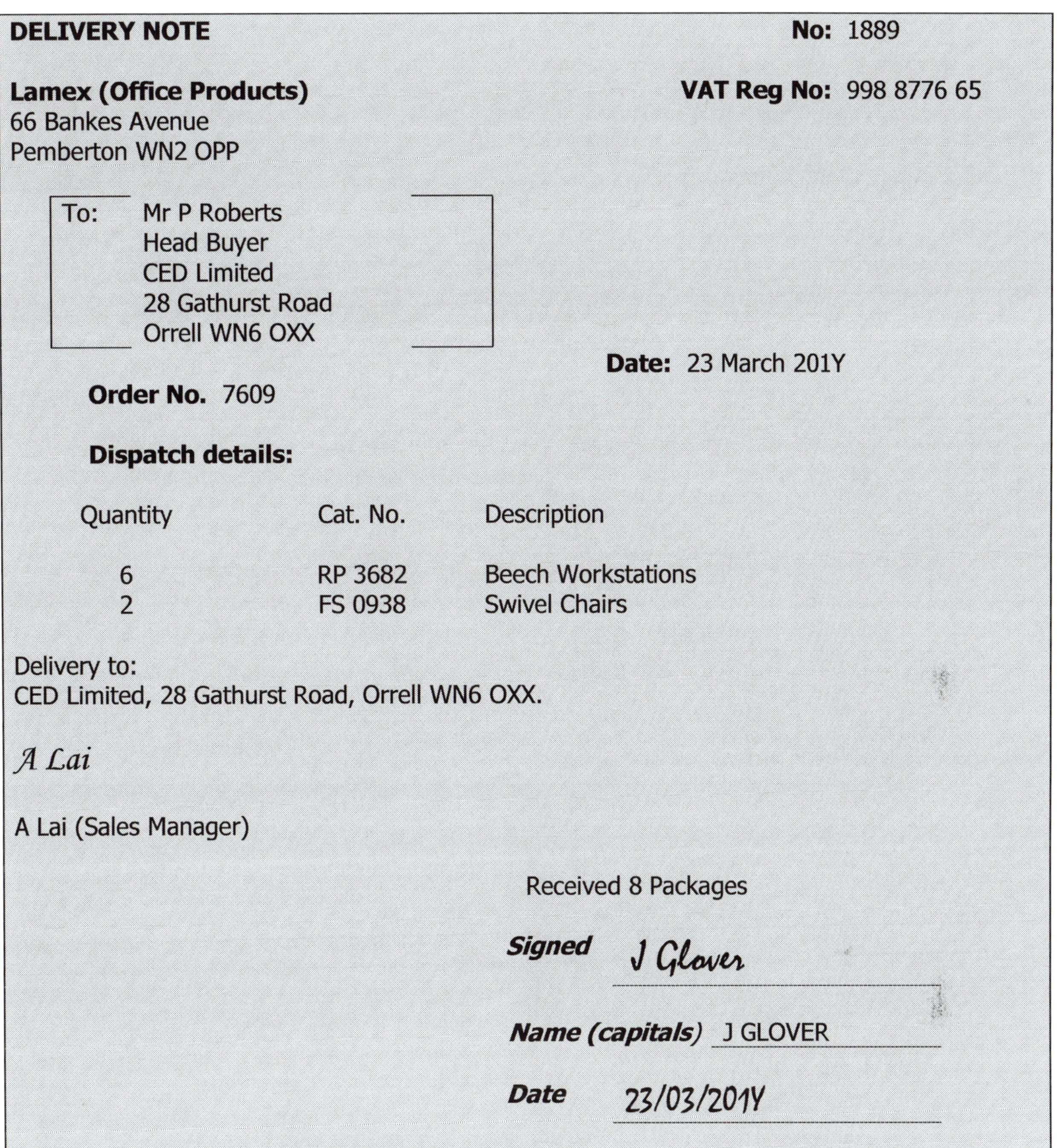

DELIVERY NOTE **No:** 1889

Lamex (Office Products) **VAT Reg No:** 998 8776 65
66 Bankes Avenue
Pemberton WN2 OPP

To: Mr P Roberts
Head Buyer
CED Limited
28 Gathurst Road
Orrell WN6 OXX

Date: 23 March 201Y

Order No. 7609

Dispatch details:

Quantity	Cat. No.	Description
6	RP 3682	Beech Workstations
2	FS 0938	Swivel Chairs

Delivery to:
CED Limited, 28 Gathurst Road, Orrell WN6 OXX.

A Lai

A Lai (Sales Manager)

Received 8 Packages

Signed J Glover

Name (capitals) J GLOVER

Date 23/03/201Y

Invoices issued – most business-to-business transactions (where one business supplies goods or supplies services to another business) are credit based. This means the supplier gives the customer a period of time in which to pay for the goods or services supplied, a period of 30 day's credit is common. When goods or services are supplied on credit the supplier supports the transaction by issuing an invoice to the customer.

The following is an example invoice sent by Lamex (Office Products) to the accounts office of CED Limited on 24 March 201Y charging them for goods delivered to them the previous day:

INVOICE

Lamex (Office Products)
66 Bankes Avenue
Pemberton WN2 OPP

To: Accounts Department
CED Limited
28 Gathurst Road
Orrell WN6 OXX

INVOICE No: 2145

Account: 886 CED

Order No: 7609 **Invoice date (tax point):** 24 March 201Y

Quantity	Description	Catalogue No	Unit Price £	Unit Price p	VAT Rate %	Goods Total £	Goods Total p
6	Beech Workstations	RP 3682	125	00	20	750	00
2	Swivel Chairs	FS 0938	70	00	20	140	00
		Goods Total				890	00
		VAT @ 20%				178	00
		Invoice Total				1,068	00

Terms: Net 30 days
Carriage paid

E&OE **VAT Reg No:** 998 8776 65

The supplier keeps an account in the name of each of its credit customers in its ledger, and the sales transaction is recorded in the accounting system from the invoice.

Where invoices issued to customers are generated using the computerised package the postings required to record the sales on credit transaction are processed automatically by the system. However, if the accounting software is not used to generate the sales invoice, i.e. the invoice is created independently of the computerised system, a copy of the invoice issued to the customer needs to be coded and the transaction postings are input from the coded invoice.

Transactions to record a sale on credit include a posting in a sales account, a posting in an account known as the VAT sales tax account (where the supplier is registered for VAT), and a posting in the account of the customer.

Credit notes issued – if a credit customer returns goods to a supplier, or has been overcharged on a sales invoice, then to reduce the value of the original invoice, the supplier will issue a credit note to the customer.

The following is an example of a credit note issued by Lamex (office Products) on 28 March 201Y to CED Limited when they returned a swivel chair invoiced to them on 24 March 201Y.

CREDIT NOTE **No: 152**

From: **Lamex (Office Products)**
66 Bankes Avenue
Pemberton WN2 OPP

To: CED Limited
28 Gathurst Road
Orrell WN6 OXX

Account: 886 CED
Date/Tax point: 28 March 201Y
Invoice No: 68868

Quantity	**Description**	**Catalogue Number**	**Unit Price**		**VAT Rate %**	**Total Amount**	
			£	**p**		**£**	**p**
1	Swivel Chair	FS 0938	70	00	20.0	70	00
			Goods Total			70	00
			VAT @ 20%			14	00
			Total Credit			84	00

Reason for credit:

Chair faulty – gas lift defective.

VAT Reg No: 998 8776 65

Credit notes generated using the computerised package are processed automatically by the system. However, if the accounting software is not used to generate the credit note, i.e. the credit note is created independently of the computerised system, a copy of the credit note issued to the customer has to be coded and the postings are input from the coded credit note.

Transactions to record goods returned by a customer, or to correct an overcharge on an invoice, include a posting in a sales returns account, a posting in the VAT sales tax account (where the supplier is registered for VAT and the transaction is subject to VAT), and a posting in the account of the customer.

Invoices received – where a business purchases goods for resale on credit, or is supplied with services on credit, they will receive an invoice from the supplier.

A business should keep an account in the name of each of its credit suppliers in its ledger. Invoices received from suppliers must be checked against purchase orders, delivery notes, and for arithmetic accuracy. Once these checks have been completed satisfactorily the invoice can be coded and input onto the accounting system.

Care must be taken when coding and inputting information from invoices received. For example, invoices received from suppliers in respect of goods bought specifically for resale (purchases) require a posting to a purchases account, a VAT purchase tax account (where a business is VAT registered and the supply is subject to VAT), and the account of the supplier.

Where a business is being invoiced for expenses and services, for example, repairs to a vehicle, telephone and internet charges, stationery, rates, insurances, advertising etc., then the invoice needs to be coded to the correct expense account, and postings made to the appropriate expense account, the VAT purchase tax account (where the business is VAT registered and the supply is subject to VAT), and the supplier account.

Invoices received for some services, such as general rates, water rates, telephone and internet services are often referred to as 'bills'.

Credit notes received – where a business returns goods previously purchased for resale on credit to a supplier, or has been overcharged by a supplier on an invoice, they will receive a credit note from the supplier.

Credit notes received must be checked for accuracy, coded and recorded in the accounting system. Inputting the information from the credit note includes making a posting in the appropriate account i.e. purchases returns account or expense account, making a posting in a VAT purchase tax account (where the business is VAT registered and the transaction is subject to VAT), and making a posting in the account of the supplier.

Cash register (till) receipt - a cash based transaction takes place when the customer pays the supplier immediately for any goods or services they receive.

Where customers pay by cash payment is usually made in the form of cash (notes and coins), by plastic card (debit card or credit card), or cheque. Cash transactions should be supported by a receipt issued by the supplier to the customer.

Some traders will issue a handwritten receipt to customers who pay in cash, however most traders issue a receipt generated by a cash register (till). Where traders use a till, the till will usually be used to generate a receipt for each sales transaction. The till will also generate a report at the end of each day's trading, the end of day report will give the trader a summary of the day's cash sales. Where a trader issues a receipt to another business in respect of a cash sale it will normally issue the business customer with a VAT receipt.

Hand written or till generated receipts are used by the supplier to record the receipt of cash, cash sales, and VAT sales tax (where a business is registered for VAT) in their accounting system. Businesses making payment by cash will need to collect a receipt from the supplier and use it as the source document from which the cash payment is recorded in their accounting system.

Other documents – in addition to the documents above there may be other documents and files which are used by a business when preparing outgoing documentation and checking incoming documentation. The following fall into this category:

Petty cash vouchers – some businesses keep a petty cash float i.e. a small amount of cash in the form of notes and coins, from which payments for some business expenses are made.

When payment is made from the petty cash float a receipt should be collected from the supplier. Details are copied from the receipt on to a petty cash voucher. The petty cash voucher is then coded and used as the source document to record the petty cash expenditure in the accounting system.

The following is an example of a petty cash voucher made out by the Kerry Carson, the petty cashier at Lamex (Office Products), from a receipt submitted by one of its employees, Jason Roberts, who recently attended a business meeting at the premises of a supplier and took a taxi from the supplier's premises to the station. The expenditure was authorised by the Lei Wu, Jason's line manager at Lamex (Office Products).

As the taxi company used by Jason is VAT registered the fare they charged is inclusive of VAT. Lamex (Office Products) are able to claim back the VAT they have paid.

Speedy Taxi Co **Receipt** **Date:** 29/3/201Y	
	AMOUNT **£**
Received with thanks	12.00
(includes VAT)	
Signed: B Johnson **Driver Speedy Taxi Co** VAT Reg No: 458 4387 69	

	No: 20
Lamex (Office Products) **Petty Cash Voucher**	
	Date: 29/3/201Y
	AMOUNT £
Taxi fare	10.00
VAT	2.00
Total	12.00
Claimant:	*Jason Roberts*
Authorised by:	*Lei Wu*
Petty Cashier:	*Kerry Carson*

Entries to record the petty cash expenditure in the accounting system will be posted from the petty cash voucher to the travel expenses account, VAT purchase tax account and petty cash account.

Most businesses which keep a petty cash float operate a petty cash system known as the **imprest system**. Under this system a petty cash float, sufficient to make payments from petty cash for a given period of time (say a week, or a month), is agreed upon.

The level of the petty cash imprest float is likely to vary from business to business. At the end of the agreed period the petty cash float is 'topped-up' to the agreed imprest balance. For example:

Lamex (Office Products) Limited has set a petty cash imprest balance of £100.00. It has been agreed that the petty cash float be restored at the end of each week. On Friday 31 March 201Y, there was £12.50 remaining in the petty cash box, therefore the float was topped up to the original imprest balance of £100.00 by adding an amount of £87.50 to restore the balance.

It should be noted that the amount required to restore a petty cash balance under the imprest system to the agreed imprest amount is always the amount spent out of petty cash when making petty cash payments. As can be seen in the example above the petty cash expenditure in the week was £87.50 and this was the amount that had to be put back into the petty cash box to restore the float to the agreed imprest amount of £100.00.

Cheque book counterfoils – where a payment is made by cheque details from the cheque should be copied onto the cheque book counterfoil/stub. Some businesses will use their cheque book counterfoils as the source document for processing payments made by cheque, particularly in circumstances where the transaction lacks any other form of documentation. For example, drawings taken by the owner of a business from the business bank current account are often processed from the cheque book counterfoil.

The following is an example of a cheque book counterfoil completed by David Vogel, the owner of Lamex (Office Products), when he withdrew £2,000.00 from the business bank account on 30 March 201Y as personal drawings:

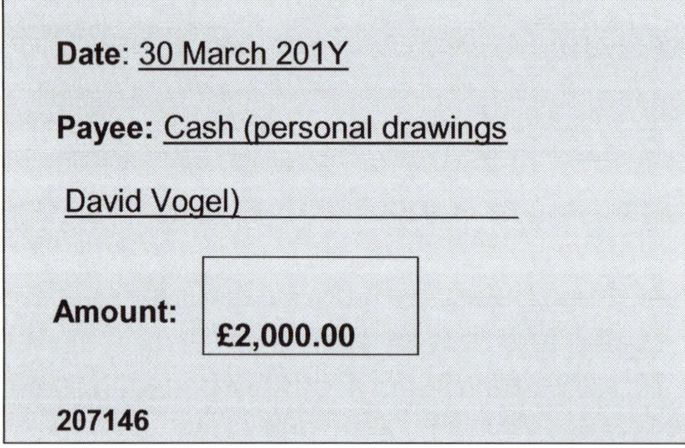

Date: 30 March 201Y

Payee: Cash (personal drawings David Vogel)

Amount: **£2,000.00**

207146

Paying-in slips **–** some businesses will record all amounts they receive by cash or cheque in a cash account in their accounting system until the cash and cheques are banked. Then, on banking the cash and cheques, they record the cash going out of the cash account and into the bank account.

The transfer of cash to the bank account is known as a 'contra entry' and in a computerised accounting system a transfer function, usually found in bank accounts area, is used to transfer amounts from the cash account to the bank account. You will be shown how this function is used as you progress with your studies.

The paying-in slip is the document completed when monies are paid over the counter of the bank into a bank current account. It is also the source document from which the transaction to transfer monies from the cash account to the bank account is input onto the computerised accounting system.

The following is an example of a paying-in slip completed when cash and cheques were paid into the bank current account of Lamex (Office Products) on 31 March 201Y. Using the paying-in slip as the source document entries will be made in the cash account and bank account in the accounting system of Lamex (Office Products) to account for the cash paid into the bank account:

Paying-in slip:

Date: 31 March 201Y		
Credit: 74547066		
£50 notes		
£20 notes	250	00
£10 notes	150	00
£5 notes	60	00
£2/£1	20	00
50p		
20p		
10p, 5p		
Bronze		
Total Cash	480	00
Total cheques etc	3,525	00
£	4,005	00

bank giro credit

Date: 31/3/201Y

Cashier's stamp and initials

Code No 30-40-50
Bank: **Northern Bank Plc**
Branch: Pemberton

Credit: Lamex (Office Products)
Account No: 74547066

Number of Cheques 8

Paid in by: Anna Vogel

£50 notes		
£20 notes	250	00
£10 notes	150	00
£5 notes	60	00
£2/£1	20	00
50p		
20p		
10p, 5p		
Bronze		
Total Cash	480	00
Total cheques etc	3,525	00
£	4,005	00

Supplier statement of account **–** it is common practice for a supplier to send each of its credit customers a statement of account at the end of each month. The statement of account is a copy of the account of the customer as it appears in the ledger of the supplier and summarises in date order the transactions which have taken place between the two parties during the previous month.

On receipt of the statement of account the customer should compare the postings on the statement with those on the supplier account in his own ledger to ensure that the statement and his own records are up-to-date and correct. Having reconciled the statement of account postings with the postings on the supplier account in his own ledger the customer will then use the statement of account to determine the amount due for payment.

The following is the account of CED Limited in the accounting system of Lamex (Office Products) at the month end 31 March 201Y:

CED Limited								
201Y	**Details**	**Debit**		**Credit**		**Balance**		**DR/CR**
		£	**p**	**£**	**p**	**£**	**p**	
24 March	Invoice 2145	1,068	00			1,068	00	DR
28 March	Credit note 152			84	00	984	00	DR

The following is an example statement of account issued by Lamex (Office Products) to CED Limited at the month end 31 March 201Y:

STATEMENT OF ACCOUNT

Lamex (Office Products) Limited
66 Bankes Avenue
Pemberton WN2 OPP

To: Accounts Department
CED Limited
28 Gathurst Road
Orrell WN6 OXX

Date: 31 March 201Y

Account: 886 CED

201Y	**Details**	**Debit**		**Credit**		**Balance**	
		£	**p**	**£**	**p**	**£**	**p**
24 March	***Invoice 2145***	***1,068***	***00***			***1,068***	***00***
28 March	***Credit Note 152***			***84***	***00***	***984***	***00***
	Amount now due				**£**	***984***	***00***

VAT Reg No: 998 8776 65

Remittance advice – common forms of payment, where one business pays another business for goods or services supplied on credit, include BACS (Bankers' Automated Clearing Service), cheque, or nowadays, over the telephone or internet using a business's debit card or credit card.

The BACS system is ideal where bulk payments of varying amounts are made. Therefore, it is mainly used where a business regularly makes payments to a number of suppliers. Businesses making payments to suppliers by BACS will often do so by means of a 'BACS run', say once a month.

Where a business makes only a small number of payments to suppliers, for example, by paying invoices daily as they fall due, will usually make payment by cheque, or over the telephone or internet using a debit card or credit card.

Where a business makes payment to suppliers by BACS or cheque then it should send the supplier a document known as a 'remittance advice'. The remittance advice gives details of the payment being made, and confirms that payment has been made. The customer issuing the remittance advice, and the supplier receiving the remittance advice, should use the remittance advice as the supporting document from which the payment made and received can be recorded on their accounting system.

A supplier receiving payment by BACS should check their bank statement to verify that the payment the customer claims to have made has in fact been received by their bank before recording the receipt in their books.

The following is the remittance advice sent to Lamex (Office Products) by CED Limited on 3 June 201Y when they settled their account balance, paying by BACS.

REMITTANCE ADVICE

No: 747
Date: 3 June 201Y
Account: 886 CED

CED Limited
28 Gathurst Road
Orrell WN6 OXX

To: Lamex (Office Products)
66 Bankes Avenue
Pemberton WN2 OPP

Details	Amount £	p
Payment – invoice 2145	***1,068***	***00***
Less – credit note 152	***84***	***00***
Payment by BACS	***984***	***00***

VAT Reg No: 987 6543 21

Bank statement - The bank will periodically issue each current account holder with a statement of account. The bank statement is a summary, of the transactions which, according to the records kept by the bank, have passed through the account holders current account during a given period of time, usually the previous month.

When a business receives a bank statement it is routine practice to check that the transactions recorded on the bank statement correspond to those recorded by the business in the bank current account in its own accounting system, and to reconcile the balance on the bank statement with the balance on the bank current account in its own records.

The reconciliation process will identify any items, receipts and payments, which appear on the bank statement but which have not been recorded by the business at the time of receiving the statement. The bank statement is often used as the source document from which such receipts and payments are recorded in the business's accounting system.

For example, amounts received for a business from credit customers directly by the bank by BACS are often posted to the accounting system of the business from the bank statement. The amounts received should be checked against the amounts per remittance advices received from customers notifying the business that payment has been made by BACS, before they are recorded in the accounting system.

The charges made by the bank to the business for the running of its current account are also usually recorded in the business's accounting system using the bank statement as the source document, as are any interest charged by the bank should the business overdraw on its bank current account.

The following is an example of a bank statement. The statement was received by Lamex (Office Products) from the Northern Bank at the month end 31 March 201Y. The three items highlighted in bold type on the bank statement are posted by the bookkeeper of Lamex (Office Products) into the accounting system directly from the bank statement i.e. using the bank statement as the source document:

Northern Bank PLC **STATEMENT OF ACCOUNT**
Pemberton Branch

Account title: Lamex (office Products) **Date:** 31 March 201Y
Account number: 74547066

201Y	**Details**	**Payments £**	**Receipts £**	**Balance £**
1 March	Balance b/f			4,725 C
4 March	Counter credit		3,960	8,685 C
9 March	Cheque 207144	2,980		5,705 C
10 March	BACS credit – Ronaldo & Co		2,750	8,455 C
13 March	Counter credit		2,145	10,600 C
14 March	**SO – Rates (SMBC)**	**1,200**		9,400 C
14 March	Cheque 207143	2,840		6,560 C
15 March	Counter credit		4,160	10,720 C
21 March	Counter credit		3,290	14,010 C
24 March	Cheque 207145	3,480		10,530 C
28 March	Counter credit		4,320	14,850 C
31 March	**Bank charges**	**20**		14,830 C
31 March	**DD – Heat & light (Solarplus)**	**360**		14,470 C
31 March	Cheque 207146	2,000		12,470 C
31 March	Counter credit		4,005	16,475 C
31 March	BACS – wages and salaries	10,240		6,235 C

D = Debit (overdrawn balance) C = Credit

DD = Direct debit SO = Standing order

Payroll records **-** where a business employs staff, either on a full-time or casual (part-time) basis, and makes a payment to them in the form of a wage or salary, then it must keep wages/salaries records.

The basic record from which information is taken for the purpose of accounting for the cost of wages and salaries of a business are its payroll. The payroll provides a record of all employees giving details of the amounts they earn, the amounts they are paid, deductions made from their pay, and contributions made on their behalf by their employer.

The following is the payroll analysis sheet prepared by the bookkeeper of Auto Spares at the month end 31 March 201Y

AUTO SPARES - PAYROLL ANALYSIS SHEET

Week Ending: 31 March 201Y

		Earnings				**Employee Deductions**					
Number	**Name**	**Basic** £	**Overtime** £	**Bonus** £	Total Gross Pay £	**PAYE (Income Tax)** £	**National Insurance** £	**Other Voluntary Deductions** £	**Total Deductions** £	**Net Pay** £	**Employer's National Insurance** £
1	K Atkins	175.00	10.00		185.00	26.17	13.91		40.08	144.92	12.98
2	P Logan	240.00	25.00		265.00	41.17	21.91		63.08	201.92	27.08
3	J Richards	225.00		25.00	250.00	36.92	20.41		57.33	192.67	25.55
4	L Windle	200.00		20.00	220.00	34.42	17.41		51.83	168.17	22.49
	TOTALS	840.00	35.00	45.00	920.00	138.68	73.64		212.32	707.68	88.10

Although you are **not** required to make payroll calculations in this unit you will be required to process payroll information i.e. net pay, deductions from pay and employer on-costs. It is important, therefore, that you understand the following terms:

Wages – the term used to describe payments made to employees who are paid weekly.

Salaries – the term used to describe payments made to employees who are paid monthly.

Gross pay - this is the amount of pay to which the employee is entitled before any deductions are made from their pay.

Net pay- this is gross pay less all deductions from pay. Net pay is often referred to as 'take home pay'.

Deductions from pay - there are two types of deductions which are made from wages and salaries i.e. statutory and voluntary deductions.

Statutory deductions - these are deductions which an employer has to make by law (statute) from the gross pay of employees. Statutory deductions consist of:

- Income Tax (PAYE – Pay as You Earn)
- National Insurance Contributions

Voluntary deductions - voluntary deductions are deductions made from pay at the employee's request and include payments into a pension scheme and payments to a trade union.

Employer costs - the cost of employment is affected not only by paying employees what they earn, but also by other employment costs incurred directly by the employer. The most common of these additional costs tend to be employer National Insurance Contributions and pension fund payments.

In an assessment you may be required to account for wages, salaries and employer costs from an entry in a journal. It is essential therefore that you acquire the skills to prepare the necessary journal entry and to process the entry from the journal.

***Internally generated notes* –** in some instances there may be a lack of documentation to support a transaction, in which case documentation in the form of a 'note' to the bookkeeper would be appropriate to support the transaction.

For example, a business has cash sales and the proprietor of the business regularly takes money in the form of cash (notes and coins) from the till for personal use i.e. drawings. There is nothing wrong with the taking of drawings, however, unless the drawings are documented the bookkeeper will be unaware that cash is 'missing' from the till. The drawings could be documented by simply making out a note stating the date on which the cash was taken from the till, indicating the amount that was taken, and that the cash was taken as personal drawings.

If the note is then passed on to the bookkeeper the transaction can be recorded in the cash account and drawings account in the ledger.

In addition to the documents above there may also be other documents and files used by a business when preparing documents to be issued, or when checking the accuracy of documents received. The following is an example of such documents and files:

- customer and supplier files
- catalogues and price lists
- goods received notes
- goods returned notes

Customer and supplier files - businesses will usually set up files for each of their customers and suppliers. The following shows an example of the type of information a business is likely to keep on file.

Customer Files	Supplier Files
Customer trading name and business address	Supplier trading name and business address
Contact name(s) within the organisation	Contact name(s) within the organisation
Trade and bank references	Agreed credit limit
Agreed credit limit	Terms of trade agreed
Terms of trade agreed	Agreed method of payment
Agreed method of payment	Supplier account number/code
Customer account number/code	

Catalogues and price lists - catalogues and price lists are issued by suppliers to customers, and provide information relevant to the raising and checking of purchase orders, invoices and credit notes. Information within the catalogue or price list is likely to include:

- A brief item/product description
- An item/product code or reference number
- The item/product price

It is important that catalogues and price lists are kept up-to-date. Therefore, they may need to be revised and reissued to customers on a regular basis.

Orders received from customers should be checked to ensure that the customer has used information extracted from the current catalogue or price list.

Invoices and credit notes issued to customers should refer to information (descriptions, codes and prices) taken from current catalogues or price lists.

Catalogues and price lists received from suppliers need to be kept 'on file', with old catalogues and price lists being destroyed once new ones have been received.

Purchase orders placed with suppliers should be prepared using information (descriptions, codes and prices) extracted from current catalogues and price lists.

Goods received note - a goods received note is an internal document used by the buyer to record and monitor the delivery of goods. Details from the delivery note are copied onto the goods received note.

When goods are delivered, if the quantity delivered is less than the quantity ordered then this should be noted on a goods received note, to ensure that the supplier charges only for goods delivered.

Goods returned note - this is used by the seller to record details of any goods returned by customers. It is then used as the basis of raising a credit note. The information recorded on the goods returned note is likely to include:

- Customer details (trading name and address)
- Date goods were returned
- Details and quantities of items returned
- Reason for return

HMRC rules for retaining source data – Her Majesty's Customs and Excise (HMRC) require that businesses keep data for a specific period of time, so that information is available to them if they should decide to inspect a business's records.
HMRC stipulate that data, other than payroll records, should be retained for a minimum period of six years. Payroll data must be kept for at least three years.

The journal - the journal is often described as a 'diary', and is a further source from which transactions are posted into the bookkeeping system. The journal is mainly used to document transactions that lack appropriate business documentation, usually because they are decision based, or are of a complicated and/or unusual nature.

A journal entry provides the following information to those who are responsible for posting the entry from the journal into the bookkeeping system:

a The date of the transaction to be processed

b The code of the account to be debited and the amount to be posted.

c The code of the account to be credited and the amount to be posted.

A brief narrative should be given to explain the journal entry in the details field.

At this level of your studies you will be required to demonstrate competence in the use of the journal in the following circumstances:

- To input opening balances when setting-up a double entry bookkeeping system for a new or existing business
- To account for a decision based transaction e.g the write off of a bad debt and the claim for VAT bad debt relief
- To support transactions to account for wages and salaries based on information collected from a payroll analysis or wages book
- To correct bookkeeping errors (errors of omission, commission, principle and original entry)

Bookkeeping errors

There are several reasons why bookkeepers make errors. Quite often its due to a lack of knowledge and understanding, which results in the bookkeeper incorrectly classifying a transaction. On other occasions, it is due to carelessness, often resulting from the bookkeeper working under pressure to process a high volume of transactions in order to meet strict deadlines.

The following are types of error which can be made by bookkeepers using a computerised accounting system:

Error of omission - such an error occurs when a transaction is missed completely from the books of account. For example, an invoice or bill is mislaid and the transaction to which the invoice or bill relates is not processed. As a result, the bookkeeping system is not a complete record of the transactions for the accounting period. However, once the error is discovered the missing transactions must be added to the system.

Error of commission – this error results in an entry being recorded in the correct class of account, but the transaction is posted to a wrong account within its class.

Errors of commission are quite common when there are two accounts within the same class with similar account titles. For example, a payment of £1,960 is made from the bank account of a business to a supplier Clayman & Co. The bookkeeper codes the credit entry for the transaction to the bank account, but in error codes the debit entry for the to the account of a supplier trading in the name of Clayworth & Co. Overall, as a result of this error, the total amount owed to trade suppliers is correct, however the balance on one supplier account (Clayman & Co) is overstated by £1,960, with the balance on the account of another supplier (Clayworth & Co), understated by £1,960.

Error of principle – this error is very similar to the error of commission. Here double entry is maintained as the transaction is posted with corresponding debit and credit entries, however one of the 'legs' of the transaction is posted to an incorrect account, but on this occasion one of the accounts used is of an entirely different class of account to the class of account to which the posting should have been made. This type of error usually occurs when the bookkeeper confuses capital and revenue expenditure. For example:

A laptop is bought at a cost of £1,200 (inclusive of VAT at 20%), the laptop is paid for by cheque. The payment of £1,200 is correctly coded to the bank account and the VAT element of the transaction (£200) is correctly coded to the purchase tax account. However, the cost of the laptop (£1,000) is coded to the purchases account instead of the office equipment account.

Error of original entry – this type of error occurs when the amounts posted from the originating document are extracted and processed incorrectly, but are posted observing double entry principles. For example, a business makes a payment for rates on its premises of £1,000 directly from the business bank account. In error the transaction is posted as:

Debit - rates account £100

Credit - bank account £100

The bookkeeper has made an error when recording both the debit and credit entries in the bookkeeping system. Both the accounts used are the correct accounts, however, the bookkeeper has understated the amounts recorded in each of the accounts by £900 when posting from the rates bill. Despite the error as the bookkeeper has recorded corresponding debit and credit entries in the accounts and arithmetic accuracy has been maintained.

Lesson 6 Practice Questions

Question 6.1

Which **one** of the following documents is issued by a supplier to a customer when goods are sold on credit?

	✓
Invoice	✓
Credit note	
Statement of account	

Question 6.2

Which **one** of the following documents is sent by a supplier to a credit customer, usually at the end of each month, summarising the transactions between to two businesses during the month and indicating the balance on the customer account in the books of the supplier at the month end?

	✓
Advice note	
Delivery note	
Statement of account	✓

Question 6.3

Which **one** of the following documents is sent by a customer to a supplier informing them that a payment has been made to them by BACS or cheque?

	✓
Credit note	
Remittance advice	✓
Delivery note	

Question 6.4

At the end of each week the proprietor of a shop takes cash from the till for personal use. Which **one** of the following is the source document from which proprietor drawings are most likely to be recorded in the shops bookkeeping system?

	✓
Till receipt	
Note from the proprietor placed in the till	✓
Paying-in slip	

Question 6.5

A list of several source documents from which transactions are recorded in a bookkeeping system is provided below:

- **Credit note**
- **Remittance advice**
- **Paying-in slip**
- **Cheque book stub**
- **Bank statement**
- **Till receipt**

The following table refers to four business transactions. From the list of documents above enter in the column headed 'source document' the document from which each transaction would be recorded in a business's bookkeeping system.

Transaction Details	Source Document
1 Cash and cheques paid from the cash account into the business bank account	Paying-in slip
2 Cash sales processed through a cash register	Till receipt
3 Gas and electricity bills paid by direct debit	Bank statement
4 Goods retuned by a customer because they are found to be damaged on delivery	Credit note

Question 6.6

Which **one** of the following is the source from which the decision to write off the balance on a customer account as a bad debt is recorded in a business's bookkeeping system?

	✓
Bank statement	
Remittance advice	
Journal	✓

Question 6.7

Which **one** of the following bookkeeping errors is an error of principle?

	✓
The purchase of an item of machinery for use in the factory is incorrectly coded and as a result is posted to the purchases account	
An invoice from a garage for repairs to a delivery vehicle is misplaced and as a result the transaction is not recorded in the bookkeeping system	
A payment of £250 from the bank account by direct debit for heat and light is debited to the heat and light account as £25 and credited to the bank account as £25	✓

Question 6.8

Which **one** of the following is the term used to describe an employee's take home pay?

	✓
Net pay	✓
Gross pay	
Minimum wage	

Lesson 7

Principles of Value Added Tax

Principles of Value Added Tax

Objectives:

By the end of this lesson you should be able to:

- *Understand how VAT is collected and passed on and Identify the government agency responsible for administration of the VAT system*
- *Understand the rules for registering for VAT and recognise the responsibilities of businesses once registered for VAT*
- *Recognise the terms 'taxable supplies', 'input tax' and 'output tax'*
- *Identify rates of VAT and understand the terms 'exempt' and 'outside the scope'*
- *Understand how the following VAT schemes operate - standard scheme, annual accounting scheme, cash accounting scheme and flat rate scheme*
- *Recognise VAT codes*
- *Recognise the HMRC rules for the keeping of VAT records, the preparation and presentation of VAT invoices, the treatment of VAT where trade and prompt payment discounts are offered, invoicing options where prompt payment discounts are offered, the use of VAT tax points, accounting for VAT bad debt relief*
- *Understand the significance of the VAT date and tax point,*
- *Make VAT calculations*
- *Understand the purpose of the VAT purchase tax and sales tax accounts, and the process of periodically clearing these account balances to a VAT control account*
- *Understand the purpose of the VAT return (VAT 100)*
- *Understand the purpose of control visits and recognise that there are penalties for failing to register for VAT, submitting late VAT returns, and the misdeclaration of information*

Lesson 7 – Principles of Value Added Tax

Introduction

Taxation is the principle source of a Governments income and is defined as 'any compulsory levy from private sector households and businesses to the Government in the form of **direct** or **indirect taxes'**

Direct taxes are paid directly to the Government by the individual taxpayer and the tax liability cannot be passed on to someone else. The main sources of direct tax the UK Government are those of:

- income tax
- National insurance contributions
- Corporation tax

Indirect taxes are taxes that are levied on goods and services produced and supplied which are then passed on by the producer or supplier to the **consumer**. As a result, an indirect tax is often referred to as 'a tax on spending'. A tax such as Value Added Tax (VAT) or a sales tax is, therefore, a prime example of an indirect tax.

Value Added Tax (VAT)

VAT is a Government tax on the supply of goods and services and is charged on most business-to-business and business-to-consumer transactions in the UK. VAT is also charged on goods and some services imported from countries outside the European Union (EU) and on goods and some services coming into the UK from other EU countries.

In the UK the government department given responsibility for the management and administration of the VAT scheme is HM Revenue & Customs (HMRC)

The VAT system

Businesses that are registered for VAT act as tax collectors on behalf of HMRC.

A business registered for VAT is required to collect VAT from its customers by charging them VAT at the appropriate rate on its taxable supplies (sales and services it provides) – this is known as the **OUTPUT TAX** of the business making the supply. In a computerised accounting system a business's output tax is recorded in a **SALES TAX** account.

Where a business is registered for VAT it can reclaim from HMRC any VAT it pays on the goods and services it buys in (purchases etc.). This is known as the **INPUT TAX** of the business. In a computerised accounting system a business's input tax is recorded in a **PURCHASE TAX** account.

Periodically if output tax (sales tax) exceeds input tax (purchase tax) the business pays over the difference between its output tax (sales tax) and input tax (purchase tax) to HMRC. However, if input tax (purchase tax) exceeds output tax (sales tax) in the VAT period the business reclaims the difference between its input tax (purchase tax) and output tax (sales tax). For example:

Output Tax (Sales Tax) Collected	Input Tax (Purchase Tax) Paid	Difference	Treatment
£15,000.00	£10,000.00	£5,000.00	Pay £5,000.00 to HMRC
£10,000.00	£13,000.00	£3,000.00	Claim a refund of £3,000.00 from HMRC

Rates of VAT

Three rates of VAT are currently applicable to taxable supplies. The rates are:

- standard rate – 20%
- reduced rate (also known as lower rate) – 5%
- zero rate – 0%

Standard rate – most goods and services are subject to VAT at the standard rate. It is the default rate i.e. the rate of VAT to be applied unless specified otherwise. Currently the standard rate of VAT is 20%.

Reduced rate – The reduced rate of VAT, also known as the lower rate, is currently 5%. Examples of reduced rate items include:

- Domestic fuel and power
- Solar panels
- Installation of energy saving materials
- Children's car seats
- Residential conversions
- Women's sanitary products
- Contraceptive products

Zero rate – Zero rated supplies are taxable, but at a rate of 0%. A business trading exclusively in zero rated items can register for VAT but will not collect output tax from customers on its supplies. It will, however, be able to reclaim from HMRC any VAT it pays on any of its inputs which fall into the standard rate category. Examples of zero rated items include:

- Food (with exceptions) – see notes below
- Books, newspapers and magazines
- Children's clothing and shoes
- Public transport
- Maps

Food - for some items classification for the purposes of VAT can be confusing, food for example, is one of the most difficult and contentious areas of VAT to deal with.

The VAT Act 1994 (Schedule 8) zero rates food, however, the Act does make reference to several exemptions as follows:

- Foodstuffs – a number of foodstuffs are specifically excluded from the zero rate category; these include:

    - Ice cream, ice lollies, frozen yogurts etc.
    - Sweets, chocolate and chocolate biscuits (cakes and non-chocolate biscuits, however, are zero rated)
    - Beverages other than milk, tea, cocoa, coffee and meat extract drinks such as Oxo or Bovril
    - Snacks which are made from potato (such as crisps), swelled cereals (such as popcorn) and nuts (other than nuts in a shell)

- Catering – this is regarded as a standard rated service. Many of the foodstuffs/ingredients purchased by caterers from their suppliers are zero rated but become standard rated when supplied to their customers.

Catering is defined as 'any supply of food for consumption on the premises on which it is supplied' and is often regarded as being a supply of 'food with service'. Meals served in a cafe or restaurant are clearly within the definition of catering, as is the supply of food and service say at an event such as a wedding reception, birthday party, Christmas party etc.

- Hot takeaways - hot meals to be taken and eaten away from the premises where they are prepared, are treated as catering, and are subject to VAT at the standard rate

Exempt and outside the scope

There are some goods and services on which VAT is not charged. These are either exempt from VAT, or outside the scope of the VAT scheme. Exempt items include:

- Royal Mail stamps and postage
- Insurance and providing finance or credit
- Education and training
- Fund raising events by charitable organisations
- Subscriptions to membership organisations such as trade unions and professional bodies
- Some services from doctors and dentists
- Burial and cremation
- Betting, gaming and lotteries
- Works of art
- Cultural services - for example, entrance fees to art galleries, museums and zoos

Items which are 'outside the scope of VAT' include:

- Goods supplies by, or purchased from, a business that is not registered for VAT
- Local authority rates
- Wages and salaries
- Donations to charity
- Statutory fees and services e.g. MOT testing and congestion charges

There is a crucial difference between zero rated goods and services and exempt goods and services. If a business supplies only zero rated goods and services it can register for VAT but would collect no VAT on its supplies, it would, however, be able to claim back any VAT on its purchases. If a business supplies only exempt items, it cannot register for VAT and does not collect VAT on its supplies or claim back VAT on its purchases.

Note - special rules exist for businesses which supply a combination of taxable and exempt items, but these rules are not within the assessment criteria at this level of your studies.

Registering for VAT

'Persons' in business, making what are known as 'taxable supplies', are faced with either registering for VAT on a compulsory basis, or registering for VAT voluntarily.

For the purpose of VAT registration, a 'person' is regarded by HMRC as being any business organisation i.e. a sole trader, partnership, limited company, club or association which is, or may be, required to register for VAT. A 'taxable supply' is regarded by HMRC as being any supply of goods or services made in the UK which fall into the standard rate, reduced rate or zero rate category of VAT.

Compulsory registration

Whether 'persons' in business **must** register for VAT depends upon the level of their turnover and the nature of the goods or services they supply. A business must register for VAT where it makes taxable supplies and its turnover in taxable supplies exceeds the **VAT annual turnover threshold.**

'Persons' in business can apply two tests to determine whether or not they **must** register for VAT. The tests are known as the 'historic test' and the 'future test'. Registration is compulsory if, having carried out the tests, **either** of the following conditions apply:

- **Historic test** – the value of taxable supplies the business makes in the previous 12 months exceeds the **VAT annual turnover threshold**

- **Future test –** the value of taxable supplies made in the next 30 days will on their own exceed the **VAT annual turnover threshold**

The term '**VAT annual turnover threshold**' applies to the turnover of a business excluding VAT.

The VAT registration turnover threshold changes from time-to-time, usually at the 1 April each year. To check the latest turnover figure for registration you are advised to look on the HMRC (VAT) website, or contact your local HMRC office.

When applying the **historic test** measure the year (previous 12 month's period) is taken to be the most recent 12 month's period on a 'rolling year' basis. This means that at the end of each month the turnover for that month is added to the previous 12 month's turnover figure, the turnover figure for month 1 of the previous 12 month's period is then deducted, to give the annual turnover for the most recent 12 month's period.

Voluntary registration

Some businesses may, in circumstances where their taxable supplies are less than the VAT turnover limit, choose to register for VAT voluntarily. There are several advantages attached to voluntary registration, these include:

- Where a business sells only zero rated items and buys standard rated items it would receive a VAT refund from HMRC and does not have to pass the VAT on to its customers
- Where a business is being set up and has not yet sold anything, or a business doesn't sell anything within a particular VAT accounting period, it can still claim VAT back on its purchases
- It often aids cash flow. The business has the use of the VAT collected from its customers before it has to make payment of the difference between its output tax and its input tax to HMRC
- VAT registration is often seen as giving a business a degree of credibility. In business-to-business transactions businesses that are themselves registered for VAT often prefer to deal with other businesses that are also registered for VAT.

Whether registration is compulsory or voluntary a business can register for VAT by downloading a simple form (VAT 1) from the HMRC website which can be filled in by hand and submitted by post, or completed and submitted online. HMRC prefer applicants to use their online service. The online service is more secure, quicker, easier (online help guides the applicant through the form) and certain, as applicants get immediate acknowledgement that their form has been received.

Once the VAT registration process has been completed a business is issued with a registration certificate containing full details of registration, including the VAT registration number allocated to them by HMRC. The VAT registration number must be quoted on all invoices issued by the business, and should also be quoted in all communications the business has with HMRC.

Once registered for VAT a business is responsible for ensuring it:

- Charges VAT at the correct rate
- Charges the right amount of VAT to its customers
- Keeps appropriate VAT records
- Pays over any VAT due to HMRC on time

Deregistration

There may be circumstances when a business will want, or need, to deregister from the VAT scheme. As with registration, deregistration can either be compulsory or voluntary.

It is compulsory for a business to deregister if it ceases to make taxable supplies and has no intention of making taxable supplies.

Deregistration is an option if the turnover of a business, in term of its taxable supplies, falls below, or is likely to fall below, the annual VAT deregistration threshold. As is the case with the VAT registration threshold, the deregistration threshold changes from time-to-time, the current deregistration threshold can be found on the HMRC VAT website.

The use of coding

Coding is widely used in accounting and is an important aspect of accounting for VAT. The process of setting up a computerised accounting system requires the user of the system to ensure that VAT codes are correctly set-up.

Sage automatically includes default TAX (VAT) codes, known as 'T codes', which are suitable for use by most businesses, but these can be amended by a user should wish to do so. The Sage 50 default VAT codes are set as follows:

T0	Applied to zero rated transactions
T1	Applied to standard rated transactions which should currently be set at 20%. Sage will automatically default to this code when required
T2	Applied to exempt transactions
T4	Applied to sales to VAT registered customers in the EC
T5	Applied to reduced rate transactions which should currently be set at 5%
T7	Applied to zero rated purchases from suppliers in the EC
T8	Applied to standard rated purchases from suppliers in the EC
T9	Applied to transactions that are outside the scope of the VAT system and should not be included on a VAT return

VAT accounting schemes

Several schemes are available for use by businesses to account for VAT. Some of the schemes, in particular the annual accounting scheme, flat rate scheme and cash accounting scheme, are specifically designed for use by small businesses. The main intention of such schemes is to simplify the record keeping of the business, reduce paperwork and benefit the business in terms of cash flow.

Businesses are recommended to choose the scheme which is most suitable to their needs.

Standard scheme

The standard scheme is based on a system known as the accruals system, with VAT being paid quarterly. The output tax declared by the business in a quarter includes VAT collectable on **all** goods and services supplied in the quarter, regardless of whether or not the VAT has actually been collected from the customer. Likewise, the input tax declared in the same quarter includes **all** VAT payable, regardless of whether or not the VAT has actually been paid over to the supplier. The application of this scheme requires detailed record keeping.

Annual accounting scheme

This scheme requires a business to pay VAT on account throughout the year in nine monthly or three quarterly instalments. The VAT liability is estimated by HMRC and is likely to be based on the VAT the business paid in the previous year. Where a business has been trading for less than a year the instalments are based on an estimate of the likely VAT liability.

Under the annual accounting scheme, the business submits only one VAT return at the end of the year which is filled in with the full year's details. Traders have 2 months after their VAT year end to complete the return. If the instalments paid throughout the year fall short of the amount paid on account, then the balancing figure is paid to HMRC. If the business has overpaid a refund is claimed.

The annual accounting scheme does not remove the requirement to keep VAT records and accounts, however the scheme has several advantages for small businesses. For example, it reduces paperwork as businesses using the scheme need to complete only one annual VAT return instead of four quarterly returns. For a business which would regularly need to make VAT payments to HMRC, because their output tax exceeds their input tax, the flat rate scheme is beneficial in terms of cash flow

Cash accounting scheme

The cash accounting scheme requires that VAT is accounted for on a payment only basis. This means that a business only declares the output tax it has actually collected from customers in the VAT period, and only reclaims any input tax it has actually paid to suppliers in the same VAT period.

Other than for businesses which buy the majority of their supplies on credit, the cash accounting scheme is beneficial to cash flow. It also allows the keeping of simplified records.

Where a trader uses the cash accounting scheme to account for VAT they submit a quarterly return to HMRC.

Flat rate scheme

The flat rate scheme is the easiest of the VAT schemes to operate. The scheme was introduced to simplify VAT for small businesses and applies only to businesses with taxable turnover of £150,000 (or less) per year (tax exclusive).

Under this scheme, businesses are not required to identify and record every single VAT transaction instead they simply calculate the VAT they pay to HMRC as a flat rate of their VAT inclusive turnover. Businesses using this scheme must still issue VAT invoices to their customers showing VAT added to the net value of goods and/or services at the standard rate. However, no VAT is reclaimed on purchases as the input tax is taken into account in calculating the flat rate percentage applied. The flat rate varies for businesses within different trade sectors and the current flat rate percentages can be found on the HMRC VAT website.

Once the trade sector a business falls into has been established the relevant flat rate percentage for that sector is applied to its tax inclusive turnover to arrive at the calculation of VAT due to HMRC. The percentages are set so that in theory the VAT payable equates to the amount that would be paid if the business kept detailed records for every transaction and accounted for VAT on the basis of output tax less input tax.

The following is an example of a flat rate percentage calculation made by a trader who is VAT registered and is self-employed with a small workshop where he repairs motor vehicles. In this example it is assumed that the flat rate percentage for the trade sector in which the trader operates is 8.5%:

Records kept by the trader show that his supplies in VAT quarter, inclusive of VAT, total £15,200. Therefore, the traders VAT liability is £1,292, i.e. £15,200 x 8.5% = £1,292 (VAT liability)

Traders using the flat rate scheme are required to submit a quarterly VAT return to HMRC.

VAT schemes for retailers

HMRC have designed several VAT schemes specifically for use by retailers. Although your understanding of such schemes will not be assessed by the IAB, it is thought necessary that you are made aware that such schemes are available for use.

Using the standard VAT accounting scheme, if a business is VAT registered, then it must record the VAT on each sale in its accounting records. However, with the VAT retail schemes, the retailer works out the value of total VAT taxable sales for a period, for example, a day, and the proportions of that total that are taxable at different rates of VAT (standard, reduced and zero) according to the scheme they are using. They then apply the appropriate VAT fraction to that sales figure to calculate the VAT due. The retail scheme can only be used for supplies that are by way of retail sales, and the trader must still issue a VAT invoice to any VAT registered customer who requests one.

Any scheme a retailer chooses to use must, in the opinion of HMRC, give a fair and reasonable result in the amount of VAT paid.

Retail schemes available for use include:

- apportionment schemes
- direct calculation schemes
- the point of sale scheme

Within the retail schemes there are special arrangements for:

- caterers and catering
- chemists (retail pharmacists)
- florists

Making VAT calculations

The task of keeping VAT records includes an ability not only to process business transactions which include VAT, but also to make VAT calculations

The work of a bookkeeper often requires them to make VAT calculations where:

- VAT is calculated given a net value of goods and services (the value of goods and services excluding VAT)
- VAT is calculated given the gross value of goods and services (the value of goods and services including VAT)

The formula for calculating VAT to be added to the net total of goods sold is:

VAT amount = net value of goods x VAT percentage rate

The formula for working out VAT at standard rate already included in a total amount paid is:

$$\text{VAT amount} = \frac{20}{120} \times \text{total amount paid (gross amount)}$$

If a product has a **net price** of, say £200 and VAT is to be added at standard rate, then it is just a question of working out 20% of £200.

VAT = £200 x 20% = £40

The **gross price** of the product is therefore £200 + £40 = £240. **It is always true that gross price = net price + VAT**.

	£
Purchaser pays gross price	240
HM Revenue & Customs take VAT	40
Seller keeps net price	200

Where the VAT calculation involves pence then the rule you should apply is to **round down to the nearest penny**. For example:

	£
Net price	99.99
VAT at 20% (£99.99 x 20% = £19.998)	19.99
	119.98

If a gross amount (a value including VAT) is given, for example a gross amount of £240, you can work out the VAT content (assuming that VAT has been added to the net value at the standard rate of 20%), as follows:

£240 ÷ 120 x 20 = £40

Alternatively, the VAT exclusive price (net goods value) can be found by simply dividing the gross amount by 1.20. For example:

£240 ÷ 1.20 = £200

You can of course use what is known as the 'VAT fraction' to calculate the VAT content of a VAT inclusive figure. Where the standard rate of VAT is 20% the VAT fraction is $1/6^{th}$. For example:

$1/6^{th}$ of £240 = £40 (VAT)
Net goods value £240 less £40 = £200

A computerised accounting system generally offers the user a facility known as a 'calc net' function. The system will calculate the VAT content of a VAT inclusive amount (gross amount).

VAT and discounts

Several types of discount are used in business, usually where one business trades with another business. These include:

Trade discount: A trade discount is normally given when the buyer and the seller are in the same trade. For example, a small shop purchasing stationery for resale from a major stationery supplier, might be given a trade discount of, say, 30%. It is usually offered as a formality between one trader and another.

Some businesses specifically offer a trade discount when an order exceeds a certain figure. For example, all orders received which amount to more than £1,000 will be allowed a 5% quantity discount. This is a form of trade discount but is often referred to as a 'bulk discount'. Bulk discounts are often 'tiered' i.e. the higher the value of the order the higher the level of the bulk discount. Trade/bulk discounts are offered to encourage a trader to buy in large quantities. Trade discounts have no effect on the VAT charges on an invoice as the discount is deducted from the price of the goods before the VAT is added to the invoice.

Prompt payment discount – a prompt payment discount is used by suppliers to encourage customers to which they have given credit to settle invoices quickly.

For example, a supplier quotes the following terms of trade to a customer:

Terms: 2.5% 14 days or net 30 days

The terms above indicate that a prompt payment discount (also known as a settlement or cash discount) of 2.5% is on offer if the customer settles the invoice within 14 days of invoice date, otherwise the invoice must be settled in full in 30 days.

HMRC VAT legislation requires that where prompt payment discounts are offered by a supplier to a customer the invoice issued by the supplier must show:

- VAT calculated on the full price of the goods/services supplied

- The rate of the prompt payment discount offered

On issuing a VAT invoice the supplier must enter the invoice into their records and show the VAT on the full price of the goods/services supplied.

For example, on 1 May 201Y a business (Beta Ltd) sell goods on credit to a customer (Able & Co) for £1,500, the goods are subject to VAT at the standard rate of 20%. Beta Ltd offers Able & Co the following terms of trade:

- Trade discount 33.3%
- Prompt payment discount of 5% if the invoice is settled within 10 days of invoice date, otherwise payment in full in 30 days.

Let us assume that invoice 1234 was issued by Beta Ltd to Able & Co, the invoice would show:

Invoice 1234
From: Beta Ltd
To: Able & Co
Date: 1 May 201Y

	£
Goods total	1,500
Less trade discount 33.3%	500
Net goods	1,000
VAT @ 20%	200
Invoice total	**1,200**

Terms 5% 10 days or net 30 days

Beta Ltd (the supplier) would record the invoice issued to Able & Co in their accounting system as follows:

Sales account £1,000 (credit)
VAT sales tax account £200 (credit)
Able & Co (customer account) £1,200 (debit)

At the time of issuing the invoice to the customer the supplier will not know whether the invoice will be settled within the period of time which allows the customer to take advantage of the prompt payment discount on offer, or whether the customer will settle the invoice in full.

Therefore, having initially issued an invoice with VAT calculated on the full price of the goods/services supplied, should the customer choose to pay the discounted price the supplier will have to adjust their records to show the payment received, the discount allowed to the customer, and the output VAT actually received.

Making a VAT adjustment

Where prompt payment discounts are offered by a supplier to a customer a VAT adjustment is necessary to account for an adjustment on the original invoice in situations where the customer takes-up the prompt payment discount on offer.

HMRC VAT legislation requires that the supplier **must** choose**, before** issuing an invoice, the process they will adopt to adjust their accounting records in order to account for the VAT adjustment. Two options are offered by HMRC as follows:

Option 1 – in addition to their initial invoice the supplier is allowed to issue a credit note as the basis of accounting for the reduction in the invoice goods value (prompt payment discount) and the VAT adjustment.

For example, using the example above, if we now assume that it is the policy of Beta Ltd to issue a credit note to customers where they take-up the offer of a prompt payment discount, and it is assumed that on 9 May 201X Alpha & Co settle invoice 1234 received from Beta Ltd on 1 May 201Y by cheque, they would send a payment of £1,140 to Beta Ltd (£1,200 less 5%). On receipt of the cheque the transaction would be recorded by Beta Ltd in their accounting system as follows

Bank account £1,140 (debit)
Alpha & Co £1,140 (credit)

Beta Ltd would then issue a credit note to account for the discount on the net value of the goods and adjust the VAT charged on the original invoice (see summary credit note number 55 issued by Beta Ltd below).

Credit Note 55
From: Beta Ltd
To: Able & Co
Date: 9 May 201Y

	£
Discount allowed	50
VAT	10
Credit note total	**60**

Beta Ltd would record the credit note issued to Able & Co in their accounting system as follows:

Discounts allowed £50 (debit)
Sales tax account £10 (debit)
Able & Co (customer account) £60 (credit)

Option 2 – If a supplier prefers not to issue a credit note to account for a VAT adjustment, HMRC VAT legislation requires that the supplier **must** issue an invoice containing the following information (in addition to the normal invoice requirements):

- the terms of the prompt payment discount offered
- a statement that the customer can only recover as VAT input tax the VAT paid to the supplier

HMRC also suggest that it may be helpful for invoices to show the following information, although including this information in the invoice is optional:

- the discounted net goods price payable if the prompt payment discount is taken
- The VAT on the discounted price of the goods
- The total amount due if the prompt payment discount is taken

The following is an example of an invoice issued by a supplier (Fine Furniture Limited) to a credit customer (Globe Restaurant) on 2 March 201Y. Fine Furniture Limited, offered Globe Restaurant a prompt payment discount of 5% for settlement of the invoice within 14 days of invoice date, otherwise payment must be made in full within 30 days.

Fine Furniture Limited have opted **not** to issue a credit note to account for the VAT adjustment should the customer take up the offer of the prompt payment discount.

Note how the VAT on the invoice is calculated on the full value of the goods invoiced and how the invoice includes a note showing the settlement terms and explaining that the customer can only recover from HMRC the VAT they pay. Note also how the invoice shows the amount to be paid and the VAT on the amount paid if the offer of the discount is taken-up.

INVOICE **No: 1455**

Fine Furniture Limited
Unit 5 Ash Tree Trading Estate
Ashford AF9 8RD

To: Accounts Department
Globe Restaurant
5 High Street
Ashford AF1 4RD

Account No: GLR/110
Order No: GR 1288

Invoice date (tax point): 2 March 201Y

Quantity	Description	Product Code	Unit Price £	Unit Price p	VAT Rate %	Goods Total £	Goods Total p
72	Atlanta stacking chairs (claret and gold) - light oak	SC 110	50	00	20	3,600	00
15	Atlanta dining tables - light oak	DT 120	120	00	20	1,800	00
Terms: a discount of 5% of the full price applies if payment is made within 14 days. Otherwise payment is required in full within 30 days. No credit note will be issued. Following payment, you must ensure you have recovered only the VAT actually paid.		Net goods total				5,400	00
		VAT @ 20%				1,080	00
		Invoice total				**6,480**	**00**

Discounted price for payment within 14 days		£	P
	Net goods	5,130	00
	VAT	1,026	00
	Total	**6,156**	**00**

E & O E **V AT Reg No**: 225 5564 88

HMRC require that copies of invoices and credit notes used for the purpose of accounting for prompt payment discounts and VAT adjustments must be kept on file by both the supplier issuing such documents and the customer receiving the documents.

HMRC also require that where a prompt payment discount is taken up by the customer, both the customer and the supplier retain evidence of the fact that an amount less than the original amount invoiced was paid and received. HMRC state that entries on a bank statement can be used by customers and suppliers to show evidence of amounts paid and received.

The VAT invoice

The VAT invoice is an important document within the VAT scheme as it is the source document used to account for output tax charged by suppliers to their credit customers and, in business-to-business transactions, input tax paid by businesses to their credit suppliers.

There is no standard format regarding the presentation of invoices, however, HMRC stipulate the minimum information the invoice must contain. HMRC VAT legislation also requires that suppliers who offer prompt payment discounts to their customers must choose a process by which they will account for the VAT adjustment required where customers take a prompt payment discount and, therefore, pay an amount which is less than the original amount invoiced.

There is also a strict time limit imposed by HMRC on the issuing of VAT invoices. A business must normally issue a VAT invoice within 30 days of the goods or services being supplied.

The following is an example of an invoice issued by a business which is registered for VAT. Note that the business has **not** offered a prompt payment discount to the customer:

INVOICE **No:** 68868

Intec (Office Products) Limited
66 Station Road
Aberdeen, AB2 4EN

To: Accounts Department
CED Limited
28 Kings Road
Aberdeen, AB6 7EN

VAT Reg No: 987 1538 78

Account No: 886 CED
Order No: CED 7609
Invoice date (tax point): 24 March 201X

Quantity	**Description**	**Catalogue No**	**Unit Price**		**VAT Rate**	**Goods Total**	
			£	**p**	**%**	**£**	**p**
6	Beech Workstations	RP 3682	125	00	20	750	00
2	Swivel Chairs	FS 0938	70	00	20	140	00
Terms: Net 30 days. Carriage paid		Goods Total				890	00
		VAT @ 20%				178	00
		Invoice Total				1,068	00

E & E O

Note how on the invoice above all the requirements of a VAT invoice are met. Although all goods on the invoice are subject to VAT at the standard rate the VAT % rate has been shown for each of the items supplied. Doing so is optional unless there are mixed supplies (supplies at different rates of VAT).

Less detailed VAT invoices

In circumstances where goods or services are supplied at a value of £250 or less (including VAT) a less detailed VAT invoice can be issued by the supplier. The invoice must include a minimum of information as follows:

- The trading name and address of the supplier
- The date of the invoice (tax point)
- Details of the goods or services supplied
- The total amount payable for each item invoiced inclusive of VAT

Modified invoices

If the supplier and customer are in agreement a modified invoice can be issued. The modified invoice can be issued for goods and services to any value (there is no minimum or maximum amount stipulated by HMRC). The invoice will show the VAT inclusive amount for each item supplied. However, the invoice must also display summarised information as follows. The information is usually shown on the bottom of the invoice:

- The overall VAT inclusive amount
- The VAT content of the VAT inclusive amount
- The goods or services net value (value excluding VAT)
- The total value of any zero and/or exempt supplies on the invoice

Proforma invoices

A proforma invoice is usually issued by the supplier in advance of the goods or services actually being delivered /carried out. The invoice is an invitation to the customer to make payment prior to delivery and the invoice is therefore seen as a 'demand for payment'.

The proforma invoice gives full details of the goods or services to be supplied i.e. goods/services description, unit prices, net goods value, VAT payable and total amount payable. However, HMRC require that the invoice must be described as a proforma invoice and that the invoice must clearly display the words 'this is not a VAT invoice'.

The proforma invoice is not a 'live' invoice and cannot be used for the purpose of reclaiming VAT input tax. Where a sale results from the issue of a proforma invoice a separate VAT invoice must then be issued by the supplier, and used as the basis of accounting for VAT by the supplier (output tax/sales tax) and customer (input tax/purchase tax). The following is an example of a proforma invoice:

PROFORMA SALES INVOICE **Invoice No**: 1348

CONSORT LTD
Floor 2, Consort House
High Street, Andover AN1 3PR

VAT Reg No: 876 1298 21

To: Rontec Ltd
21 Pond Street
Andover, AN11 6TY

Date/Tax Point: 2 June 201Y
Your Order No: R128

Item Code	Quantity	Description	Unit Price £	p	VAT Rate %	Goods Total £	p
5375	2	Display calculator (Casio)	27	95	20	55	90
1901	1	Executive computer workstation (Hazel)	139	99	20	139	99
1903	1	Economy tower workstation (Hazel)	85	75	20	85	75
0701	2	Senior manager chair, swivel (Blue)	155	00	20	310	00
0703	4	Visitors chair, cantilever (Blue)	99	50	20	398	00
		This is not a VAT invoice A VAT invoice will be issued following settlement of this proforma invoice	GOODS TOTAL			989	64
			VAT @ 20%			197	92
		E & O E	**TOTAL DUE**			1,187	56

The VAT date and tax point

The 'time of supply' is often referred to as 'the tax point' and is the date, for VAT purposes, on which a transaction takes place.

Normally VAT must be accounted for on the VAT return (VAT 100), which relates to the date in which the tax point occurs, and the rate of VAT applied to the transaction by the supplier must be the relevant rate in force at the tax point date.

The basic tax point (the date on which the supply is made) is usually determined as being the date on which:

- The supplier sends the goods to the customer
- The customer collects the goods from the supplier
- The goods (which are not either sent or collected) are made available to the customer - for example the supplier is assembling something at the premises of the customer

For services the basic tax point is regarded as being:

- The date when the service is completed i.e. when the service is carried out and all the work is finished

There are some circumstances when the basic tax point can be overridden by a different date which is known as 'the actual tax point' (the date on which the transaction is recognised for VAT purposes). For example:

- For transactions where a VAT invoice is issued and payment is received in advance, the time of supply (actual tax point) is the date on which payment is received or the date on which the invoice was issued whichever is the earlier

- If the supplier receives payment in full before the date on which supply takes place, and no VAT invoice has yet been issued, the time of supply (actual tax point) is the date payment is received

- If the supplier issues a VAT invoice more than 14 days after the date when supply took place, the time of supply (actual tax point), will be the date on which the supply was issued

The following are examples of the use of tax points in practice:

Details	Tax Point
Goods are sent by the supplier to the customer on 5 May, the invoice is issued on 12 May and payment is received on 1 June	12 May is the actual tax point as the invoice was issued within 14 days of the time of supply (basic tax point)
Goods are sent by the supplier to the customer on 8 May, the invoice is issued on 27 May and payment is received on 7 June	8 May is the actual tax point as the invoice is issued more than 14 days after the time of supply (basic tax point)
Goods are sent by the supplier to the customer on 10 May, the invoice is issued on 20 May and payment was received on 18 May	18 May is the actual tax point as payment was received before the invoice was issued (basic tax point)
Goods are sent by the supplier to the customer on 20 May, the invoice is issued on 15 May and payment was received on 10 June	15 May is the actual tax point as the invoice was issued before the basic tax point (time of supply)

The taking of deposits

There are some circumstances in which it is possible to have more than one tax point for the same supply, an example being when a supplier takes a deposit from a customer prior to the goods or service being delivered.

For example, a customer orders some bedroom furniture from a supplier on 1 April 201Y at a cost of £4,800 (inclusive of VAT at standard rate of 20%) and pays a deposit of 10% (£480) on placing the order. On 1 May 201Y the supplier delivers the bedroom furniture and invoices the customer on 6 May 201Y for the balance outstanding (£4,320). The customer pays the invoice on 12 May 201Y.

In the above situation the tax point for the deposit would be 1 April 201Y i.e. the date on which the deposit was received. The supplier of the bedroom furniture would account for output tax of £80 as at that date. The tax point for the balance of £4,320 outstanding would be 6 May 201Y as the supplier had invoiced the customer within 14 days of the date of supply (the basic tax point), the supplier would account for output tax of £720 at that date (the VAT content of the outstanding balance).

It should be noted that if the supplier in the above example had a VAT period which ended on 30 April 201Y, the output tax of £80 collected on the deposit and the output tax of £720 in the balance outstanding would be accounted for on different VAT returns and would be paid to HMRC on different dates.

Accounting for imports and exports

Accounting for VAT on imports and exports, and on transactions where businesses trade with suppliers and customers within the European Union (EU) is a very complex subject area. For example, there are different rules for accounting for VAT on transactions taking place between suppliers and customers within the EU and those outside the EU.

As this is a very complex and specialised matter it is one of the areas of the VAT system on which businesses (unless they already employ a relevant expert) may need to seek guidance from HMRC – particularly if they are considering importing and exporting for the first time.

On this basis, this area of the VAT scheme is not within the current IAB Level 2 qualification specifications and your knowledge or understanding of this complex area will not be assessed by the IAB.

VAT bad debt relief – A bad debt occurs when an amount due from a credit customer is believed to be uncollectable. At this point in time the business has given up trying to collect the debt and recognises that a loss has been incurred i.e. that the amount due from the customer will not be collected, and any goods or services supplied will not be recovered. Once this conclusion has been reached it is common practice to write-off the amount uncollectable as a bad debt.

Where an amount written off as a bad debt includes VAT a business can claim VAT bad debt relief in respect of the VAT content of the loss, subject to the following conditions being met:

- The business must have accounted for the VAT and paid the output VAT to HMRC
- More than six months must have elapsed since the date of supply and the due date of the invoice
- The debt must have been written off in the books of the business as a bad debt

Any bad debt relief claimed is added into the input tax figure which is entered on the VAT return submitted at the end of a VAT period.

As mentioned in Lesson 6 of this study text the write off of the balance on the account of a customer as a bad debt and the claiming of VAT bad debt relief is processed from a journal entry. You must acquire the skill to prepare and process such journal entries, as tasks relating to the writing off of a debt as bad, and the claiming of VAT bad debt relief, often appear in IAB assessments.

Keeping VAT records

HMRC require businesses that are registered for VAT to keep adequate records and accounts of all transactions to support both output VAT charged (sales tax) and input VAT reclaimable (purchase tax). The main records to be kept include:

- Purchase orders and delivery notes
- Sales invoices received and copies of sales invoices issued
- Credit notes received and copies of credit notes issued
- Records of any daily cash takings e.g. till rolls
- Bank statements, cheque book counterfoils and paying-in slips
- Journal – a variety of information relating to VAT can be found in the Journal, this includes – VAT on the purchase or sale of fixed assets and VAT bad debt relief
- Where a business trades internationally documentation relating to foreign sales or purchases or goods or services, imports or exports outside the EU or buying or selling within the EU
- Any correspondence relating to VAT
- VAT accounts (purchase tax, sales tax and VAT control account)

Information must be kept on file for a period of at least six years and must be kept in such a way that the records:

- Are complete and up to date
- Allow the correct calculation of VAT payable to or reclaimable from HMRC at the VAT period end
- Are easily accessible and the figures used in keeping VAT accounts and completing VAT returns can be easily found.

If a business is registered for VAT it must periodically submit a VAT return (VAT 100) to HMRC. Most businesses are required to complete the VAT return online. The VAT return is used to calculate, at the end of each VAT period, the amount of VAT to be paid over to HMRC or reclaimed from them. The Sage 50 system has a function which allows the user to automatically produce the VAT return for each specific VAT period.

The following is an example of VAT purchase tax and sales tax accounts showing some of the VAT transactions you will be required to account for at this level of your studies. You will learn more about accounting for VAT in the lesson Introduction to Double Entry Processing (lesson 9 in this study text).

Purchase Tax

DR	**CR**
VAT goods purchased for resale	VAT on purchase returns
VAT on the purchase of fixed assets	VAT adjustments required when prompt payment discounts are received from credit suppliers
VAT on expenses/services	

Sales Tax

DR	**CR**
VAT on sales returns	VAT on sales of goods or supplies of services
VAT adjustments required when prompt payment discounts are allowed to credit customers	VAT on the sale of fixed assets
VAT bad debt relief	

Periodically the balances on the purchase tax account and sales tax account are transferred to an account known as the 'VAT control account'. Journal entries are prepared from which the balances on the purchase tax and sales tax accounts are cleared, following which the purchase tax and sales tax accounts will each carry a nil balance, whereas the VAT control account will carry either a debit or a credit balance. For example:

- If the debit balance on the purchase tax account (VAT reclaimable from HMRC) exceeds the credit balance on the sales tax account (VAT payable to HMRC), the VAT control account will carry a debit balance representing a refund to be claimed from HMRC.

- If the credit balance on the sales tax account (VAT payable to HMRC) exceeds the debit balance on the purchase tax account (VAT reclaimable from HMRC), the VAT control account will carry a credit balance representing an amount to be paid over to HMRC.

Later in this study text the lesson Introduction to Double Entry Processing will show you how to process a range of transactions using double entry processing principles. The processing will include accounting for VAT.

Control visits

HMRC officers may want to visit the premises of VAT registered businesses to carry out what is known as a 'control visit'.

The main aim of a control visit is to ensure that the correct amount of VAT has been paid by the business and that adequate records are being kept. The visiting officer will most probably also take the opportunity to discuss various aspects of the business with its owner(s)/manager(s) and give guidance in the form of help and advice. The visit can also be used by owner(s)/manager(s) for the purpose of seeking advice from the control officer on particular issues and discussing specific problem areas with them. It is essential that where information or advice is given by the control officer during the visit that such information and advice is confirmed in writing.

The visit will entail the visiting officer inspecting the accounting records of the business and testing the accuracy of the VAT returns submitted by the business. The control officer will highlight any errors discovered during the inspection and, where under-declarations of VAT are discovered by the control officer, this may lead to the issue of an assessment of under-declared VAT and could also result in interest and penalties being charged.

VAT penalties for mistakes and delays

A range of penalties and charges are made by HMRC where a trader:

- Is late in registering for VAT
- Submits a late return, or is late in making a VAT payment
- Submits an incorrect VAT return, or accepts a VAT assessment which has underestimated the VAT due

The late registration penalty – when a business is late in notifying HMRC that it should be registered for VAT a late registration penalty is charged. The late registration penalty is a percentage of the net tax due (output tax less input tax) from the date when the business should have registered to the date that HMRC receive notification of registration (the period of default). There is a minimum penalty and a sliding scale of penalty charges, therefore, the longer the business delays informing HMRC that it should be registered for VAT the higher the penalty.

The default surcharge – where a VAT return is submitted late or a payment of VAT is late then the trader may be charged a default surcharge.

On each occasion a default occurs HMRC issue a Surcharge Liability Notice to the trader, the notice is effective for a period of 12 months (the surcharge period). A further default during the 12 months' period results in the trader being liable to the payment of a default surcharge, HMRC will also issue them with a Surcharge Liability Notice Extension extending the surcharge period for a further twelve months from the end of the quarter in which the second default occurred.

The amount of surcharge is a percentage of the VAT paid late and is levied in addition to the unpaid VAT. The percentage charged depends on previous defaults in the current surcharge period, with the percentage rate applied increasing each time, within the surcharge period, that the trader is in default.

Small businesses i.e. those with a taxable turnover of less than £150,000, may be subject to special arrangements by HMRC if they have difficulty in paying their VAT on time. On the first occasion that they default they are sent a letter offering help and support to help them sort out any short term problems they may have. However, if they default again during the following 12 months' period they will be sent a Surcharge Liability Notice.

Misdeclaration penalties – these penalties were introduced by HMRC in an effort to get businesses to submit accurate VAT returns. Two penalties apply to the misdeclaration of information, these are:

- Misdeclaration Penalty - which applies to **large** misdeclarations
- Repeated Misdeclaration Penalty – which applies to large repeated misdeclarations

HMRC may issue a penalty to a business whenever there has been a significant or repeated lack of care in preparing VAT Returns that leads to errors in the true amount of tax payable or repayable.

For both penalties a percentage rate is applied to the amount of the misdeclaration for the period in question.

Changes in VAT rules and rates

Those responsible for running a business must closely monitor any changes in VAT legislation and rates, and bring such changes to the attention of others within the organisation who are directly involved in accounting for VAT on behalf of the business. Monitoring changes includes watching for HMRC information releases and regularly visiting the HMRC (VAT) website to look at changes that might directly affect their business.

Where a computerised accounting package is used for the purpose of invoicing and processing transactions it is quite possible that a new version of the software will be issued following a change in the rate of VAT, the software will have to be installed and be operational from the time any change comes into force. For a business using its own bespoke software, a change in the rate of VAT would require an updating of the software.

Lesson 7 Practice Questions

Question 7.1

Which **one** of the following government departments responsible for the administration of the VAT system?

	✓
Department or Work and Pensions (DWP)	
HM Revenue and Customs (HMRC)	✓
HM Treasury	

Question 7.2

Which **one** of the following statements best describes the requirement for a business to register for VAT?

	✓
All businesses must register for VAT within six months of starting trading	
Whether a business must register for VAT depends on the level of its sales (turnover)	
Only businesses trading in standard rated supplies must register for VAT	
Whether a business must register for VAT depends on the level of its sales (turnover) and the nature of the goods/services it supplies	✓

Question 7.3

Which **one** of the following statements best describes VAT?

	✓
VAT is a tax on profit	
VAT is an indirect tax	✓
VAT is a direct tax	

Question 7.4

VAT paid by a trader and reclaimable from HMRC is known as:

	✓
Input tax (purchase tax)	✓
Output tax (sales tax)	

Question 7.5

Calculate the VAT at standard rate (20%) to be added to the net goods prices for each of the following, also calculate the total gross goods price:

	£ : p
Net goods price	418.00
Add VAT @ 20%	83.60
Gross goods price	501.60

Net x 0,20 = VAT

Net + VAT = Gross

	£ : p
Net goods price	1,356.50
Add VAT @ 20%	271.30
Gross goods price	1,627.80

	£ : p
Net goods price	2,752.25
Add VAT @ 20%	550.45
Gross goods price	3,302.70

Question 7.6

Calculate the VAT element at standard rate (20%), already included in the total gross goods prices of each of the following, also calculate the net goods price:

	£ : p
Net goods price	1,317.75
Add VAT @ 20%	263.55
Gross goods price	1,581.30

Gross/6 = VAT
or
Gross/1.2 = Net

	£ : p
Net goods price	2,420.50
Add VAT @ 20%	484.10
Gross goods price	2,904.60

	£ : p
Net goods price	6,012.50
Add VAT @ 20%	1,202.50
Gross goods price	7,215.00

Question 7.7

Which **one** of the following forms is submitted to HMRC when making a payment of VAT, or reclaiming VAT?

	✓
VAT 100	✓
VAT Notice 700	
VAT 1	

Question 7.8

Which **one** of the following types of discount is offered by suppliers to customers to encourage them to settle invoices quickly?

	✓
Prompt payment discount	✓
Trade discount	
Bulk discount	

Question 7.9

Tiles Direct offers a discount to its credit customers of 20% on orders over the value of £2,500. A further 10% discount is offered by Tiles Direct to those customers who place orders over the value of £5,000.

Which **one** of the following types of discount is Tiles Direct offering to customers?

	✓
Trade discount	
Prompt payment discount	
Bulk discount	✓

Tömeges kedvezmény

Question 7.10

A business invoices goods to a credit customer at a value of £12,500.00 (excluding VAT). The goods are a mixed supply of standard rated and zero rated goods. The net value of the zero rated goods invoiced is £4,200.00. The business offers the customer a settlement discount of 5% for payment of the invoice in 10 days, otherwise payment must be made in full in 30 days.

Given the above information which one of the following represents the VAT which should be charged on the invoice (assuming the standard rate of VAT is 20%)?

	✓
£2,500.00	
£2,375.00	
£1,660.00	✓
£1,577.00	

£12.500
− £ 4.200
8.300 x 0,20 = 1,660.-

Question 7.11

Office Supplies is registered for VAT. They recently received the following order from Ink Spot, one of their credit customers.

Order Number 636

Goods Ordered

Quantity	Description	Unit Price	
3	Desk	£175.50	= 526,50
4	Cabinet	£96.25	= 385
6	Chair	£75.50	= 453
4	Shredder	£58.50	= 234
			1,598,50

The business does not offer a trade discount to customers. Its payment terms are 5% discount for settlement of invoices within 10 days of invoice date, or net payment in 30 days. Where prompt payment discounts are taken-up by customers Office Supplies issues a credit note to the customer to account for the discount and the VAT adjustment on the discount.

The following boxes have been extracted from the invoice to be issued by Office Supplies to Ink Spot, you are required to complete each of the boxes.

	£	p
Goods total (Net Goods)	1,598	50
VAT @ 20%	319	70
Invoice Total	1,918	20

Question 7.12

Using appropriate words from the following list complete the gaps in the sentences below:

- cash accounting scheme
- misdeclaration penalties
- annual accounting scheme
- default surcharges
- flat rate scheme
- standard accounting scheme

1. The accounting scheme that allows a business to submit one VAT return each year is the annual acc. scheme.

2. The cash acc scheme allows a business to account for VAT based only on payments received and payments made in the VAT period.

3. The standard acc. scheme requires a business to keep detailed VAT records and submit a quarterly VAT return.

4. The penalty payments introduced by HMRC in an effort to get businesses to submit accurate VAT returns are known as misdeclaration penalties.

Question 7.13

Which **one** of the following balances would you expect to find on the VAT sales tax account?

	✓
Debit balance	
Credit balance	✓

Question 7.14

A business is registered for VAT. Indicate whether the VAT element of **each** of the transactions listed in the table below would be recorded as a debit entry or credit entry in the VAT account kept by the business.

Transaction	**DR** ✓	**CR** ✓
VAT on sales to credit customers		✓
VAT on Purchases from credit suppliers	✓	
VAT on purchases returned to credit suppliers		✓
VAT on sales returned by credit customers	✓	
VAT on cash sales		✓
VAT on cash purchases	✓	
VAT on payments of business expenses	✓	
VAT on the purchase of fixed assets	✓	

Question 7.15

A business is registered for VAT. At the end of a recent VAT period the VAT purchase tax account in its nominal ledger carried a closing balance of £7,644.00. At the end of the same period the same period the VAT sales tax account carried a closing balance of £10,188.00.

Given the information above which **one** of the following statements is correct?

	✓
At the end of the VAT period the business must make a payment of £2,544.00 to HMRC	✓
At the end of the VAT period business must claim a refund of £2,544.00 from HMRC	

Question 7.16

The following is a list of three default VAT Tax codes (T codes) used within a computerised accounting system:

T1
T2
T9

In the table below are three business transactions which took place recently. Indicate, using the column in the table headed-up 'T code', which of the T codes on the above list should be allocated to each of the transactions.

Nominal ledger account title	T code
Paid business rates by direct debit (exempt from VAT)	T2
Filled the delivery van with fuel, the payment was inclusive of VAT at standard rate (20%)	T1
Paid casual wages (outside the scope of VAT)	T9

Lesson 8

Classification and Coding

Classification and Coding

Objectives:

By the end of this lesson you should be able to:

- *Define the terms 'capital income', 'revenue income', 'capital expenditure', and 'revenue income'*
- *Classify business transactions and appreciate the consequences of incorrect classification*
- *Understand the use of account codes and the purpose of the chart of accounts*

Introduction

The main duties of the bookkeeper are those of processing business transactions and checking the accuracy of their processing.

To be able to process business transactions accurately bookkeepers need to be able to identify, classify and code transactions.

Classifying transactions

Business income and expenditure can be classified as follows:

- Income
  - Capital
  - Revenue
- Expenditure
  - Capital
  - Revenue

The above classifications can be defined as follows:

Capital income – income **'borrowed'** by the business and invested in the business for the long term. Capital income includes capital invested by the owner(s) of the business or finance provided to the business by lenders such as banks.

Revenue income – income **earned** by the business, generated from either its trading or non-trading activities. Examples here include income from the sale of goods to customers, bank interest received, rental income received from sub-letting premises, commissions received for providing services etc.

Capital expenditure is defined as expenditure which has a long-term effect on the profit-making capacity of the business. Capital expenditure includes the initial cost of acquiring fixed assets (items purchased for use in the business over a number of accounting periods), together with other costs incurred when installing, modifying and improving fixed assets.

Revenue expenditure is expenditure which has only a short-term effect on the profit-making capacity of the business. Benefit is derived from such expenditure for one accounting period only and includes – purchases of goods for resale, rent, rates, insurances, repairs to fixed assets, wages and salaries, gas and electricity, stationery, postage, insurances etc.

Errors made by a bookkeeper in classifying a transaction will most probably lead to the transaction being incorrectly coded and recorded in the accounting system. This can then result in the profit or loss of a business being under or overstated and the financial position of the business being incorrectly reported.

For example - A business buys an item of machinery at a cost of £5,000. The machine is intended for use in the workshop over a period of several years. The bookkeeper of the business is inexperienced and in error classifies the machine as a purchase i.e. an item bought for resale. As a result, the cost of the machine is recorded in the purchases account. As the machine was bought for use in the business it is regarded as a fixed asset (an item bought specifically for use in the business rather than for resale) and therefore, should be classified as an asset and its cost should be recorded in the appropriate fixed asset account.

Due to the transaction being incorrectly classified, the balance on the purchases account is overstated by £5,000, whereas the balance on a fixed asset account, most probably the machinery cost account, is understated by £5,000. As the purchases account is used in the calculation of profit or loss when preparing the profit and loss account, the fact that purchases are overstated will have the effect of reducing the profit for the period by £5,000. As the balance on the machinery cost account (a fixed asset) would be used when preparing the balance sheet the financial position of the business would be misstated with the value of fixed assets being understated by £5,000.

The following is an example of classifying various items of business income and expenditure:

Item	Income		Expenditure	
	Capital	Revenue	Capital	Revenue
Payment to purchase plant and equipment			✓	
Receipt of a loan from a bank	✓			
Payment of a telephone bill				✓
Income received from the bank on a deposit account		✓		
Payment of insurance				✓
Payment to purchase a motor van			✓	
Income from sales to customers		✓		
Payment of staff wages and salaries				✓
Receipt of funds invested by the owner of the business (capital)	✓			
Payment to purchase goods for resale				✓
Payment to purchase fixtures and fittings			✓	
Payment of business rates				✓
Income received as rent on property sub-let by the business		✓		

Coding transactions

Coding is widely used in computerised accounting. Coding systems are usually based on codes made up from numbers, letters or a combination of both numbers and letters.

Codes which consist only of numbers are knowns as **numeric codes.** Where codes consist only of letters they are known as **alphabetic codes**.

The system of coding where codes consist of a combination of letters and codes is known as **alpha-numeric coding**.

The chart of accounts

A computerised accounting system provides the user with a listing of all the nominal accounts within the system, this is referred to as a **'chart of accounts'.**

In a Sage system nominal codes are numeric codes and the system is set-up with a range of codes known as default codes. The default codes presented will vary depending on the type of business for which the system is being set-up. The term 'default' in this context means 'pre-arranged' i.e. the codes are pre-arranged within the system, although you can amend default codes should you wish to do so. Amending default codes is known as 'editing'.

When setting-up a computerised accounting system for a new business the setting up process involves selecting the business type for which the system is being set-up. It is important that you select the correct business type, as this will determine the range of default nominal account codes pre-set within the system.

Some of the default codes pre-set by the system for a sole trader type entity are likely to vary from the default codes pre-set where a computerised accounting system is set-up for a partnership or limited company. For example, the default codes for sole trader and partnerships will include a capital account and a drawings account for the trader, or in a partnership, each of the partners. The default accounts for a partnership will also include an account for each partner known as a 'current account', an account which is not used in accounting for either sole traders or limited companies. In accounting for limited companies there are number of accounts pre-set such as share capital accounts, reserve (undistributed profit) accounts and dividend accounts which are not used in accounting for sole traders or partnerships.

Within a computerised accounting system, the default nominal ledger codes within the chart of accounts are pre-arranged within a series of categories which group the accounts to facilitate the preparation of financial statements (the profit and loss account and the balance sheet), and are, therefore, directly affected by the classification given to a transaction.

To facilitate the preparation of the profit and loss account the Sage 50 chart of accounts uses the following categories:

4000 - 4999	Sales	Codes used to record income from sales of goods and/or services
5000 - 5999	Purchases	Codes used to record the purchase of goods for resale, or materials used in the manufacture of products for sale. Changes in stock levels are also recorded in this category
6000 - 6999	Direct expenses	Codes used to record expenses (other than the purchase of materials) incurred in the direct production of goods for sale
7000 - 9999	Overheads	Codes used to record expenses incurred in running the business

Listed within overheads within the Sage 50 chart of accounts are code 9998 Suspense and 9999 Mispostings. These accounts are not used in the preparation of financial statements and at the time of preparing financial statements should have zero balances.

The codes used within a Sage 50 package to facilitate the preparation of the balance sheet are as follows:

0001 - 0999	Fixed assets	Codes used to record the cost of items bought for use in the business over several accounting periods
1000 - 2099	Current assets	Codes used to record cash or near cash items (balances which will be converted into cash in the short-term – usually within days or weeks)
2100 - 2299	Current liabilities	Codes used to record amounts owed by a business which will be repaid in the short-term (within the next 12 months)
2300 - 2399	Long term liabilities	Codes used to record amounts owed by the business which are not due to be repaid in the next 12 months
3000 - 3999	Capital and reserves	Codes used to record investment by the owner(s) in their business

Lesson 8 Practice Questions

Question 8.1

Which **one** of the following statements describes the accounting term 'revenue expenditure'?

	✓
Expenditure which has only a short-term effect on the profit- making capacity of a business. The business benefits from such expenditure in one accounting period	
Capital invested by the owner in the business, or monies borrowed to help set-up a business or expand it	
Expenditure which has a long-term effect on the profit-making capacity of a business. It includes payments made to buy fixed asset as well as payments made to install, modify and improve fixed assets	

Question 8.2

Paula is the owner of a shop selling greetings cards. Which **one** of the following is an example of capital income to her business?

	✓
Income received by the business from sales to its customers	
A payment made to purchase new shelving for the shop	
Additional money to be used to expand the business transferred by Paula from her private business account into the business bank account	

Question 8.3

Classify each of the items listed in the table below as being examples of capital income or expenditure, or revenue income or expenditure.

Item	Capital		Revenue	
	Income ✓	Expenditure ✓	Income ✓	Expenditure ✓
Receipt of funds invested by the owner of a business				
Payment made to purchase goods for resale				
Income received from sales to customers				
Payment of a heat and light bill				
Receipt of a loan from a bank				
Payment made to purchase office machinery for use in the business				
Payment made for repairs to property				
Payment made to purchase a vehicle for use in the business				
A receipt of interest from the bank on funds in a deposit account				
Payment made for advertising				
Payment made for business rates				

Question 8.4

Using appropriate words from the following list complete the gaps in **each** of the sentences below.

- default
- coding menu
- alpha-numeric
- chart of accounts
- numeric

1. In a computerised accounting system, nominal ledger account codes are found in a ________________________________.

2. Codes made up only of numbers are known as __________ codes.

3. In a computerised accounting system, nominal codes which are pre-arranged within the system are known as __________ codes.

Question 8.5

Which **one** of the following is an example of an alpha-numeric code?

	✓
1056215	
IAB/660	
ARB/FTP	

Question 8.6

Within a computerised accounting system in which **one** of the following range of account codes would you find the code for a fixed asset cost account such as office equipment?

	✓
4000 - 4999	
0001 - 0999	
7000 - 8299	

Question 8.7

Within a computerised accounting system in which **one** of the following range of account codes would you find the code for the bank current account?

	✓
1000 - 2099	
5000 - 5999	
6000 - 6999	

Question 8.8

Within a computerised accounting system in which **one** of the following range of account codes would you find the code for the bank charges account?

	✓
2300 - 2399	
3000 - 3999	
7000 -9999	

Question 8.9

Within a computerised accounting system in which **one** of the following range of account codes would you find the code for a sales account?

	✓
7000 - 9999	
4000 - 4999	
5000 - 5999	

Question 8.10

The following is a list of nominal ledger account codes taken from a computerised accounting systems chart of accounts:

0050
4001
7005
5002

Using the column in the table headed-up 'Nominal code' allocate each of the codes on the list above to the appropriate nominal ledger account title.

Nominal ledger account title	Nominal code
Purchases - materials	
Motor vehicles	
Cash sales	
Rent on workshop	

Lesson 9

Introduction to Double Entry Processing

Introduction to Double Entry Processing

Objectives:

By the end of this lesson you should be able to:

- *Recognise the form of leger 'T' accounts and running balance accounts*

- *Understand how the concepts of business entity, dual aspect, money measurement and historic cost are applied by bookkeepers*

- *Identify the elements within the accounting equation, make missing term calculations and understand how the accounting equation related to the principle of double entry bookkeeping*

- *Understand the terms 'assets' (fixed and current assets), 'capital' and 'liabilities' (long-term and current liabilities)*

- *Recognise the terms 'real time' and 'batch' processing and understand how these techniques are used to process business transactions*

- *Understand the use of the following in a computerised accounting system – ledger accounts, the nominal ledger, debtor and creditor control accounts*

- *Process a range of business transaction using appropriate ledger accounts and applying double entry principles*

- *Recognise the format of a trial balance and understand its purpose*

Introduction

The objective of this lesson is to introduce you to the principles of double entry bookkeeping i.e. the system on which computerised accounting systems are based.

Where a business is using a computerised accounting system it is the responsibility of the bookkeeper to classify and code transactions and enter them onto the system, however, the software package then automatically makes the appropriate accounting entries in the system.

In a manual accounting system, the bookkeeper is responsible not only for classifying and coding transactions, but is also required to record the transactions in the accounting system.

Studying the basics of double entry by looking at the process of manually recording transactions will help you understand the workings of a computerised accounting package and the principles of double entry bookkeeping.

Basic accounting concepts

Bookkeepers and accountants in keeping financial records and preparing financial statements are required to work within a set of generally accepted rules or principles. The knowledge that this is the case should give some reassurance to the reader and user of financial information that such information represents a true and fair account of a business's financial transactions, operating performance, and financial standing.

The rules and principles applied are commonly referred to as **accounting concepts** and include the following, which particularly apply to the function of bookkeeping:

- Business Entity Concept
- Dual Aspect Concept
- Money Measurement Concept
- Historic Cost Concept

Business entity concept

Closely linked to the process of bookkeeping and accounting is the basic concept of business entity. The convention adopted by bookkeepers and accountants is that of treating each business, regardless of its legal status, as though it were an independent unit. This means that each business is in fact treated as though it were a 'living person' with its own identity quite separate to that of its owner or owners.

Based on this assumption books of account are kept in the name in which the business trades, and financial statements are prepared in that name.

Bookkeeping information is restricted to the business entity. Transactions recorded in the books relate only to the activities of the entity and do not account for the private affairs of the owner(s) of the business, except in circumstances where their actions affect the entity, for example where the owner(s) invest in or introduce capital to the business, or take drawings from the business.

Dual aspect concept

Duality is the foundation of the system of bookkeeping known as double entry. The concept requires that we recognise that there are two aspects to accounting. One representing the items of value or assets of a business, the other being claims against those assets, known as capital (the owner's claim,) or liabilities (the claims of other providers of funds). The two aspects must always be equal i.e. what the business entity **owns** (its assets) must be equal to what it **owes** (capital and liabilities). This relationship is expressed by what is commonly referred as 'the accounting equation' i.e.:

Assets = Capital + Liabilities

The above equation reflects the assumption that for each business transaction there is a 'giver' and a 'receiver'. The double entry system of bookkeeping is an expansion of this assumption which results in each transaction being recorded in the books of account twice. One entry is made to the left hand side of an account (debit side) with a corresponding entry of equal monetary value being made to the right hand side of an account (credit side).

Money measurement concept

As bookkeeping is the classification and recording of monetary transactions it follows that in keeping financial records and preparing financial statements we must concern ourselves only with business events to which a monetary value can be attached. However, there are many aspects of business life which cannot be expressed in monetary terms.

For example, the books and accounts will not reflect the flair, motivation or expertise of the owner(s), managers and workforce of the business, or evaluate relationships between owner(s), managers and the workforce, or relationships employees of the business may have with the outside world (customers in particular).

On the basis that we would have difficulty in accounting for the more qualitative or intangible factors of business life we must confine ourselves to accounting for transactions which can be translated into the common unit of money.

Historic cost concept

The quantitative information recorded in the books of account can be influenced by the person recording it or by what the information is required for. As a result, the historic cost concept has been adopted, whereby assets are valued at their original cost to the business. Transactions recorded in the books of account are in the main documented by the invoice as proof of the amount paid to acquire an asset, in payment of an expense, or of the amount received when goods are sold.

The books of account are therefore a historic record of the value at which goods and services (or the promise of goods and services) originally changed hands.

Accounting terms - assets, capital and liabilities

As referred to above, the fundamental principle of double entry bookkeeping is based on the dual aspect concept and the accounting equation:

$$\text{Assets} = \text{Capital} + \text{Liabilities}$$

You should note that wherever we know two of the terms within the accounting equation (Assets = Capital + Liabilities) we can calculate the missing term. For example:

If we are told that the assets of a business have a value of £250,000, and its liabilities are £50,000, we can calculate that the capital contribution of the owner of the business must be £200,000 (assets £250,000 less liabilities £50,000 = capital £50,000).

If we are told that the assets of a business have a value of £300,000 and the capital contribution of the owner to the business is £225,000, we can calculate that the liabilities of the business must be £75,000 (assets £300,000 less capital £225,000 = liabilities £75,000).

Given the information that the capital contribution of the owner to the business is £500,000 and that its liabilities are £100,000, we can calculate that its assets must have a value of £600,000 (capital £500,000 plus liabilities £100,000 = assets £600,000.

It is important that those individuals who are to process business transactions, and/or prepare financial statements, are able to recognise the assets, capital and liabilities of a business entity and be able to make a missing entry calculation if called upon to do so. You will see later in your studies how the missing term calculation is used when setting-up a double entry bookkeeping system.

The following is an explanation of the above terms which should prove suitable for the purpose of your studies at this level of the IAB qualification:

Assets:

These are items of value owned by a business, or amounts owing to the business. Assets can be further classified as being either Fixed or Current.

Fixed assets – are items of value which form the basis or framework of the business. Such items are held for the purpose of providing a service to the business in the long term and are not held for resale in the normal course of trading.

Examples of fixed assets include:

Land and buildings, fixtures, fittings and office equipment, plant and machinery, motor vehicles etc.

Current assets – these are items of value which are either in the form of liquid funds (cash and bank) or which are held for conversion into liquid funds in the normal course of trading. Examples of current assets include:

Stocks, debtors (customers who owe the business money for goods or services supplied on credit), short term investments, and liquid funds (cash on hand and in a bank account).

Capital:

Capital represents the funds provided to the business entity by its owner(s).

Liabilities:

Liabilities are the financial obligations of a business to individuals or organisations other than its owner(s). Whilst all claims on the assets of a business represent a liability we tend to make a distinction between the claim of the owner(s) (capital) and the claims of other providers of funds. Liabilities are further classified as being either Long-Term Liabilities or Current Liabilities.

Long-term liabilities – these are financial obligations which are repayable in the longer term. Long-term liabilities are claims on the business which do not fall due for payment within the next twelve months. Long-term liabilities include:

Loan stock (a method of raising funds used by a limited company), bank loans or other methods of raising finance from organisations or individuals where repayment is made over several years.

Current liabilities – are claims which are repayable in the short-term. They are financial obligations which fall due for payment within the next twelve months and include:

Creditors (amounts due to the suppliers of goods and services supplied on credit), a bank overdraft (meant to be a short-term borrowing facility).

The effect of transactions on the accounting equation

Having dealt with the identification of businesses Assets, Capital and Liabilities we can now relate this information to the effect of transactions on the accounting equation.

Consider the following scenario and note the effect each transaction has on the accounting equation (Assets = Capital + Liabilities).

Alan is a qualified metalworker and recently decided to set-up his own business making ornamental gates and fencing, the business is to trade in the name Iron Works.

On 1 March 201X Alan invested £40,000 of his own funds in the business, by transferring £40,000 from his personal bank account into a bank current account opened in the name of the business. At the same date, Alan borrowed £20,000 from the bank (repayable over 6 years) for the purpose of financing the setting-up of the business. The loan from the bank was transferred by the bank directly into the business bank current account.

The following balance sheet shows the financial position of Iron Works, i.e. its assets, capital and liabilities, at 1 March 201X:

Iron Works
Balance Sheet at 1 March 201X

	£
Current assets	
Cash at Bank	60,000
Total assets	60,000
Financed by:	
Capital	40,000
Long-term liabilities	
Bank Loan	20,000
Total capital and liabilities	60,000

Over the period 2 March to 7 March 201X the following five business transactions took place. Note in this example exercise VAT has been ignored.

201X

2 March	**Transaction 1** - Purchased a workshop on a local trading estate at a cost of £40,000, making payment from the business bank account.
3 March	**Transaction 2** - Purchased equipment for use in the business making a payment of £7,500 from the business bank account.
4 March	**Transaction 3** - Purchased a stock of materials at a cost of £2,500. The supplier, Steel Supplies, has invoiced Iron Works with the goods supplied, and has given the business 30 days in which to pay the invoice.
5 March	**Transaction 4** - Alan repaired a pair of gates and perimeter fencing for a local firm and charged £1,000 for the work. Alan invoiced the firm (Building Supplies Ltd) with the repairs and gave them 7 days in which to pay the invoice. When repairing the gates and fencing Alan took materials from his stock of materials which had cost him £400, and made a profit of £600 on the repair work.
7 March	**Transaction 5** - Purchased a transit van for use in the business at a cost of £10,000. The vehicle was paid for from the business bank account.

The following table shows the effect of each of the five transactions above on the accounting equation:

Iron Works

Details	1 March Opening financial position	2 March	3 March	4 March	5 March	7 March
(Transaction number)		**(1)**	**(2)**	**(3)**	**(4)**	**(5)**
Fixed assets						
Premises		***40,000***	40,000	40,000	40,000	40,000
Equipment			***7,500***	7,500	7,500	7,500
Vehicle						***10,000***
Total fixed assets		40,000	47,500	47,500	47,500	57,500
Current assets						
Stock of materials				***2,500***	***2,100***	2,100
Trade debtor (Building Supplies Ltd)					***1,000***	1,000
Cash at bank	60,000	***20,000***	***12,500***	12,500	12,500	***2,500***
Total current assets	60,000	20,000	12,500	15,000	15,600	5,600
Total assets	60,000	60,000	60,000	62,500	63,100	63,100
Capital	40,000	40,000	40,000	40,000	40,000	40,000
Profit					***600***	600
Long-term liabilities						
Bank loan	20,000	20,000	20,000	20,000	20,000	20,000
Current Liabilities						
Trade creditor (Steel Supplies)				***2,500***	2,500	2,500
Total capital and liabilities	60,000	60,000	60,000	62,500	63,100	63,100

The effect of each of the five transactions on the financial position of the business can be explained as follows:

Transaction 1 - This transaction is classified as capital expenditure. The value of a current asset (cash at bank) is reduced by £40,000, and the business now has a fixed asset (business premises at a cost of £40,000).

Transaction 2 - This transaction is also classified as capital expenditure. The value of a current asset (cash at bank) is reduced by £7,500, and the business now has a further fixed asset (equipment at a cost of £7,500).

Transaction 3 - This transaction is classified as revenue expenditure. The value of the current assets of the business has increased by £2,500 as the business now holds a stock of materials. However, the business now also has a current liability (trade creditor), as the business has taken 30 day's credit from Steel Supplies the supplier of the parts.

Transaction 4 - This transaction is classified as revenue income. Overall current assets have increased in value by £600 and the increase, which is profit on a job on completed for Building Supplies Ltd, has been claimed by Alan and increases his capital. The table shows that the value of the stock of materials (a current asset) has decreased by £400, and that the business now has a further current asset of £1,000 i.e. the amount owed to the business by Building Supplies Ltd. Alans claim on the assets of the business has increased by £600.

Transaction 5 - This transaction is classified as capital expenditure. The value of a current asset (cash at bank) is reduced by £10,000, and the value of fixed assets is increased as the business has acquired a transit van at a cost of £10,000

The financial position of Alan's business as at 7 March 201X, is presented below in the form of a further balance sheet:

Iron Works
Balance Sheet at 7 March 201X

	£	£
Fixed assets		
Premises	40,000	
Equipment	7,500	
Vehicle	10,000	
		57,500
Current assets		
Stock of parts	2,100	
Trade debtor (Building Supplies Ltd)	1,000	
Cash at Bank	2,500	
		5,600
Total assets		63,100
Financed by:		
Capital	40,000	
Add Profit	600	
		40,600
Long-term liabilities		
Bank loan		20,000
Current Liabilities		
Trade creditor (Steel Supplies)		2,500
Total capital and liabilities		63,100

Businesses are likely to be faced with having to account for a high volume of transactions taking place each day. It wouldn't be possible to show the effect of each transaction on the financial position of a business by simply adjusting figures on a table, or to calculate whether the business is making a profit or loss after each transaction.

Keeping a record of business transactions is the purpose of the bookkeeping system. Calculating whether a business has made a profit or loss during an accounting period and showing its financial position at the end of an accounting period is the purpose of accounting and the preparation and presentation of financial statements.

Double entry bookkeeping

In a double entry bookkeeping system transactions are recorded in accounts known as 'ledger accounts'. Traditionally accounts were paper based and transactions were processed manually, the term 'ledger' was used to describe a book in which accounts were kept. In a computerised bookkeeping system double entry takes place in a ledger known as the 'nominal ledger'.

In a manual bookkeeping system 'T accounts' are usually kept. The following is an example of a ledger account in 'T' account format. The 'T' account allows the bookkeeper to record each transaction in either the debit side or credit side of each account, each transaction date, details and amount is recorded:

DR			**Account Title**		**CR**
Date	**Details**	**£**	**Date**	**Details**	**£**

One disadvantage of a 'T' account is that the balance on the account (by how much the value of transactions posted to one side of the account exceeds the value of transactions posted to the opposite side of the account), cannot be seen without balancing off the account. Balancing off can be a lengthy process, particularly where there are a large number of accounts each containing several postings.

The following is an example of a customer account (XYZ Trading) extracted from the ledger of a business. The account is in 'T' account format and shows several transactions recorded in the account. The example also shows the account balanced off to show the closing balance on the account.

DR		XYZ Trading			CR
201Y	**Details**	**£**	**201Y**	**Details**	**£**
2 May	Sales	2,800	6 May	Sales returns	400
20 May	Sales	1,200	31 May	Bank	2,400
			31 May	Balance c/d	1,200
		4,000			4,000
31 May	Balance b/d	1,200			

An alternative format for a ledger account is to present the account as a 'running balance' account. Just like the 'T' account, the running balance account has columns for entering transaction dates and details, but the debit (DR) and credit (CR) columns are shown side-by-side, the account then has a column where a running balance, which is adjusted following the recording of each transaction, is entered. By adding a further column to the account, we can indicate whether the running balance is a debit or credit balance.

The following is an example of a ledger account shown in running balance format.

Account Title

Date	Details	Debit		Credit		Balance		DR/CR
		£	p	£	p	£	p	

The account of the customer (XYZ Trading), previously shown in in 'T' account format is now represented below in running balance format.

XYZ Trading

Date	Details	Debit		Credit		Balance		DR/CR
		£	p	£	p	£	p	
2 May	Sales	2,800	00			2,800	00	DR
6 May	Sales returns			400	00	2,400	00	DR
20 May	Sales	1,200	00			3,600	00	DR
31 May	Bank			2,400	00	1,200	00	DR

Lesson 9 – Introduction to Double Entry Processing

The double entry system of bookkeeping requires that the 'giver' and 'receiver' element of each transaction (which is the basis of the dual aspect concept and the accounting equation), is recognised and accounted for.

This results in each business transaction being recorded with a left hand or **Debit (DR)** entry in a suitable ledger account, with a corresponding entry of equal monetary value also being recorded in the right hand side or **Credit (CR)** side of another suitable ledger account.

Suitable accounts are those accounts which will provide a business with an analysis of its transactions.

On setting-up a bookkeeping system for a new business assets are recorded as debit entries within ledger accounts, with capital and liabilities being recorded as credit entries (see the diagram below). If all transactions are recorded with a debit entry and corresponding credit entry, then arithmetic accuracy within the books of account will always be maintained i.e. debit entries will always be equal in value to credit entries.

See the diagram below:

Once a business starts to trade, ledger accounts will be used not only to record the changes in assets, liabilities and capital, but also the business's costs, expenses, income earned from its trading and/or non-trading activities, and any proprietor drawings. At the end of an accounting period debit and credit balances on ledger accounts are likely to represent:

*Costs are associated with making and buying, expenses are associated with the selling, distribution and the administration of a business.

The following entries are made within ledger accounts to increase or decrease debit and credit balances on the accounts:

– To increase a debit balance on a ledger account, debit the account

– To decrease a debit balance on a ledger account, credit the account

- To increase a credit balance on a ledger account, credit the account

- To decrease a credit balance on a ledger account, debit the account

Real time and batch processing

Two methods of processing are in general use by businesses as the basis of recording transactions in their accounting system. These methods are known as 'real time' and 'batch' processing'

Real time processing, or 'single transaction processing' as it is also known, is a method of processing whereby individual transactions are processed as they take place. The main advantage from real time processing is that the bookkeeping system is always up-to-date. However single transaction processing the system is much slower than the system of processing known as 'batch processing'. Real time processing also tends to be less accurate than batch processing, and generally is only suitable where a low volume of transactions is to be processed.

Batch processing is a method of processing whereby all transactions of the same 'nature' or 'type' are batched for a given period of time. At the end of the agreed time period the transactions are then processed collectively. Batch processing is extensively used when an accounting system is computerised.

In practice, it is quite common to batch sales invoices, purchase invoices, credit notes issued and received, and receipt and payment transactions. The batching period usually depends on the volume of transactions to be processed. Some organisations will batch and post on say a weekly cycle, others may batch and post say every two / three days, or even on a daily basis where there is an extremely high volume of transactions to process.

The advantages of batch processing include speed and accuracy, the main disadvantage, however, is that the books of account lag behind real time events whilst information is being batched and awaiting posting.

Double entry processing

Before you move on to process transactions using a computerised accounting package it is recommended that you learn more about the principles of double entry bookkeeping. The theory being that an insight into the mechanics of processing will better help you understand the basis on which a computerised bookkeeping system operates.

- When recording a transaction in the debit side of a ledger account the information recorded in the details column usually makes reference to the account being credited. Likewise, the information recorded in the details column on the credit side of a ledger account usually refers to the ledger account being debited. However, it is not uncommon to enter document references in the details column when recording transactions.

- Where a business trades i.e. buys and sells goods, a stock account is kept in the nominal ledger. Stock is the accounting term used to describe the goods a business holds for resale. However, this account is **only** used at the beginning and end of an accounting period when the value of the opening and closing stock of a business is recorded and used in the preparation of the profit and loss account. The following ledger accounts are used to account for increases and decreases in stock in an accounting period:

- The cost of goods bought for resale and put into stock in an accounting period is recorded in a purchases account.
- Income from goods sold and taken from stock in an accounting period is recorded in a sales account.
- Goods returned to suppliers and taken out of stock in an accounting period are recorded in a purchase returns account.
- Goods returned by customers and put back into stock in an accounting period are recorded in a sales returns account.

- Where goods are sold on credit to customers an account is opened in the name of each customer. The business needs to know who owes it money, and how much they owe. Customers which owe the business money are known as debtors.
- Where goods are purchased on credit from suppliers an account is opened in the name of each supplier. The business needs to know who it owes money to, and how much they owed. Suppliers to which the business owes money are known as creditors.
- Expenses incurred in running the business are posted (debited) to relevant expense accounts. Although a detailed analysis of expenses is recommended, some expense transactions may be grouped together under one account title. For example, road tax, vehicle insurance, petrol, diesel and vehicle repairs are usually posted (debited) to a vehicle expenses account
- Separate cash and bank accounts are usually kept for the purpose of accounting for cash and bank receipts and payments. Receipts are debited to the cash or bank account and payments credited to the accounts
- Where the business borrows money from say a bank or other financial institution a loan account is kept and the amount borrowed is credited to the account
- Amounts in cash taken from a cash box, cash register, or from the business bank account by the owner of the business for private purposes, or goods taken by the owner from stock by the owner for private use must be recorded in the books and posted (debited) to a drawings account

The use of control accounts

The term 'debtors' is used in accounting to collectively describe all credit customers of a business. The term 'creditors' is used to collectively describe all credit suppliers of a business. In a computerised accounting system, in addition to keeping accounts in the name of individual customers (debtors) and suppliers (creditors) accounts known as 'control accounts' are also kept.

Control accounts are 'total accounts'. The debtors control account is an account for total debtors, and the creditors control account is an account for total creditors. In a computerised bookkeeping system control accounts are within the double entry system and are kept in the nominal ledger, whereas the accounts of individual customers (debtors) and suppliers (creditors) are kept in separate subsidiary ledgers which are outside the double entry system, these accounts are often referred to as 'customer and supplier records'. The accounts of individual customers are kept in a subsidiary ledger known as the 'sales ledger', and the accounts of individual suppliers are kept in a subsidiary ledger known as the 'purchase ledger'.

When recording transactions in the accounts of individual credit customers and credit suppliers, in addition to recording the transaction in the account of the customer in the sales ledger, or supplier in the purchase ledger, the system will also automatically record the transaction in the debtors control account or creditors control account in the nominal ledger Therefore, at any point in time:

- The balance on the debtors control account in the nominal ledger should be equal to the total of all balances on the individual accounts of credit customers in the customers record i.e. the balance on the debtors control account represents the total amount a business is owed by its debtors at any point in time

- The balance on the creditors control account in the nominal ledger should be equal to the total of all balances on the individual accounts of credit suppliers in the purchase ledger i.e. the balance on the creditors control account represents the total amount a business owes to its creditors at any point in time

Whereas in a manual bookkeeping system a transaction may have to be entered more than once in different parts of the accounting system, computerised accounting packages are integrated. This means that a transaction is entered on the system once and the accounting package then makes all the required entries within the system. For example:

Invoices issued – nominal ledger (within the double entry system)

An invoice is issued to a credit customer Kane & Co, the system will automatically:

DR the gross amount invoiced to the debtors control account

CR the net value of the goods sold to the sales account

CR the VAT element of the transaction to the VAT sales tax account

Invoices issued – customer record (outside the double entry system)

DR the gross amount invoiced to the account of Kane & Co

Credit notes issued – nominal ledger (within the double entry system)

A credit note is issued to a credit customer Kane & Co, the system will automatically:

CR the gross amount on the credit note to the debtors control account

DR the net amount of the goods returned to the sales returns account

DR the VAT element of the transaction to the VAT sales tax account

Credit notes issued – customer record (outside the double entry system)

CR the gross amount on the credit note to the account of Kane & Co.

Remittance advices and payments received – nominal ledger (within the double entry system)

A payment is received by BACS from a credit customer Kane & Co, the system will automatically:

CR the amount received to the debtors control account

DR the amount received to the bank account

Remittance advices received and payments received – customer record (outside the double entry system)

CR the amount received to the account of Kane & Co

The following 'account' summarises the recording a business's transactions with its credit customers in the debtors control account in the nominal ledger:

Nominal Ledger

DR **Debtors Control** **CR**

Transaction	Source of posting	Transactions	Source of posting
Sales on credit	*Invoices issued to customers*	*Sales returns*	*Credit notes issued to customers*
		Payments received from credit customers	*Remittance advices and amounts received from customers*

Invoices received – nominal ledger (within the double entry system)

A business receives an invoice from a credit supplier Baker & Sons, the system will automatically:

CR total gross amount invoiced to the creditors control account

DR the net amount to the purchases account

DR the VAT to the VAT purchase tax account

Invoices received – supplier record (outside the double entry system)

CR the gross amount invoiced to the account of Baker & Sons

Credit notes received – nominal ledger (within the double entry system)

A business receives a credit note from Baker & Sons a credit supplier, the system will automatically:

DR the gross amount on the credit note to the creditors control account

CR the net goods amount of the goods purchased to the purchase returns account

CR the VAT element of the transaction to the VAT purchase tax account

Credit notes received – supplier record (outside the double entry system)

DR the gross amount on the credit note to the account of Baker & Sons

Remittance advices issued and payments made – nominal ledger (within the double entry system)

A business makes a payment from its bank account to Baker & Sons a credit supplier, the system will automatically:

DR the amount paid to the creditors control account

CR the amount paid to the bank account

Remittance advices issued and payments made – supplier record (outside the double entry system)

DR the amount paid to the account of Baker & Sons

The following 'account' summarises the recording a business's transactions with its credit suppliers in the creditors control account in the nominal ledger:

Nominal Ledger

DR **Creditors Control** **CR**

Transaction	Source of posting	Transactions	Source of posting
Purchase returns	***Credit notes received from suppliers***	***Purchases on credit***	***Invoices received from suppliers***
Payments made to credit suppliers	***Remittance advices and amounts paid to suppliers***		

Double entry processing – worked example

The following is worked example intended to introduce you to the basics of double entry processing. The example shows how a range of transactions would are recorded in ledger accounts in a manual bookkeeping system. Each transaction has been given a transaction number and is processed through appropriate ledger accounts relevant to that transaction, the running balance on ledger accounts used are recalculated as each transaction is entered.

At the end of the processing exercise all the accounts used in the example are reproduced in alphabetical order and the accuracy of the processing is verified by preparing a trial balance.

Alice has recently decided to set-up her own business. The business is to supply stationery and educational supplies on both a credit and cash-and-carry basis. The business is to trade from a unit on a local business park, and will trade in the name of Select Stationery.

Alice has already agreed terms with several local schools, colleges and businesses to supply them with goods on credit. She has also agreed credit terms with several suppliers of stationery and office furniture products.

The business is registered for VAT. The following transactions took place in the first week of trading i.e. 1 May 201X to 7 May 201X.

201X	**Transaction number 1 (TR1)**
1 May	Alice transferred £50,000 from her private bank account into a bank current account opened in the name of the business as her capital contribution on setting-up the business. The transaction is not subject to VAT.
DR	Bank account (receiver account)
CR	Capital account (giver account)

Select Stationery – Nominal Ledger (extract)

		Bank						
201X	**Details**	**Debit**		**Credit**		**Balance**		**DR/CR**
		£	**p**	**£**	**p**	**£**	**p**	
1 May	*Capital (TR1)*	*50,000*	*00*			*50,000*	*00*	*DR*

Capital								
201X	**Details**	**Debit**		**Credit**		**Balance**		**DR/CR**
		£	**p**	**£**	**p**	**£**	**p**	
1 May	***Bank (TR1)***			***50,000***	***00***	***50,000***	***00***	***CR***

201X	**Transaction number 2 (TR2)**
1 May	Alice borrowed £25,000 from the bank to help her finance the setting up of the business. The loan, which is repayable over 5 years, was transferred by the bank directly into the business bank current account. The transaction is not subject to VAT.
DR	Bank account (receiver account)
CR	Loan account (giver account)

Select Stationery – Nominal Ledger (extract)

Bank								
201X	**Details**	**Debit**		**Credit**		**Balance**		**DR/CR**
		£	**p**	**£**	**p**	**£**	**p**	
1 May	Capital (TR1)	50,000	00			50,000	00	DR
1 May	***Loan (TR2)***	***25,000***	***00***			***75,000***	***00***	***DR***

Loan								
201X	**Details**	**Debit**		**Credit**		**Balance**		**DR/CR**
		£	**p**	**£**	**p**	**£**	**p**	
1 May	***Bank (TR2)***			***25,000***	***00***	***25,000***	***00***	***CR***

201X	**Transaction number 3 (TR3)**
1 May	Paid rent of £4,500 for three months on the warehouse unit from which the business operates. Payment was made from the business bank current account by cheque. The transaction is not subject to VAT.
DR	Rent account (receiver account)
CR	Bank account (giver account)

Select Stationery – Nominal Ledger (extract)

Rent								
201X	**Details**	**Debit**		**Credit**		**Balance**		**DR/CR**
		£	**p**	**£**	**p**	**£**	**p**	
1 May	***Bank (TR3)***	***4,500***	***00***			***4,500***	***00***	***DR***

Bank								
201X	**Details**	**Debit**		**Credit**		**Balance**		**DR/CR**
		£	**p**	**£**	**p**	**£**	**p**	
1 May	Capital (TR1)	50,000	00			50,000	00	DR
1 May	Loan (TR2)	25,000	00			75,000	00	DR
1 May	***Rent (TR3)***			***4,500***	***00***	***70,500***	***00***	***DR***

201X	**Transaction number 4 (TR4)**
1 May	Bought racking and shelving to fit out the warehouse unit at a cost of £9,600. Payment was made from the business bank current account by cheque. The transaction is inclusive of VAT at the standard rate of 20% (£1,600).
DR	Warehouse Fixtures & Fittings account (receiver account)
DR	VAT purchase tax account (receiver account – the VAT is reclaimable from HMRC)
CR	Bank account (giver account)

Select Stationery – Nominal Ledger (extract)

Warehouse Fixtures & Fittings								
201X	**Details**	**Debit**		**Credit**		**Balance**		**DR/CR**
		£	**p**	**£**	**p**	**£**	**p**	
1 May	***Bank (TR4)***	***8,000***	***00***			***8,000***	***00***	***DR***

VAT Purchase Tax								
201X	**Details**	**Debit**		**Credit**		**Balance**		**DR/CR**
		£	**p**	**£**	**p**	**£**	**p**	
1 May	***Bank (TR4)***	***1,600***	***00***			***1,600***	***00***	***DR***

Bank								
201X	**Details**	**Debit**		**Credit**		**Balance**		**DR/CR**
		£	**p**	**£**	**p**	**£**	**p**	
1 May	Capital (TR1)	50,000	00			50,000	00	DR
1 May	Loan (TR2)	25,000	00			75,000	00	DR
1 May	Rent (TR3)			4,500	00	70,500	00	DR
1 May	***Warehouse fixtures & fittings and VAT (TR4)***			***9,600***	***00***	***60,900***	***00***	***DR***

201X	Transaction number 5 (TR5)
1 May	Bought a delivery van for use in the business £18,000, making payment from the business current account by debit card. The transaction is inclusive of VAT at the standard rate of 20% (£3,000).
DR	Vehicles account (receiver account)
DR	VAT purchase tax account (receiver account – the VAT will be reclaimed from HMRC)
CR	Bank account (giver account)

Select Stationery – Nominal Ledger (extract)

Vehicles

201X	Details	Debit £	p	Credit £	p	Balance £	p	DR/CR
1 May	***Bank (TR5)***	***15,000***	***00***			***15,000***	***00***	***DR***

VAT Purchase Tax

201X	Details	Debit £	p	Credit £	p	Balance £	p	DR/CR
1 May	Bank (TR4)	1,600	00			1,600	00	DR
1 May	***Bank (TR5)***	***3,000***	***00***			***4,600***	***00***	***DR***

Bank

201X	Details	Debit £	p	Credit £	p	Balance £	p	DR/CR
1 May	Capital (TR1)	50,000	00			50,000	00	DR
1 May	Loan (TR2)	25,000	00			75,000	00	DR
1 May	Rent (TR3)			4,500	00	70,500	00	DR
1 May	Warehouse fixtures & fittings and VAT (TR4)			9,600	00	60,900	00	DR
1 May	***Vehicles and VAT (TR5)***			***18,000***	***00***	***42,900***	***00***	***DR***

201X	Transaction number 6 (TR6)
1 May	Purchased goods for resale on credit from Office Supplies Ltd £15,600 (invoice OS1040). The supplier gave Select Stationery 7 days in which to settle the invoice. The transaction is inclusive of VAT at the standard rate of 20% (£2,600).
DR	Purchases account (receiver account)
DR	VAT purchase tax account (receiver account – the VAT will be reclaimed from HMRC)
CR	Creditors control account (giver account – within the double entry bookkeeping system). Credit also the account of Office Supplies Ltd in the purchase ledger (giver account – supplier record outside the double entry bookkeeping system)

Select Stationery - Nominal Ledger (extract)

Purchases

201X	Details	Debit £	p	Credit £	p	Balance £	p	DR/CR
1 May	***Creditors control (TR6)***	***13,000***	***00***			***13,000***	***00***	***DR***

VAT Purchase Tax

201X	Details	Debit £	p	Credit £	p	Balance £	p	DR/CR
1 May	Bank (TR4)	1,600	00			1,600	00	DR
1 May	Bank (TR5)	3,000	00			4,600	00	DR
1 May	***Creditors control (TR6)***	***2,600***	***00***			***7,200***	***00***	***DR***

Creditors Control

201X	Details	Debit £	p	Credit £	p	Balance £	p	DR/CR
1 May	***Purchases and VAT (TR6)***			***15,600***	***00***	***15,600***	***00***	***CR***

Select Stationery – Purchase Ledger/Supplier Record (extract)

Office Supplies Ltd								
201X	**Details**	**Debit**		**Credit**		**Balance**		**DR/CR**
		£	**p**	**£**	**p**	**£**	**p**	
1 May	***Invoice OS1040 (TR6)***			***15,600***	***00***	***15,600***	***00***	***CR***

201X	**Transaction number 7 (TR7)**
1 May	Alice presented a cheque for £100 to the bank, the cheque was made payable to 'cash'. The cash she received was put into a petty cash box. The transaction is not subject to VAT.
DR	Petty Cash account (receiver account)
CR	Bank account (giver account)

Select Stationery - Nominal Ledger (extract)

Petty Cash								
201X	**Details**	**Debit**		**Credit**		**Balance**		**DR/CR**
		£	**p**	**£**	**p**	**£**	**p**	
1 May	***Bank (TR7)***	***100***	***00***			***100***	***00***	***DR***

Bank								
201X	**Details**	**Debit**		**Credit**		**Balance**		**DR/CR**
		£	**p**	**£**	**p**	**£**	**p**	
1 May	Capital (TR1)	50,000	00			50,000	00	DR
1 May	Loan (TR2)	25,000	00			75,000	00	DR
1 May	Rent (TR3)			4,500	00	70,500	00	DR
1 May	Warehouse fixtures & fittings and VAT (TR4)			9,600	00	60,900	00	DR
1 May	Vehicles and VAT (TR5)			18,000	00	42,900	00	DR
1 May	***Petty cash (TR7)***			***100***	***00***	***42,800***	***00***	***DR***

201X	Transaction number 8 (TR8)
1 May	Paid road tax and insurance on delivery van £1,200, making payment directly from the business bank current account. The transaction is not subject to VAT.
DR	Vehicle expenses account (receiver account)
CR	Bank account (giver account)

Select Stationery - Nominal Ledger (extract)

Vehicle expenses								
201X	**Details**	**Debit**		**Credit**		**Balance**		**DR/CR**
		£	**p**	**£**	**p**	**£**	**p**	
1 May	***Bank (TR8)***	***1,200***	***00***			***1,200***	***00***	***DR***

Bank								
201X	**Details**	**Debit**		**Credit**		**Balance**		**DR/CR**
		£	**p**	**£**	**p**	**£**	**p**	
1 May	Capital (TR1)	50,000	00			50,000	00	DR
1 May	Loan (TR2)	25,000	00			75,000	00	DR
1 May	Rent (TR3)			4,500	00	70,500	00	DR
1 May	Warehouse fixtures & fittings and VAT (TR4)			9,600	00	60,900	00	DR
1 May	Vehicles and VAT (TR5)			18,000	00	42,900	00	DR
1 May	Petty cash (TR7)			100	00	42,800	00	DR
1 May	***Vehicle expenses (TR8)***			***1,200***	***00***	***41,600***	***00***	***DR***

201X	Transaction number 9 (TR9)
1 May	Filled van with diesel £90, making payment from the bank current account by debit card. The transaction is inclusive of VAT at standard rate 20% (£15).
DR	Vehicle expenses account (receiver account)
DR	VAT purchase tax account (receiver account – the VAT will be reclaimed from HMRC)
CR	Bank account (giver account)

Select Stationery - Nominal Ledger (extract)

Vehicle Expenses								
201X	**Details**	**Debit**		**Credit**		**Balance**		**DR/CR**
		£	**p**	**£**	**p**	**£**	**p**	
1 May	Bank (TR8)	1,200	00			1,200	00	DR
1 May	***Bank (TR9)***	***75***	***00***			***1,275***	***00***	***DR***

VAT Purchase Tax								
201X	**Details**	**Debit**		**Credit**		**Balance**		**DR/CR**
		£	**p**	**£**	**p**	**£**	**p**	
1 May	Bank (TR4)	1,600	00			1,600	00	DR
1 May	Bank (TR5)	3,000	00			4,600	00	DR
1 May	Purchase ledger control (TR6)	2,600	00			7,200	00	DR
1 May	***Bank (TR9)***	***15***	***00***			***7,215***	***00***	***DR***

Bank								
201X	**Details**	**Debit**		**Credit**		**Balance**		**DR/CR**
		£	**p**	**£**	**p**	**£**	**p**	
1 May	Capital (TR1)	50,000	00			50,000	00	DR
1 May	Loan (TR2)	25,000	00			75,000	00	DR
1 May	Rent (TR3)			4,500	00	70,500	00	DR
1 May	Warehouse fixtures & fittings and VAT (TR4)			9,600	00	60,900	00	DR
1 May	Vehicles and VAT (TR5)			18,000	00	42,900	00	DR
1 May	Petty cash (TR7)			100	00	42,800	00	DR
1 May	Vehicle expenses (TR8)			1,200	00	41,600	00	DR
1 May	***Vehicle expenses and VAT (TR9)***			***90***	***00***	***41,510***	***00***	***DR***

201X	**Transaction number 10 (TR10)**
2 May	Sold goods to the value of £1,800 on credit to the Midlands College (invoice 0001), allowing them 7 days in which to pay for the goods. The goods sold are inclusive of VAT at the standard rate of 20% (£300).
DR	Debtors control account (receiver account – within the double entry bookkeeping system). Debit also the account of Midlands College in the sales ledger (receiver account – customer record outside the double entry bookkeeping system)
CR	Sales account (giver account)
CR	VAT Sales tax account (giver account – the VAT will be paid over to HMRC)

Select Stationery - Nominal Ledger (extract)

Debtors Control								
201X	**Details**	**Debit £**	**p**	**Credit £**	**p**	**Balance £**	**p**	**DR/CR**
2 May	*Sales and VAT (TR10)*	*1,800*	*00*			*1,800*	*00*	*DR*

Sales								
201X	**Details**	**Debit £**	**p**	**Credit £**	**p**	**Balance £**	**p**	**DR/CR**
2 May	*Debtors control (TR10)*			*1,500*	*00*	*1,500*	*00*	*CR*

VAT Sales Tax								
201X	**Details**	**Debit £**	**p**	**Credit £**	**p**	**Balance £**	**p**	**DR/CR**
2 May	*Debtors control (TR10)*			*300*	*00*	*300*	*00*	*CR*

Select Stationery – Sales Ledger/Customer Record (extract)

Midlands College								
201X	**Details**	**Debit £**	**p**	**Credit £**	**p**	**Balance £**	**p**	**DR/CR**
2 May	*Invoice 0001 (TR10)*	*1,800*	*00*			*1,800*	*00*	*DR*

201X	**Transaction number 11 (TR11)**
2 May	Bought office stationery £12, making the payment in cash taken from the petty cash box. The payment is inclusive of VAT at the standard rate of 20% (£2)
DR	Stationery & postage account (receiver account)
DR	VAT purchase tax account (receiver account – the VAT will be reclaimed from HMRC)
CR	Petty cash account (giver account)

Select Stationery - Nominal Ledger (extract)

Stationery & Postage								
201X	**Details**	**Debit**		**Credit**		**Balance**		**DR/CR**
		£	**p**	**£**	**p**	**£**	**p**	
2 May	***Petty cash (TR11)***	***10***	***00***			***10***	***00***	***DR***

VAT Purchase Tax								
201X	**Details**	**Debit**		**Credit**		**Balance**		**DR/CR**
		£	**p**	**£**	**p**	**£**	**p**	
1 May	Bank (TR4)	1,600	00			1,600	00	DR
1 May	Bank (TR5)	3,000	00			4,600	00	DR
1 May	Creditors control (TR6)	2,600	00			7,200	00	DR
1 May	Bank (TR9)	15	00			7,215	00	DR
2 May	***Petty cash (TR11)***	***2***	***00***			***7,217***	***00***	***DR***

Petty Cash								
201X	**Details**	**Debit**		**Credit**		**Balance**		**DR/CR**
		£	**p**	**£**	**p**	**£**	**p**	
1 May	Bank (TR7)	100	00			100	00	DR
2 May	***Stationery, and VAT (TR11)***			***12***	***00***	***88***	***00***	***DR***

201X	**Transaction number 12 (TR12)**
3 May	Paid business rates £1,200, making the payment from the bank current account by direct debit. The transaction is not subject to VAT.
DR	Rates account (receiver account)
CR	Bank account (giver account)

Rates								
201X	**Details**	**Debit**		**Credit**		**Balance**		**DR/CR**
		£	**p**	**£**	**p**	**£**	**p**	
3 May	***Bank (TR12)***	***1,200***	***00***			***1,200***	***00***	***DR***

Bank								
201X	**Details**	**Debit**		**Credit**		**Balance**		**DR/CR**
		£	**p**	**£**	**p**	**£**	**p**	
1 May	Capital (TR1)	50,000	00			50,000	00	DR
1 May	Loan (TR2)	25,000	00			75,000	00	DR
1 May	Rent (TR3)			4,500	00	70,500	00	DR
1 May	Warehouse fixtures & fittings and VAT (TR4)			9,600	00	60,900	00	DR
1 May	Vehicles and VAT (TR5)			18,000	00	42,900	00	DR
1 May	Petty cash (TR7)			100	00	42,800	00	DR
1 May	Vehicle expenses (TR8)			1,200	00	41,600	00	DR
1 May	Vehicle expenses and VAT (TR9)			90	00	41,510	00	DR
3 May	***Rates (TR12)***			***1,200***	***00***	***40,310***	***00***	***DR***

201X	**Transaction number 13 (TR13)**
4 May	Received a credit note number OS0120 from Office Supplies Ltd, credit note total £360. Goods purchased from Office Supplies Ltd on 1 May 201X (TR6) were returned to them as they were not as ordered. The credit note included VAT at the standard rate of 20% (£60).
DR	Creditors control (receiver account). Debit also the account of Office Supplies Ltd in the purchase ledger reduce the balance on their account (giver account – supplier record outside the double entry bookkeeping system)
CR	Purchase returns account (giver account)
CR	VAT purchase tax account (giver account the VAT reclaimable from HMRC and accounted for on a previous invoice now has to be reduced)

Select Stationery - Nominal Ledger (extract)

Creditors Control								
201X	**Details**	**Debit**		**Credit**		**Balance**		**DR/CR**
		£	**p**	**£**	**p**	**£**	**p**	
1 May	Purchases and VAT (TR6)			15,600	00	15,600	00	CR
4 May	***Purchase returns and VAT (TR13)***	***360***	***00***			***15,240***	***00***	***CR***

Purchase Returns								
201X	**Details**	**Debit**		**Credit**		**Balance**		**DR/CR**
		£	**p**	**£**	**p**	**£**	**p**	
4 May	***Creditors control (TR13)***			***300***	***00***	***300***	***00***	***CR***

VAT Purchase Tax								
201X	**Details**	**Debit**		**Credit**		**Balance**		**DR/CR**
		£	**p**	**£**	**p**	**£**	**p**	
1 May	Bank (TR4)	1,600	00			1,600	00	DR
1 May	Bank (TR5)	3,000	00			4,600	00	DR
1 May	Creditors control (TR6)	2,600	00			7,200	00	DR
1 May	Bank (TR9)	15	00			7,215	00	DR
2 May	Petty cash (TR11)	2	00			7,217	00	DR
4 May	***Creditors control (TR13)***			***60***	***00***	***7,157***	***00***	***DR***

Select Stationery – Purchase Ledger/Supplier Record (extract)

Office Supplies Ltd								
201X	**Details**	**Debit**		**Credit**		**Balance**		**DR/CR**
		£	**p**	**£**	**p**	**£**	**p**	
1 May	Invoice OS1040 (TR6)			15,600	00	15,600	00	CR
4 May	***Credit note OS0120 (TR13)***	***360***	***00***			***15,240***	***00***	***CR***

201X	**Transaction number 14 (TR14)**
4 May	Purchased goods for resale on credit from Stationery World £7,200 (invoice SW0752). The supplier gave Select Stationery 30 days in which settle the invoice. The transaction is inclusive of VAT at the standard rate of 20% (£1,200).
DR	Purchases account (receiver account)
DR	VAT purchase tax account (receiver account – the VAT will be reclaimed from HMRC)
CR	Creditors control account (giver account – within the double entry bookkeeping system). Credit also the account of Stationery World in the purchase ledger (giver account – supplier record outside the double entry bookkeeping system)

Select Stationery - Nominal Ledger (extract)

Purchases								
201X	**Details**	**Debit**		**Credit**		**Balance**		**DR/CR**
		£	**p**	**£**	**p**	**£**	**p**	
1 May	Creditors control (TR6)	13,000	00			13,000	00	DR
4 May	***Creditors control (TR14)***	***6,000***	***00***			***19,000***	***00***	***DR***

VAT Purchase Tax								
201X	**Details**	**Debit**		**Credit**		**Balance**		**DR/CR**
		£	**p**	**£**	**p**	**£**	**p**	
1 May	Bank (TR4)	1,600	00			1,600	00	DR
1 May	Bank (TR5)	3,000	00			4,600	00	DR
1 May	Creditors control (TR6)	2,600	00			7,200	00	DR
1 May	Bank (TR9)	15	00			7,215	00	DR
2 May	Petty cash (TR11)	2	00			7,217	00	DR
4 May	Creditors ledger control (TR13)			60	00	7,157	00	DR
4 May	***Creditors control (TR14)***	***1,200***	***00***			***8,357***	***00***	***DR***

Creditors Control								
201X	**Details**	**Debit £**	**p**	**Credit £**	**p**	**Balance £**	**p**	**DR/CR**
1 May	Purchases and VAT (TR6)			15,600	00	15,600	00	CR
4 May	Purchase returns and VAT (TR13)	360	00			15,240	00	CR
4 May	***Purchases and VAT (TR14)***			***7,200***	***00***	***22,440***	***00***	***CR***

Select Stationery – Purchase Ledger/Supplier Record (extract)

Stationery World								
201X	**Details**	**Debit £**	**p**	**Credit £**	**p**	**Balance £**	**p**	**DR/CR**
1 May	***Invoice SW0752 (TR14)***			***7,200***	***00***	***7,200***	***00***	***CR***

201X	**Transaction number 15 (TR15)**
5 May	Sold goods to the value of £1,500 on credit to G & K Office Supplies (invoice 0002), allowing them 7 days in which to pay for the goods. The goods sold are inclusive of VAT at the standard rate of 20% (£250).
DR	Debtors control account (receiver account – within the double entry bookkeeping system). Debit also the account of G & K Office Supplies in the sales ledger (receiver account – customer record outside the double entry bookkeeping system)
CR	Sales account (giver account)
CR	VAT Sales tax account (giver account – the VAT will be paid over to HMRC)

Select Stationery - Nominal Ledger (extract)

Debtors Control								
201X	**Details**	**Debit £**	**p**	**Credit £**	**p**	**Balance £**	**p**	**DR/CR**
2 May	Sales and VAT (TR10)	1,800	00			1,800	00	DR
5 May	***Sales and VAT (TR15)***	***1,500***	***00***			***3,300***	***00***	***DR***

Sales								
201X	**Details**	**Debit**		**Credit**		**Balance**		**DR/CR**
		£	**p**	**£**	**p**	**£**	**p**	
2 May	Debtors control (TR10)			1,500	00	1,500	00	CR
5 May	***Debtors control (TR15)***			***1,250***	***00***	***2,750***	***00***	***CR***

VAT Sales Tax								
201X	**Details**	**Debit**		**Credit**		**Balance**		**DR/CR**
		£	**p**	**£**	**p**	**£**	**p**	
2 May	Debtors control (TR10)			300	00	300	00	CR
5 May	***Debtors control (TR15)***			***250***	***00***	***550***	***00***	***CR***

Select Stationery – Sales Ledger/Customer Record (extract)

G & K Office Supplies								
201X	**Details**	**Debit**		**Credit**		**Balance**		**DR/CR**
		£	**p**	**£**	**p**	**£**	**p**	
5 May	***Invoice 0002 (TR15)***	***1,500***	***00***			***1,500***	***00***	***DR***

201X	**Transaction number 16 (T16)**
5 May	Bought postage stamps £20, making the payment in cash taken from the petty cash box. The transaction is not subject to VAT.
DR	Stationery and postage account (receiver account)
CR	Petty cash account (giver account)

Select Stationery - Nominal Ledger (extract)

Stationery & Postage								
201X	**Details**	**Debit**		**Credit**		**Balance**		**DR/CR**
		£	**p**	**£**	**p**	**£**	**p**	
2 May	Petty cash (TR11)	10	00			10	00	DR
5 May	***Petty cash (TR16)***	***20***	***00***			***30***	***00***	***DR***

Petty Cash								
201X	**Details**	**Debit**		**Credit**		**Balance**		**DR/CR**
		£	**p**	**£**	**p**	**£**	**p**	
1 May	Bank (TR7)	100	00			100	00	DR
2 May	Stationery, and VAT (TR11)			12	00	88	00	DR
5 May	***Postage (TR16)***			***20***	***00***	***68***	***00***	***DR***

201X	**Transaction number 17 (TR17)**
6 May	Made payment of £15,240 to Office Supplies Ltd. The payment was made over the telephone from the business bank current account by debit card. The transaction is not subject to VAT
DR	Creditors control account (receiver account – within the double entry bookkeeping system). Debit also the account of Office Supplies Ltd in the purchase ledger (receiver account – supplier record outside the double entr bookkeeping system)
CR	Bank account (giver account)

Note: VAT on the above transaction was accounted for when the goods were invoiced by the supplier.

Select Stationery – Nominal Ledger (extract)

Creditors Control								
201X	**Details**	**Debit**		**Credit**		**Balance**		**DR/CR**
		£	**p**	**£**	**p**	**£**	**p**	
1 May	Purchases and VAT (TR6)			15,600	00	15,600	00	CR
4 May	Purchase returns and VAT (TR13)	360	00			15,240	00	CR
4 May	Purchases and VAT (TR14)			7,200	00	22,440	00	CR
6 May	***Bank (TR17)***	***15,240***	***00***			***7,200***	***00***	***CR***

Bank								
201X	**Details**	**Debit**		**Credit**		**Balance**		**DR/CR**
		£	**p**	**£**	**p**	**£**	**p**	
1 May	Capital (TR1)	50,000	00			50,000	00	DR
1 May	Loan (TR2)	25,000	00			75,000	00	DR
1 May	Rent (TR3)			4,500	00	70,500	00	DR
1 May	Warehouse fixtures & fittings and VAT (TR4)			9,600	00	60,900	00	DR
1 May	Vehicles and VAT (TR5)			18,000	00	42,900	00	DR
1 May	Petty cash (TR7)			100	00	42,800	00	DR
1 May	Vehicle expenses (TR8)			1,200	00	41,600	00	DR
1 May	Vehicle expenses and VAT (TR9)			90	00	41,510	00	DR
3 May	Rates (TR12)			1,200	00	40,310	00	DR
6 May	***Creditors control (TR17)***			***15,240***	***00***	***25,070***	***00***	***DR***

Select Stationery – Purchase Ledger/Supplier Record (extract)

Office Supplies Ltd								
201X	**Details**	**Debit**		**Credit**		**Balance**		**DR/CR**
		£	**p**	**£**	**p**	**£**	**p**	
1 May	Invoice OS1040 (TR6)			15,600	00	15,600	00	CR
4 May	Credit note OS0120 (TR13)	360	00			15,240	00	CR
6 May	***Bank (TR17)***	***15,240***	***00***			***0***	***00***	

201X	Transaction number 18 (TR18)
7 May	Paid monthly instalment of £480 for gas and electricity from the business bank current account by direct debit. The payment is inclusive of VAT at the standard rate of 20% (£80)
DR	Heat & light account (receiver account)
DR	VAT purchase tax account (receiver account – the VAT will be reclaimed from HMRC)
CR	Bank account (giver account)

Select Stationery – Nominal Ledger (extract)

Heat and Light

201X	Details	Debit £	p	Credit £	p	Balance £	p	DR/CR
7 May	***Bank (TR18)***	***400***	***00***			***400***	***00***	***DR***

VAT Purchase Tax

201X	Details	Debit £	p	Credit £	p	Balance £	p	DR/CR
1 May	Bank (TR4)	1,600	00			1,600	00	DR
1 May	Bank (TR5)	3,000	00			4,600	00	DR
1 May	Creditors control (TR6)	2,600	00			7,200	00	DR
1 May	Bank (TR9)	15	00			7,215	00	DR
2 May	Petty cash (TR11)	2	00			7,217	00	DR
4 May	Creditors control (TR13)			60	00	7,157	00	DR
4 May	Creditors control (TR14)	1,200	00			8,357	00	DR
7 May	***Bank (TR18)***	***80***	***00***			***8,437***	***00***	***DR***

Bank								
201X	**Details**	**Debit**		**Credit**		**Balance**		**DR/CR**
		£	**p**	**£**	**p**	**£**	**p**	
1 May	Capital (TR1)	50,000	00			50,000	00	DR
1 May	Loan (TR2)	25,000	00			75,000	00	DR
1 May	Rent (TR3)			4,500	00	70,500	00	DR
1 May	Warehouse fixtures & fittings and VAT (TR4)			9,600	00	60,900	00	DR
1 May	Vehicles and VAT (TR5)			18,000	00	42,900	00	DR
1 May	Petty cash (TR7)			100	00	42,800	00	DR
1 May	Vehicle expenses (TR8)			1,200	00	41,600	00	DR
1 May	Vehicle expenses and VAT (TR9)			90	00	41,510	00	DR
3 May	Rates (TR12)			1,200	00	40,310	00	DR
6 May	Creditors control (TR17)			15,240	00	25,070	00	DR
7 May	***Heat & light and VAT (TR18)***			***480***	***00***	***24,590***	***00***	***DR***

201X	**Transaction number 19 (TR19)**
7 May	Alice presented a cheque for £600 to the bank, the cheque was made payable to 'cash'. The cash she received was taken by Alice as her personal drawings. The transaction is not subject to VAT
DR	Drawings account (receiver account)
CR	Bank account (giver account)

Select Stationery – Nominal Ledger (extract)

Drawings								
201X	**Details**	**Debit**		**Credit**		**Balance**		**DR/CR**
		£	**p**	**£**	**p**	**£**	**p**	
7 May	***Bank (TR19)***	***600***	***00***			***600***	***00***	***DR***

Bank								
201X	**Details**	**Debit**		**Credit**		**Balance**		**DR/CR**
		£	**p**	**£**	**p**	**£**	**p**	
1 May	Capital (TR1)	50,000	00			50,000	00	DR
1 May	Loan (TR2)	25,000	00			75,000	00	DR
1 May	Rent (TR3)			4,500	00	70,500	00	DR
1 May	Warehouse fixtures & fittings and VAT (TR4)			9,600	00	60,900	00	DR
1 May	Vehicles and VAT (TR5)			18,000	00	42,900	00	DR
1 May	Petty cash (TR7)			100	00	42,800	00	DR
1 May	Vehicle expenses (TR8)			1,200	00	41,600	00	DR
1 May	Vehicle expenses and VAT (TR9)			90	00	41,510	00	DR
3 May	Rates (TR12)			1,200	00	40,310	00	DR
6 May	Creditors control (TR17)			15,240	00	25,070	00	DR
7 May	Heat & light and VAT (TR18)			480	00	24,590	00	DR
7 May	***Drawings (TR19)***			***600***	***00***	***23,990***	***00***	***DR***

201X	**Transaction number 20 (TR20)**
7 May	Paid wages of £1,550 to employees of the business from the business bank account by cheque. The transaction is not subject to VAT
DR	Wages account (receiver account)
CR	Bank account (giver account)

Select Stationery – Nominal Ledger (extract)

		Wages						
201X	**Details**	**Debit**		**Credit**		**Balance**		**DR/CR**
		£	**p**	**£**	**p**	**£**	**p**	
7 May	***Bank (TR20)***	***1,550***	***00***			***1,550***	***00***	***DR***

		Bank						
201X	**Details**	**Debit**		**Credit**		**Balance**		**DR/CR**
		£	**p**	**£**	**p**	**£**	**p**	
1 May	Capital (TR1)	50,000	00			50,000	00	DR
1 May	Loan (TR2)	25,000	00			75,000	00	DR
1 May	Rent (TR3)			4,500	00	70,500	00	DR
1 May	Warehouse fixtures & fittings and VAT (TR4)			9,600	00	60,900	00	DR
1 May	Vehicles and VAT (TR5)			18,000	00	42,900	00	DR
1 May	Petty cash (TR7)			100	00	42,800	00	DR
1 May	Vehicle expenses (TR8)			1,200	00	41,600	00	DR
1 May	Vehicle expenses and VAT (TR9)			90	00	41,510	00	DR
3 May	Rates (TR12)			1,200	00	40,310	00	DR
6 May	Creditors control (TR17)			15,240	00	25,070	00	DR
7 May	Heat & light and VAT (TR18)			480	00	24,590	00	DR
7 May	Drawings (TR19)			600	00	23,990	00	DR
7 May	***Wages (TR20)***			***1,550***	***00***	***22,440***	***00***	***DR***

201X	**Transaction number 21 (TR21)**
7 May	Cash sales in the form of notes and coins in the week totalled £1,860. All cash received has been paid into the business bank account. The amount received is inclusive of VAT at the standard rate of 20% (£310)
DR	Bank account (receiver account)
CR	Sales account (giver account)
CR	Sales tax account (giver account – the VAT will be paid over to HMRC)

Select Stationery – Nominal Ledger (extract)

		Bank						
201X	**Details**	**Debit**		**Credit**		**Balance**		**DR/CR**
		£	**p**	**£**	**p**	**£**	**p**	
1 May	Capital (TR1)	50,000	00			50,000	00	DR
1 May	Loan (TR2)	25,000	00			75,000	00	DR
1 May	Rent (TR3)			4,500	00	70,500	00	DR
1 May	Warehouse fixtures & fittings and VAT (TR4)			9,600	00	60,900	00	DR
1 May	Vehicles and VAT (TR5)			18,000	00	42,900	00	DR
1 May	Petty cash (TR7)			100	00	42,800	00	DR
1 May	Vehicle expenses (TR8)			1,200	00	41,600	00	DR
1 May	Vehicle expenses and VAT (TR9)			90	00	41,510	00	DR
3 May	Rates (TR12)			1,200	00	40,310	00	DR
6 May	Creditors control (TR17)			15,240	00	25,070	00	DR
7 May	Heat & light and VAT (TR18)			480	00	24,590	00	DR
7 May	Drawings (TR19)			600	00	23,990	00	DR
7 May	Wages (TR20)			1,550	00	22,440	00	DR
7 May	***Sales and VAT (TR21)***	***1,860***	***00***			***24,300***	***00***	***DR***

		Sales						
201X	**Details**	**Debit**		**Credit**		**Balance**		**DR/CR**
		£	**p**	**£**	**p**	**£**	**p**	
2 May	Debtors control (TR10)			1,500	00	1,500	00	CR
5 May	Debtors control (TR15)			1,250	00	2,750	00	CR
7 May	***Bank (TR21)***			***1,550***	***00***	***4,300***	***00***	***CR***

VAT Sales Tax								
201X	**Details**	**Debit**		**Credit**		**Balance**		**DR/CR**
		£	**p**	**£**	**p**	**£**	**p**	
2 May	Debtors control (TR10)			300	00	300	00	CR
5 May	Debtors control (TR15)			250	00	550	00	CR
7 May	***Bank (TR21)***			***310***	***00***	***860***	***00***	***CR***

201X	**Transaction number 22 (TR22)**
7 May	Cash sales in the week to customers who paid by plastic card (debit card and credit card) totalled £2,490. The card receipts reach the business bank current account automatically. The amount received is inclusive of VAT at the standard rate 0f 20% (£415)
DR	Bank account (receiver account)
CR	Sales account (giver account)
CR	Sales tax account (giver account – the VAT will be paid over to HMRC)

Select Stationery – Nominal Ledger (extract)

Bank								
201X	**Details**	**Debit**		**Credit**		**Balance**		**DR/CR**
		£	**p**	**£**	**p**	**£**	**p**	
1 May	Capital (TR1)	50,000	00			50,000	00	DR
1 May	Loan (TR2)	25,000	00			75,000	00	DR
1 May	Rent (TR3)			4,500	00	70,500	00	DR
1 May	Warehouse fixtures & fittings and VAT (TR4)			9,600	00	60,900	00	DR
1 May	Vehicles and VAT (TR5)			18,000	00	42,900	00	DR
1 May	Petty cash (TR7)			100	00	42,800	00	DR
1 May	Vehicle expenses (TR8)			1,200	00	41,600	00	DR
1 May	Vehicle expenses and VAT (TR9)			90	00	41,510	00	DR
3 May	Rates (TR12)			1,200	00	40,310	00	DR
6 May	Creditors control (TR17)			15,240	00	25,070	00	DR
7 May	Heat & light and VAT (TR18)			480	00	24,590	00	DR
7 May	Drawings (TR19)			600	00	23,990	00	DR
7 May	Wages (TR20)			1,550	00	22,440	00	DR
7 May	Sales and VAT (TR21)	1,860	00			24,300	00	DR
7 May	***Sales and VAT (TR22)***	***2,490***	***00***			***26,790***	***00***	***DR***

Sales							
201X	**Details**	**Debit**		**Credit**		**Balance**		**DR/CR**
		£	**p**	**£**	**p**	**£**	**p**	
2 May	Debtors control (TR10)			1,500	00	1,500	00	CR
5 May	Debtors control (TR15)			1,250	00	2,750	00	CR
7 May	Bank (TR21)			1,550	00	4,300	00	CR
7 May	***Bank (TR22)***			***2,075***	***00***	***6,375***	***00***	***CR***

VAT Sales Tax								
201X	**Details**	**Debit**		**Credit**		**Balance**		**DR/CR**
		£	**p**	**£**	**p**	**£**	**p**	
2 May	Debtors control (TR10)			300	00	300	00	CR
5 May	Debtors control (TR15)			250	00	550	00	CR
7 May	Bank (TR21)			310	00	860	00	CR
7 May	***Bank (TR22)***			***415***	***00***	***1,275***	***00***	***CR***

201X	**Transaction number 23 (TR23)**
7 May	Sold goods to the value of £1,590 on credit to the Midlands College (invoice 0003), allowing them 7 days in which to pay for the goods. The goods sold are inclusive of VAT at the standard rate of 20% (£265).
DR	Debtors control account (receiver account – within the double entry bookkeeping system). Debit also the account of Midlands College in the sales ledger (receiver account – customer record outside the double entry bookkeeping system)
CR	Sales account (giver account)
CR	VAT Sales tax account (giver account – the VAT will be paid over to HMRC)

Select Stationery - Nominal Ledger (extract)

Debtors Control								
201X	**Details**	**Debit**		**Credit**		**Balance**		**DR/CR**
		£	**p**	**£**	**p**	**£**	**p**	
2 May	Sales and VAT (TR10)	1,800	00			1,800	00	DR
5 May	Sales and VAT (TR15)	1,500	00			3,300	00	DR
7 May	***Sales and VAT (TR23)***	***1590***	***00***			***4,890***	***00***	***DR***

Sales								
201X	**Details**	**Debit £**	**p**	**Credit £**	**p**	**Balance £**	**p**	**DR/CR**
2 May	Debtors control (TR10)			1,500	00	1,500	00	CR
5 May	Debtors control (TR15)			1,250	00	2,750	00	CR
7 May	Bank (TR21)			1,550	00	4,300	00	CR
7 May	Bank (TR22)			2,075	00	6,375	00	CR
7 May	***Debtors control (TR23)***			***1,325***	***00***	***7,700***	***00***	***CR***

VAT Sales Tax								
201X	**Details**	**Debit £**	**p**	**Credit £**	**p**	**Balance £**	**p**	**DR/CR**
2 May	Debtors control (TR10)			300	00	300	00	CR
5 May	Debtors control (TR15)			250	00	550	00	CR
7 May	Bank (TR21)			310	00	860	00	CR
7 May	Bank (TR22)			415	00	1,275	00	CR
7 May	***Debtors control (TR23)***			***265***	***00***	***1,540***	***00***	***CR***

Select Stationery – Sales Ledger/Customer Record (extract)

Midlands College								
201X	**Details**	**Debit £**	**p**	**Credit £**	**p**	**Balance £**	**p**	**DR/CR**
2 May	Invoice 0001 (TR10)	1,800	00			1,800	00	DR
2 May	***Invoice 0003 (TR23)***	***1,590***	***00***			***3,390***	***00***	***DR***

201X	Transaction number 24 (T24)
7 May	Goods sold on credit to the G & K Office Supplies on 5 May 201X (T15), were returned by them as they were found to be damaged when unpacked. A credit note number 0001 for £240 was issued to G & K Office Supplies. The credit note included VAT at the standard rate of 20% (£40).
DR	Sales returns account (receiver account)
CR	Debtors control account (giver account). Credit also the account of G & BK Office Supplies in the sales ledger (giver account – customer record outside the double entry bookkeeping system)

Select Stationery – Nominal Ledger (extract)

Sales Returns

201X	Details	Debit £	p	Credit £	p	Balance £	p	DR/CR
7 May	***Debtors control (TR4)***	***200***	***00***			***200***	***00***	***DR***

VAT Sales Tax

201X	Details	Debit £	p	Credit £	p	Balance £	p	DR/CR
2 May	Debtors control (TR10)			300	00	300	00	CR
5 May	Debtors control (TR15)			250	00	550	00	CR
7 May	Bank (TR21)			310	00	860	00	CR
7 May	Bank (TR22)			415	00	1,275	00	CR
7 May	Debtors control (TR23)			265	00	1,540	00	CR
7 May	***Debtors control (TR24)***	***40***	***00***			***1,500***	***00***	***CR***

Debtors Control

201X	Details	Debit £	p	Credit £	p	Balance £	p	DR/CR
2 May	Sales and VAT (TR10)	1,800	00			1,800	00	DR
5 May	Sales and VAT (TR15)	1,500	00			3,300	00	DR
7 May	Sales and VAT (TR23)	1590	00			4,890	00	DR
7 May	***Sales returns and VAT (TR24)***			***240***	***00***	***4,650***	***00***	***DR***

Select Stationery – Sales Ledger/Customer Record (extract)

G & K Office Supplies								
201X	**Details**	**Debit**		**Credit**		**Balance**		**DR/CR**
		£	**p**	**£**	**p**	**£**	**p**	
5 May	Invoice 0002 (TR15)	1,500	00			1,500	00	DR
7 May	***Credit note 0001 (TR24)***			***240***	***00***	***1,260***	***00***	***DR***

Checking accuracy – the trial balance

The trial balance is a periodic listing of all balances on accounts in the double entry system. A computerised accounting system enables the user to generate a trial balance at regular intervals throughout the financial year. The trial balance is used to check the accuracy of the nominal ledger account balances and, at the financial year end, is usually the starting point from which financial statements are prepared.

All the ledger accounts in the nominal ledger, purchase ledger (supplier record) and sales ledger (customer record) of Select Stationery showing transactions processed in the week 1 May 201X to 7 May 201X are reproduced below.

The account balances within the double entry system i.e. the nominal ledger, have then been listed on the trail balance at 7 May 201X, and the trial balance debit and credit columns have been totalled.

Select Stationery – Nominal Ledger

Bank								
201X	**Details**	**Debit** £	p	**Credit** £	p	**Balance** £	p	**DR/CR**
1 May	Capital (TR1)	50,000	00			50,000	00	DR
1 May	Loan (TR2)	25,000	00			75,000	00	DR
1 May	Rent (TR3)			4,500	00	70,500	00	DR
1 May	Warehouse fixtures & fittings and VAT (TR4)			9,600	00	60,900	00	DR
1 May	Vehicles and VAT (TR5)			18,000	00	42,900	00	DR
1 May	Petty cash (TR7)			100	00	42,800	00	DR
1 May	Vehicle expenses (TR8)			1,200	00	41,600	00	DR
1 May	Vehicle expenses and VAT (TR9)			90	00	41,510	00	DR
3 May	Rates (TR12)			1,200	00	40,310	00	DR
6 May	Creditors control (TR17)			15,240		25,070	00	DR
7 May	Heat & light and VAT (TR18)			480	00	24,590	00	DR
7 May	Drawings (TR19)			600	00	23,990	00	DR
7 May	Wages (TR20)			1,550	00	22,440	00	DR
7 May	Sales and VAT (TR21)	1,860	00			24,300	00	DR
7 May	Sales and VAT (TR22)	2,490	00			26,790	00	DR

Capital								
201X	**Details**	**Debit** £	p	**Credit** £	p	**Balance** £	p	**DR/CR**
1 May	Bank (TR1)			50,000	00	50,000	00	CR

Creditors Control								
201X	**Details**	**Debit** £	p	**Credit** £	p	**Balance** £	p	**DR/CR**
1 May	Purchases and VAT (TR6)			15,600	00	15,600	00	CR
4 May	Purchase returns and VAT (TR13)	360	00			15,240	00	CR
4 May	Purchases and VAT (TR14)			7,200	00	22,440	00	CR
6 May	Bank (TR17)	15,240	00			7,200	00	CR

Debtors Control								
201X	**Details**	**Debit £**	**p**	**Credit £**	**p**	**Balance £**	**p**	**DR/CR**
2 May	Sales and VAT (TR10)	1,800	00			1,800	00	DR
5 May	Sales and VAT (TR15)	1,500	00			3,300	00	DR
7 May	Sales and VAT (TR23)	1590	00			4,890	00	DR
7 May	Sales returns and VAT (TR24)			240	00	4,650	00	DR

Drawings								
201X	**Details**	**Debit £**	**p**	**Credit £**	**p**	**Balance £**	**p**	**DR/CR**
7 May	Bank (TR19)	600	00			600	00	DR

Heat and Light								
201X	**Details**	**Debit £**	**p**	**Credit £**	**p**	**Balance £**	**p**	**DR/CR**
7 May	Bank (TR18)	400	00			400	00	DR

Loan								
201X	**Details**	**Debit £**	**p**	**Credit £**	**p**	**Balance £**	**p**	**DR/CR**
1 May	Bank (TR2)			25,000	00	25,000	00	CR

Petty Cash								
201X	**Details**	**Debit £**	**p**	**Credit £**	**p**	**Balance £**	**p**	**DR/CR**
1 May	Bank (TR7)	100	00			100	00	DR
2 May	Stationery, and VAT (TR11)			12	00	88	00	DR
5 May	Postage (TR16)			20	00	68	00	DR

Purchases								
201X	**Details**	**Debit**		**Credit**		**Balance**		**DR/CR**
		£	**p**	**£**	**p**	**£**	**p**	
1 May	Creditors control (TR6)	13,000	00			13,000	00	DR
4 May	Creditors control (TR14)	6,000	00			19,000	00	DR

Purchase Returns								
201X	**Details**	**Debit**		**Credit**		**Balance**		**DR/CR**
		£	**p**	**£**	**p**	**£**	**p**	
4 May	Creditors control (TR13)			300	00	300	00	CR

Rates								
201X	**Details**	**Debit**		**Credit**		**Balance**		**DR/CR**
		£	**p**	**£**	**p**	**£**	**p**	
3 May	Bank (TR12)	1,200	00			1,200	00	DR

Rent								
201X	**Details**	**Debit**		**Credit**		**Balance**		**DR/CR**
		£	**p**	**£**	**p**	**£**	**p**	
1 May	Bank (TR3)	4,500	00			4,500	00	DR

Sales								
201X	**Details**	**Debit**		**Credit**		**Balance**		**DR/CR**
		£	**p**	**£**	**p**	**£**	**p**	
2 May	Debtors control (TR10)			1,500	00	1,500	00	CR
5 May	Debtors control (TR15)			1,250	00	2,750	00	CR
7 May	Bank (TR21)			1,550	00	4,300	00	CR
7 May	Bank (TR22)			2,075	00	6,375	00	CR
7 May	Debtors control (TR23)			1,325	00	7,700	00	CR

Sales Returns								
201X	**Details**	**Debit**		**Credit**		**Balance**		**DR/CR**
		£	**p**	**£**	**p**	**£**	**p**	
7 May	Debtors control (TR4)	200	00			200	00	DR

Stationery & Postage								
201X	**Details**	**Debit**		**Credit**		**Balance**		**DR/CR**
		£	**p**	**£**	**p**	**£**	**p**	
2 May	Petty cash (TR11)	10	00			10	00	DR
5 May	Petty cash (TR16)	20	00			30	00	DR

VAT Purchase Tax								
201X	**Details**	**Debit**		**Credit**		**Balance**		**DR/CR**
		£	**p**	**£**	**p**	**£**	**p**	
1 May	Bank (TR4)	1,600	00			1,600	00	DR
1 May	Bank (TR5)	3,000	00			4,600	00	DR
1 May	Creditors control (TR6)	2,600	00			7,200	00	DR
1 May	Bank (TR9)	15	00			7,215	00	DR
2 May	Petty cash (TR11)	2	00			7,217	00	DR
4 May	Creditors control (TR13)			60	00	7,157	00	DR
4 May	Creditors control (TR14)	1,200	00			8,357	00	DR
7 May	Bank (TR18)	80	00			8,437	00	DR

VAT Sales Tax								
201X	**Details**	**Debit**		**Credit**		**Balance**		**DR/CR**
		£	**p**	**£**	**p**	**£**	**p**	
2 May	Debtors control (TR10)			300	00	300	00	CR
5 May	Debtors control (TR15)			250	00	550	00	CR
7 May	Bank (TR21)			310	00	860	00	CR
7 May	Bank (TR22)			415	00	1,275	00	CR
7 May	Debtors control (TR23)			265	00	1,540	00	CR
7 May	Debtors control (TR24)	40	00			1,500	00	CR

Vehicles								
201X	**Details**	**Debit**		**Credit**		**Balance**		**DR/CR**
		£	**p**	**£**	**p**	**£**	**p**	
1 May	Bank (TR5)	15,000	00			15,000	00	DR

Vehicle expenses								
201X	**Details**	**Debit**		**Credit**		**Balance**		**DR/CR**
		£	**p**	**£**	**p**	**£**	**p**	
1 May	Bank (TR8)	1,200	00			1,200	00	DR
1 May	Bank (TR9)	75	00			1,275	00	DR

Wages								
201X	**Details**	**Debit**		**Credit**		**Balance**		**DR/CR**
		£	**p**	**£**	**p**	**£**	**p**	
7 May	Bank (TR20)	1,550	00			1,550	00	DR

Warehouse Fixtures & Fittings								
201X	**Details**	**Debit**		**Credit**		**Balance**		**DR/CR**
		£	**p**	**£**	**p**	**£**	**p**	
1 May	Bank (TR4)	8,000	00			8,000	00	DR

Select Stationery – Purchase Ledger/Supplier Record

Office Supplies Ltd								
201X	**Details**	**Debit**		**Credit**		**Balance**		**DR/CR**
		£	**p**	**£**	**p**	**£**	**p**	
1 May	Invoice OS1040 (TR6)			15,600	00	15,600	00	CR
4 May	Credit note OS0120 (TR13)	360	00			15,240	00	CR
6 May	Bank (TR17)	15,240	00			0	00	

Stationery World								
201X	**Details**	**Debit**		**Credit**		**Balance**		**DR/CR**
		£	**p**	**£**	**p**	**£**	**p**	
1 May	Invoice SW0752 (TR14)			7,200	00	7,200	00	CR

Select Stationery – Sales Ledger/Customer Record

G & K Office Supplies								
201X	**Details**	**Debit**		**Credit**		**Balance**		**DR/CR**
		£	**p**	**£**	**p**	**£**	**p**	
5 May	Invoice 0002 (TR15)	1,500	00			1,500	00	DR
7 May	Credit note 0001 (TR24)			240	00	1,260	00	DR

Midlands College								
201X	**Details**	**Debit**		**Credit**		**Balance**		**DR/CR**
		£	**p**	**£**	**p**	**£**	**p**	
2 May	Invoice 0001 (TR10)	1,800	00			1,800	00	DR
2 May	Invoice 0003 (TR23)	1,590	00			3,390	00	DR

Select Stationery Trial Balance at 7 May 201X		
Ledger Account	**DR £**	**CR £**
Bank	26,790	
Capital		50,000
Creditors control		7,200
Debtors control	4,650	
Drawings	600	
Heat & light	400	
Loan		25,000
Petty cash	68	
Purchases	19,000	
Purchase returns		300
Rates	1,200	
Rent	4,500	
Sales		7,700
Sales returns	200	
Stationery & postage	30	
VAT purchase tax	8,437	
VAT sales tax		1,500
Vehicles	15,000	
Vehicle expenses	1,275	
Wages	1,550	
Warehouse fixtures & fittings	8,000	
Totals	91,700	91,700

Note: the balances on the accounts of individual debtors and creditors which are kept in the sales and purchase ledger are not listed on the trial balance as they are not within the double entry bookkeeping system. Instead, the balances on the debtors control account (total debtors) and creditors control account (total creditors), which are kept in the nominal ledger, are listed on the trial balance.

Lesson 9 Practice Questions

Question 9.1

Complete the blank box below and show the element which is missing from the accounting equation.

ASSETS = CAPITAL + [ ]

Question 9.2

Which **one** of the following statements represents a description of the accounting term 'capital'?

	✓
Funds provided to a business by its owner(s)	
Financial obligations of a business i.e. monies owed by the business to individuals or organisations other than its owner(s)	
Items of value owned by a business, or amounts owed to the business	

Question 9.3

Which **one** of the following accounting concepts is the foundation on which the principle of double entry bookkeeping is based?

	✓
Business entity	
Money measurement	
Dual aspect	
Historic cost	

Question 9.4

Which **one** of the following transactions would result in a decrease in both the assets and liabilities of a business?

	✓
A business buys a delivery vehicle at a cost of £12,500, making payment directly from the business bank current account	
A business makes payment to a supplier to clear the balance on the supplier account, payment is made directly from the business bank current account	
A business borrows £10,000 from the bank. The funds are transferred by the bank directly into the business bank current account	

Question 9.5

Using the table provided below identify each of the following as being examples of either assets or liabilities.

Item	**Asset** ✓	**Liability** ✓
A vehicle owned by the business		
Money on deposit in a business's bank account		
An amount owed by the business to a supplier who has supplied goods on credit		
A computer owned by the business		
An overdraft balance on a business bank current account		
Stock carried by a business		
A loan from a bank		
Notes and coins in the business's cash box		
An amount owed to the business by a customer who was supplied goods on credit		

Question 9.6

A vehicle bought for use by a business to deliver goods to customers is an example of a:

	✓
Current asset	
Long-term liability	
Fixed asset	
Current liability	

Question 9.7

A loan to a business from a bank repayable over a period of 5 years, is an example of a:

	✓
Current asset	
Long-term liability	
Fixed asset	
Current liability	

Question 9.8

A business has an overdrawn balance on its bank current account with the bank. This is an example of a:

	✓
Current asset	
Long-term liability	
Fixed asset	
Current liability	

Question 9.9

An amount owed to a business by one of its credit customers is an example of a:

	✓
Current asset	
Long-term liability	
Fixed asset	
Current liability	

Question 9.10

If the liabilities of a business are £100,000 and its assets have a value of £500,000, which **one** of the following represents the capital claim of the owner of the business on its assets?

	✓
£300,000	
£600,000	
£400,000	

Question 9.11

Which **one** of the following terms is used to describe suppliers to which a business owes money for goods supplied on credit?

	✓
Trade creditors	
Trade debtors	

Question 9.12

Carla recently set-up in business as a market trader. Her business is not registered for VAT. The following is a table of transactions which took place during a recent week of trading. You are required to complete the table by nominating for each transaction the account to be debited and the account to be credited, the amount to be recorded in each of the accounts you have nominated should also be stated. As an example, the first transaction has been processed for you:

Transaction	Account to be Debited	Account to be Credited
1 Paid rent on market stall £100 by cheque.	Rent £100	Bank £100
2 Purchased goods for resale costing £1,200 on credit from Clearance Products Ltd.		
3 Carla borrowed £5,000 from the bank to invest in the business. The money was transferred by the bank into the business bank account.		
4 Bought a vehicle for use in the business costing £10,000 paying by cheque.		
5 Paid assistants wages in cash £120.		
6 Returned goods previously bought on credit costing £150 to Clearance Products Ltd.		

Question 9.13

Which **one** of the following statements describes the method of processing transactions known as 'real time processing?

	✓
Transactions are processed as they take place on an individual transaction-by-transactions basis	
At the end of an agreed period of time all transactions of the same type are processed collectively from a batch	

Question 9.14

Which **one** of the following transactions would **not** be recorded in a debtors control account?

	✓
Sales on credit	
Cash sales	

Question 9.15

Listed below are three transactions which took place recently between a business and its credit customers. Indicate for **each** of the transactions whether the transaction be recorded as a debit entry or credit entry in a debtors control account.

	Debit ✓	Credit ✓
Invoice issued to a credit customer		
Credit note issued to a credit customer		
Payment received from a credit customer		

Question 9.16

Jenny is the owner of a shop. The shop is doing well and Jenny has decided to expand the business. To do so she has decided to introduce further capital into the business. Record the following transaction in the nominal ledger of Jenny's business. Ledger accounts are provided below for your use in completing this task. The accounts provided carry balances brought forward (Balance b/f) at 1 June 201Y, you are required to adjust each of the account balances following the recording of the transactions in the ledger accounts.

201Y	Transaction
1 June	Jenny transferred £10,000 from her private bank account into the business bank current account as additional capital. The transaction is not subject to VAT.

Nominal Ledger (extract)

Capital								
201Y	**Details**	**Debit**		**Credit**		**Balance**		**DR/CR**
		£	**p**	**£**	**p**	**£**	**p**	
1 June	Balance b/f					40,000	00	CR

Bank								
201Y	**Details**	**Debit**		**Credit**		**Balance**		**DR/CR**
		£	**p**	**£**	**p**	**£**	**p**	
1 June	Balance b/f					2,250	00	DR

Question 9.17

Roberta Mann is the owner of a business which manufactures ladies clothing, the business is registered for VAT and trades in the name of Mann Maid Clothing. Most of Roberta's customers are credit customers.

You are provided below with an extract from an invoice issued to a credit customer, Just Girls, on 15 May 201Y.

Invoice 0750

Mann Maid Clothing

To: Just Girls

Date: 15 May 201Y

	£ : P
Goods total	1,500. 00
VAT @ 20%	300.00
Invoice Total	1,800.00

VAT Reg No: 465 3175 66

You are required to record the invoice issued by Mann Maid Clothing to Just Girls in appropriate accounts in the nominal ledger and sales ledger which are kept for the business. Ledger accounts are provided below for your use in completing this task. The accounts provided carry balances brought forward (Balance b/f) at 1 May 201Y, you are required to adjust each of the account balances following the recording of the invoice.

Mann Maid Clothing - Nominal Ledger (extract)

Debtors Control

201Y	Details	Debit £	p	Credit £	p	Balance £	p	DR/CR
1 May	Balance b/f					6,840	00	DR

Sales								
201Y	**Details**	**Debit**		**Credit**		**Balance**		**DR/CR**
		£	**p**	**£**	**p**	**£**	**p**	
1 May	Balance b/f					36,720	00	CR

VAT Sales Tax								
201Y	**Details**	**Debit**		**Credit**		**Balance**		**DR/CR**
		£	**p**	**£**	**p**	**£**	**p**	
1 May	Balance b/f					2,140	00	CR

Mann Maid Clothing - Sales Ledger/Customer Record (extract)

Just Girls								
201Y	**Details**	**Debit**		**Credit**		**Balance**		**DR/CR**
		£	**p**	**£**	**p**	**£**	**p**	
1 May	Balance b/f	1,200	00			1,200	00	DR

Question 9.18

Pine Products is a business owned by Rob Mentz, the business is registered for VAT. The following is a summary of information appearing on a credit note received by Pine Products from one of its credit suppliers, Modus Furniture, to which it had returned goods recently.

Credit Note 176

Modus Furniture

To: Pine Products

Date: 10 May 201Y

	£ : P
Goods total	400.00
VAT @ 20%	80.00
Credit note total	480.00

VAT Reg No: 345 6783 27

Using the credit note date, record the credit note received by Pine Product in appropriate accounts in their nominal ledger and purchase ledger. Ledger accounts are provided below for your use in completing this task. The accounts provided carry balances brought forward (Balance b/f) at 1 May 201Y, you are required to adjust each of the account balances following the recording of the credit note.

Pine Products - Nominal Ledger (extract)

Creditors Control								
201Y	**Details**	**Debit** £	p	**Credit** £	p	**Balance** £	p	**DR/CR**
1 May	Balance b/f					14,760	00	CR

Purchase Returns								
201X	**Details**	**Debit**		**Credit**		**Balance**		**DR/CR**
		£	**p**	**£**	**p**	**£**	**p**	
1 May	Balance b/f					1,980	00	CR

VAT Purchase Tax								
201X	**Details**	**Debit**		**Credit**		**Balance**		**DR/CR**
		£	**p**	**£**	**p**	**£**	**p**	
1 May	Balance b/f					3,140	00	DR

Pine Products - Purchase Ledger/Supplier Record (extract)

Modus Furniture								
201X	**Details**	**Debit**		**Credit**		**Balance**		**DR/CR**
		£	**p**	**£**	**p**	**£**	**p**	
1 May	Balance b/f			2,100	00	2,100	00	CR

Question 9.19

On 3 June 201Y Motor Factors received a payment directly into its business bank current account from one of its credit customers, Motorist Discount Centre.

Listed in the table below are the accounts in the nominal ledger and sales ledger of Motor Factors in which the amount received would be recorded. Indicate for each of the accounts listed whether the payment received would be recorded as a debit or credit entry in the account.

Account	Debit ✓	Credit ✓
Nominal ledger - Debtors control		
Nominal ledger – Bank		
Sales ledger – Motorist Discount Centre		

Question 9.20

In the week ended 7 April 201Y the cash sales of Kitchen Craft, received in the form of notes and coins, totalled £3,480.00. Kitchen Craft is registered for VAT. All sales made by the business are subject to VAT at the standard rate of 20%.

Listed in the table below are the accounts in the nominal ledger of Kitchen Craft in which cash sales are recorded. Indicate for each of the accounts listed whether the transaction amount recorded in the account would be posted to the account as a debit or credit entry.

Account	Debit ✓	Credit ✓
Cash		
Sales		
VAT sales tax		

Lesson 9 – Introduction to Double Entry Processing

Section 3

(Lessons 10 to 14)

Basic Principles of Costing

Method of Assessment – Knowledge Test

Lesson 10

Cost and Cost Classification

Cost and Cost Classification

Objectives:

By the end of this lesson you should be able to:

- *Explain the nature of the organisation's business transactions in relation to its accounting systems*

- *Identify materials, labour and expenses and explain how they are classified and recorded*

- *Identify types of cost and profit centres*

Lesson 10 – Cost and Cost Classification

Introduction

Any organisation has a requirement to show how monies are received and spent. This requirement is met by using accounting systems whether the system operated is either manual or computerised. The aim of any accounting system is to provide information about how the organisation is doing financially so that its owners and managers can have a level of control over the organisation. It is necessary to be aware that accounting can have many different aspects that use the same basic recorded information. These aspects include, but are not limited to:

- Financial accounting
- Management accounting

These functions can be described as follows:

Financial accounting involves the recording of day-to-day business transactions in accounts within a bookkeeping system, as well as periodically using financial information from within the bookkeeping system in the preparation and presentation of financial statements.

The two main financial statements prepared for a business organisation are the Profit and Loss Account and the Balance Sheet. The recording and presentation of financial transactions should be consistent over time so that owners and managers of the organisation can use the information to assess its financial performance.

An organisation's Profit and Loss Account shows a summary of the income generated less the expenses incurred by the organisation over a specific period of time, usually one year. If the income generated in a period is higher than expenses incurred in the same period then the business has made a profit in the period. However if the expenses incurred by a business in a specific period are higher than the income it has generated, then the business has made a loss in that period. The Profit and Loss Account uses the information recorded on the bookkeeping system for the period under review. The transactions making up the statement are, therefore, considered historic in nature. Once produced the Profit and Loss Account provides information on what has happened in terms of income, expenses and profit or loss in an accounting period and this information can then be used by owners and managers as well as other interested parties such as government bodies, banks, investors and creditors.

The Balance Sheet is a statement providing a view on the organisations assets, liabilities and capital, but only at a specific point in time. The statement shows, in summary, how money has been used to acquire fixed assets and current assets and also shows the short and long term liabilities of the organisation as well as the amount the owner(s) of the business have invested in the form of capital.

Management accounting is the preparation, interpretation and communication of information used by management for the purpose of planning, evaluating and controlling the resources of an organisation. This means that whilst management accounting is not concerned with the routine processing of financial transactions it is concerned with analysing the transactions in order to help managers better understand where income has been generated and costs incurred. This analysis should then assist management to improve decisions about the organisations future.

It is the responsibility of those undertaking management accounting functions to be able to deal with a range of tasks including:

- Being able to utilise information to obtain details about cost. For a business manufacturing goods for resale then information relating to the cost of producing goods in a particular period of activity can be calculated. This is done in an account known as the Manufacturing Account

- Using cost information to build specific product costs so that the product costs can then be assessed against income to identify the products profitability

- Preparing budgets using cost and income information as a plan for future periods for the organisation

- Comparing budgets against actual performance in order to identify aspects of the organisation that are working as planned and those aspects that are not performing

Whilst management accounting involves generating future data it uses as its base the historical financial transactions of the organisation. Once the future data has been prepared then it should be presented to management in a form that is of use to management. Management accounting does not have any statutory requirements in terms of presentation or format and, therefore, the presentation should be one that the users of the information can easily understand.

Costs and cost classifications

All organisations will incur some form of costs. Management accounting is intended to classify and analyse how these costs have been made up. It is necessary to classify costs into various **elements**. These basic elements are materials, labour and expenses.

Material costs are those costs associated with the production of a product, for example raw material costs, and the costs of any components and other items purchased from a supplier for incorporation into a product.

Labour costs are the costs associated with employees which will include wages and salaries.

Expenses are any other costs that are not associated with materials and labour.

An example of cost classification by element – JayJay, manufacture a cooking sauce for retail through local grocers. They incur costs such as ingredients, packaging, wages of employees involved in manufacture of the product, wages of employees involved in the activities of selling and distribution and administration of the organisation, rent of the factory, insurance for the organisation, telephone costs and stationery.

If we were to classify these costs by **element** the following classification would result:

Materials – ingredient costs and packaging costs

Labour – wages of employees engaged in manufacture, selling and distribution and administration.

Expenses – rent of the factory, insurance, telephone and stationery.

This basic classification of costs can allow managers to understand how the costs of the organisation are split between materials, labour and expenses. This should then help managers in controlling costs.

Cost nature and classification

Although costs can be classified into elements it may also be necessary to classify cost according to its **nature**. To do this it is necessary to know that costs can have a direct or indirect basis.

Direct costs are those costs that can be directly related to the product or service being provided. Such direct costs would include materials going into the manufacture of the product, wages of the labour directly associated with the production of the product and direct expenses which are specific to the product for example the cost of hiring a mixing machine only required for this product.

Indirect costs are those costs that cannot directly be linked to the product or service being provided but are costs that are still incurred. Indirect costs can include indirect materials such as lubricants for machinery, wages of supervisors who may oversee several production lines and expenses such as the heat and light of the factory which produces several products. The total indirect costs of an organisation can be brought together and this is referred to as the overheads of the organisation.

Cost by element	Direct cost	Indirect cost
Materials	Direct Materials	Indirect Materials
Labour	Direct Labour	Indirect Labour
Expenses	Direct Expenses	Indirect Expenses
Total cost	Total Direct cost	*Overheads

*in practice overheads would then be split (apportioned) between those indirectly associated with the production of the product or service (production overheads) and those associated only with selling and distribution and the general administration of the business. The subject of apportionment is outside the scope of the learning objectives at this level of your studies.

The total cost can, therefore, be split into the total direct cost and the overhead cost. An example of cost classification by nature – Let us now reconsider the example of JayJay who you will recall manufacture a cooking sauce for retail through local grocers. They incur costs such as ingredients, packaging, wages of employees involved in manufacture of the product, wages of employees involved in the activities of selling and distribution and administration of the organisation, rent of the factory, insurance for the organisation, telephone costs and stationery.

If we were now to classify these costs by **nature** the classification would be as follows:

Direct materials - ingredient costs and packaging costs of the product

Direct labour - wages of employees involved in the manufacture of the product

Indirect labour - wages of employees involved in selling and distribution and administration

Indirect expenses - rent of the factory, insurance, telephone and stationery.

NB: If JayJay had incurred costs such as having to pay a fee for the use of a brand name, or had to pay royalties for the right to manufacture a particular product, then these would be direct expenses related to the manufacture of that product.

Cost per unit

A cost per unit is a cost for one unit of product or service. In manufacturing a unit may be one can of soup, a car or a television. In the service sector a unit may be a haircut, a meal served or a car service.

The cost per unit can be calculated to aid managers understand how much it costs to manufacture a product and then allow them to add a profit margin on to the cost so that a selling price for the product can be set. For example:

Cost per unit

Direct Materials

+

Direct Labour

+

Direct Expenses

= Direct Costs (or Prime Cost)

+

Production Overheads (proportion of overheads associated with production)

= Total Production Cost (or Factory Cost)

+

Non-Production Overheads (selling, distribution and administration expenses)

= Total Cost

Total cost ÷ number of units produced = cost per unit

+

Profit Margin (per unit)

= Selling price per unit

The cost of production in practice is usually calculated by means of the preparation of a Manufacturing Account. Not only would direct expenses and production overheads in a period be charged to the Manufacturing Account we would also have to make adjustments for any stock of raw materials at the beginning and end of the production period, any work in progress at the beginning and end of the production period and any finished goods at the beginning and end of the production period.

We can now put some figures into the framework shown above as follows:

Manufacturing Account

Manufacturing Account	**£**
Opening Stock of Raw Materials	55,000
Add Purchases of Raw Materials	165,000
Less Closing Stock of Raw Materials	(60,000)
DIRECT MATERIALS USED	**160,000**
Direct Labour	90,000
PRIME COST	**250,000**
Manufacturing Overheads (or Production Overheads)	70,000
FACTORY (MANUFACTURING) COST	**320,000**
Opening Stock of Work in Progress	45,000
Less Closing Stock of Work in Progress	(50,000)
FACTORY COST OF GOODS MANUFACTURED	**315,000**
Opening Stock of Finished Goods	65,000
Less Closing Stock of Finished Goods	(60,000)
COST OF GOODS SOLD	**320,000**

Cost classification by function

Managers may find that cost classification into direct and indirect is useful but would rather have a breakdown of cost by the sections within the organisation. This type of classification is known as classification by **function**.

Individual sections within the organisation may comprise many similar activities for which costs can be associated, for example a production section may include several different production machines producing different products but the costs associated with these machines can be classed as being production costs. Costs can be classified by the function they are associated with. Usually there are five main function areas that costs are categorized into:

Production costs: Costs incurred during the production of the product or products

Selling and distribution costs: Costs associated with the marketing and delivery of the product or products. Such costs will include advertising costs, wages of sales staff and delivery costs

Administration costs: Costs associated with the general running of the organisation. Such costs will include wages of accounting and administration staff

Finance costs: Costs associated with how the organisation is financed. Such costs will include overdraft interest charges, interest charges on loans and finance leases

Specialist costs: Costs associated with any additional work being undertaken by the organisation. Not all organisations would incur this type of cost. Such costs may include any cost associated with research into new and improved products and the development of those products in readiness for production.

Some organisations will not have a production function for example service industries like accounting, hair dressing and retailers. Although they may not produce products they will still need to understand how costs are have been incurred so they may use a department method of recording costs. Managers within the organisation can then better understand which departments are under spending or over spending against their budgets.

In summary costs can be classified in different ways in order to assist management better understand how costs are incurred by the organisation. The way in which costs are recorded and classified will be determined by the needs of the organisation.

Cost centres and profit centres

Cost centres

The use of cost classification by function also allows the management accountant in an organisation to bring costs together under the term **cost centre**. A cost centre is any area of the organisation where costs can be specifically identified to this area.

Cost centres can be areas such as large as a production department or just single machines within a production department.

An example of various cost centres:

Type of organisation	**Possible cost centres**
Production organization	Assembly department, Production machine 1, Production office
Service organization	Bus 15, Payroll department, High street shop, Out of town shop

It will be the needs of the information required by the management of the organisation that may well determine the cost centres used.

Profit centres

A **profit centre** is any area of the organisation where both costs and revenues can be identified.

Profit centres not only incur costs but also generate revenues to offset those costs, a profit centre can effectively produce a separate profit and loss account (income statement) for that part of the organisation. This should aid management in its understanding of how that part of the organisation is performing.

An example of a profit centre would be a retail shop where the costs would include the purchase of goods for resale, the wages of selling staff and heat and light costs and the revenues would be the sales made to customers.

Lesson 10 Practice Questions

Question 10.1

Which **two** of the following characteristics apply to Financial Accounting?

Characteristic	Financial Accounting ✓
Deals with cost information	
Used in the preparation of financial statements	✓
Provides information for internal management	
Records transactions that have already occurred	✓

Question 10.2

Classify each of the following costs according to its **element** and its **nature**:

Cost	Materials ✓	Labour ✓	Expenses ✓	Direct ✓	Indirect ✓
Wages of production workers		✓		✓	✗
Factory rent			✓		✓
Wood for use in production	✓			✓	
Factory supervisor's salary		✓		✗	✓
Royalties paid to product designer		✗	✓	✓	✗
Insurance on the factory			✓		✓

Question 10.3

Identify each of the following as being either a cost centre or a profit centre:

	Cost centre ✓	**Profit centre ✓**
A maintenance department for a factory		
A cafe in a superstore		
An administration office in a factory		

Question 10.4

You have been asked to prepare a Manufacturing Account and the following figures have been provided:

Details	**£**	**Details**	**£**
Closing Stock of Work in Progress	29,000	Closing Stock of Raw Materials	40,000
Direct Labour	35,000	Manufacturing Overheads	15,000
Opening Stock of Raw Materials	50,000	Opening Stock of Work in Progress	39,000
Closing Stock of Finished Goods	23,000	Opening Stock of Finished Goods	28,000
Purchases of Raw Materials	90,000		

A proforma Manufacturing Account is provided below and you are asked to fill in the appropriate figures and calculate the Direct Materials Used, Prime Cost, Factory Cost, Factory Cost of Goods Manufactured and Cost of Goods Sold:

Manufacturing Account	**£**
Opening Stock of Raw Materials	50,000
Add Purchases of Raw Materials	90,000
Less Closing Stock of Raw Materials	(40,000)
DIRECT MATERIALS USED	100.000
Direct Labour	35.000
PRIME COST	135.000
Manufacturing Overheads (or Production Overheads)	15.000
FACTORY (MANUFACTURING) COST	150,000
Opening Stock of Work in Progress	39.000
Less Closing Stock of Work in Progress	(29.000)
FACTORY COST OF GOODS MANUFACTURED	160,000
Opening Stock of Finished Goods	28.000
Less Closing Stock of Finished Goods	(23.000)
COST OF GOODS SOLD	165,000

Lesson 11

Cost Behaviour Patterns

Cost Behaviour Patterns

Objectives:

By the end of this lesson you should be able to:

- *Explain the purpose and structure of a costing system within an organisation*
- *Understand the relationship between the costing and accounting systems within the organisation*
- *Identify sources of income and expenditure information for historic, current and forecast periods*
- *Recognise fixed, variable and semi-variable overheads*

Introduction

In the previous lesson the concept of classifying costs was introduced and it was explained that costs can be classified as being material, labour and expenses as well as being either is direct or indirect costs. Another method of cost classification is by the behaviour pattern associated with the cost.

Different costs will have different cost behaviour patterns and part of the role of a management accountant is to work out the behaviour pattern that is associated with the cost. Once the cost behaviour pattern is identified this allows the management accountant to develop future forecasts and budgets in order to help the decision-making of management in the organisation.

The main cost behaviour patterns are:

- Variable costs
- Fixed costs
- Stepped fixed costs
- Semi-variable costs

Variable costs

A **variable cost** is one that varies in proportion with a change in the level of activity. A variable cost is usually associated with the direct costs of a product, for example the direct materials and labour costs.

Where a product requires 5kg of material at £5 per kg per unit, then to manufacture 10 units of the product would require 50kgs of materials at a cost of £250. If the product requires one hour of direct labour per unit to manufacture at a cost of £20 per labour hour, then the labour cost of manufacturing 10 units will be £200.

As you can see the total variable costs are usually calculated by taking the variable costs per unit and multiplying these by the number of units being manufactured.

This is a further example of variable cost:

G-Mex manufactures a product 'Tidy Way'. The manufacture of 'Tidy Way' requires 4kgs of material and one hour of labour per unit. The cost of the material is 25p per kg whilst labour is £12 per hour. In the next period the production manager anticipates that 1000 units of 'Tidy Way' will be manufactured. The calculation of the variable cost per unit of 'Tidy Way' and the total variable cost for the next period would be made as follows:

	Cost per unit	**Cost for 1000 units**
	£	£
Direct Materials 4kgs @ 25p per kg	1.00	1,000.00
Direct Labour 1 hour @ £12 per hour	12.00	12,000.00
Total variable cost	**13.00**	**13,000.00**

The more units that are produced the more the total variable cost will rise. Sometimes the use of bulk order discounts may affect the variable cost where a certain level of activity is reached. For example if the direct material was 25p per kg on purchases up to 50000kgs but 23p per kg for purchases of more than 50000kgs then the above calculations would apply until G-Mex purchased over 50000kgs. It seems that the bulk order discount is worth taking but the organisation must consider the savings made against other costs such as stock holding costs, wastage of the material and financing costs.

Overheads can also be a variable cost. For example oil and lubricants to keep the production machinery working are indirect materials but the more the machine is used the more of these costs will be incurred.

Fixed costs

A **fixed cost** is a cost that will stay the same no matter what level of activity is achieved.

A fixed cost is often associated with indirect costs such as rent. The organisation may well rent office space for its administration and selling staff. This rental charge will remain the same each year until the contract is renewed, thus because this cost does not change it is considered a fixed cost. The rental cost will remain the same whether 1000 or 10000 units are produced. The more the activity the more number of units the cost can be split over thus the cost per unit will decrease.

The following is an example of a fixed cost:

G-Mex manufactures a product 'Tidy Way'. The manufacture of 'Tidy Way' is undertaken in a warehouse that is rented. The cost of the rent is £400 per month and the production manager anticipates that either 1000 or 1250 units of the 'Tidy Way' will be manufactured in the next month. The production manager would like to know what the cost per unit for rent would be if these levels of production were achieved.

Rental Cost £400 per month

If 1000 units were produced the cost per unit would be:

£400 ÷ 1000 = £ 0.40 per unit.

If 1250 units were produced the cost per unit would be:

£400 ÷ 1250 = £ 0.32 per unit.

Although rent is an example of a fixed cost other examples are business rates, insurances, advertising and salaries for administration staff.

Stepped fixed costs

A **stepped fixed cost** is a cost that is usually fixed up to a certain level of activity but then the cost increases beyond that level of activity.

Although similar to a fixed cost a stepped fixed cost is associated with costs such as the wages of a production supervisor.

For example a supervisor may be able to manage a maximum of 5 production machines in the production area so if 6 machines were required an additional production supervisor would be required. The additional production supervisor would double the cost of wages of production supervisors. If 12 machines were required then 3 production supervisors would be required as per the following table:

Number of Machines	Production Supervisors Required	Cost per Supervisor @ £8000 each	Total Cost for Production Supervision
1 - 5	1	£8000	£8000
6 - 10	2	£8000 X 2	£16000
11 - 15	3	£8000 X 3	£24000

As can be seen the cost of production supervisors rises in steps once a certain activity level has been achieved.

Another example of a stepped fixed cost would be rent for storage where if more stock is being held, say in the period before Christmas, an extra rental cost may be incurred.

Semi-variable costs

A **semi-variable cost** is that type of cost which combines a fixed element and a variable element of cost.

A good example of a semi-variable cost is a telephone service where the service includes a line-rental (the fixed element), which has to be paid whether the service is used or not, and the cost of calls made (the variable element), the cost varies with the number of calls.

Other examples of a semi-variable cost include:

Sales staff wages where the sales staff have a basic salary (the fixed element) but earn commission on sales (the variable element).

Utility bills where there is a standing charge and then a cost for each unit used.

The following is an example of calculating a semi-variable cost:

G-Mex manufactures a product 'Tidy Way'. The manufacture of 'Tidy Way' requires a special machine which is powered by electricity. The last electricity bill showed that there was a standing charge of £100 per month and that each unit produced required 10kwh of electricity costing 20p per kwh. The production manager anticipates that either 1000 or 1250 units of 'Tidy Way' will be manufactured in the next month.

The calculation of the semi-variable cost (electricity) in the next month would be made as follows:

	Cost 1000 units	**Cost 1250 units**
	£	£
Fixed cost (Standing charge)	100	100
Variable cost ((10kwh X units) X 20p)	2,000	2,500
Total semi-variable cost of electricity	**2,100**	**2,600**

Cost per unit using cost behavior patterns

As can be seen from the examples above a cost per unit can also be calculated using cost behaviour patterns. The cost per unit is built up using variable and fixed costs. Remember variable costs vary with the level of activity and fixed costs do not change with the level of activity. As seen in the examples above the variable cost per unit will remain the same for each unit produced but the fixed cost per unit will decline with more units produced. For example:

G-Mex manufactures a product 'Tidy Way'. The manufacture of 'Tidy Way' incurs variable costs for material of £1.00 per unit and labour of £12 per unit. The fixed costs incurred are rent of £400 per month. In the next month the production manager anticipates that either 1000 or 1250 units of 'Tidy Way' will be manufactured. The calculation of the cost per unit of 'Tidy Way' in the next month at the different activity levels would be as follows:

	Cost 1000 units	**Cost 1250 units**
	£	£
Variable cost: Materials £1.00 per unit	1,000.00	1,250.00
Variable cost: Labour £12 per unit	12,000.00	15,000.00
Fixed cost: Rent £400	400.00	400.00
Total cost	**13,400.00**	**16,650.00**

The cost per unit can be calculated by dividing the total cost by the number of units being produced. In this case:

Total cost for 1000 units = £13400 divided by 1000 units = £13.40 per unit

Total cost for 1250 units = £16650 divided by 1250 units = £13.32 per unit

It must be remembered that cost per unit can be based on direct and indirect costs or variable and fixed costs. The basic principle is the same but do not confuse the two separate methods.

Budgets

One of the main purposes of management accounting is to help managers plan and control the resources of the organisation. To assist in this process **budgets** are prepared. A budget is a planning document prepared to show the future plans of the organisation which is expressed either in monetary terms or in number of units dependent on the type of budget being prepared.

Budgets provide a short-term plan for the organisation, usually for a period of twelve months.

Budgets are useful to management for several reasons:

- **Planning** – the routine day-to-day operation of the organisation will require resources such as raw materials and labour so a budget can provide a basis for ensuring that these resources are available. Management also will need to ensure that the plans are achievable and not unrealistic. By preparing budgets management can highlight any potential problems so that changes can be made.

- **Communication** – A budget should involve managers within the organisation that the budget is concerned with. The manager should be consulted to ensure plans are actually possible. A co-ordination process should take place to ensure that one manager is not making plans that other managers could not achieve. For example a sales manager may make plans to sell more units than can actually be produced therefore the sales and production managers should co-ordinate their plans. A budget process that does not involve communication can lead to problems within the organisation.

- **Authorisation** – The budget once agreed sets the plans of the organisation for the period of the budget. Managers within the organisation then have authorisation to meet those plans within the defined budget plan.

- **Monitoring and control** – Although a budget is a plan of what should happen the plan may need to be altered in light of unexpected changes. Thus budgets provide a base upon which to monitor actual activity and identify changes that have occurred. If a change from the budget occurs then control action may need to be made by management. Where the change is not significant then the budget should not be altered, for example a temporary machine breakdown which caused loss of production. However if the change is significant then budgets for future periods should be altered to incorporate the change, for example a permanent price rise in the cost of raw material.

- **Motivation** – if budgets are used correctly then they can be a motivational tool. If managers and staff are consulted and involved in the budget setting process they are often more motivated to ensure that the budget is achieved. However, the budget has to be based on targets which are realistic for both the manager and the organisation. Meeting achievable targets and having a rewards culture may help motivate managers and staff.

Lesson 11 Practice Questions

Question 11.1

Identify each of the following costs according to their behaviour pattern:

Details	Fixed costs ✓	Semi variable costs ✓	Variable costs ✓
Administration salaries	✓		
Telephone costs which includes a line rental		✓	
Factory rent	✓		
Wages of production workers			✓
Supervisor's salary	✓		
Insurance for the factory	✓		

Question 11.2

Which **one** of the following describes a stepped fixed cost?

Description	Stepped Fixed Cost ✓
A cost that has both a fixed and variable element	
A cost that does not change with the level of activity	
A cost that changes once a certain level of activity has been reached	✓

Question 11.3

A budget is a planning document which allows managers to show the future plans of the organisation. List **three** reasons why budgets are useful to management.

Reason
1 To make a plan
2 Communication
3 Monitoring and control

Lesson 12

Cost Coding

Cost Coding

Objectives:

By the end of this lesson you should be able to:

- *Understand the use of cost codes*
- *Identify different methods of coding data*

Introduction

Providing information to the management of a business in a format whereby they can use it for the purpose of decision making, control of the business, and planning for its future, requires a great deal of data analysis. In a manual accounting system the analysis of data to provide information which can be used effectively by management can be very time consuming. However, where a business uses a computerised accounting package a system of cost coding can be used for the purpose of analysing information. The analysis is usually done at the time of preparing financial information for processing. Source documents are normally coded, not only to include account codes so that a transactions are recorded in the correct accounts, but also to include cost codes which will give the business the analysis it requires.

A cost code is a specific code based on series of letters and/or numbers, which is used for the purpose of analysing both revenue and costs. As there is a need for management to have information relevant to their own organisation, each business will have its own coding system.

Numeric codes

These are codes that require the use of numbers only.

Often these types of code use a certain grouping of numbers to be able to identify locations, sections and type of cost. It may be that such a code is made up of the following:

The first 3 digits of the code represent factories located in Sheffield, Manchester and Hull.

The codes for these may be:

Code Number	Location
300	Sheffield
500	Manchester
900	Hull

The next digit represents the section the cost belongs to:

Code Number	Section
1	Production
2	Sales
3	Administration

And the final two digits represent the type of cost:

Code Number	Type of cost
21	Direct Material
22	Direct Labour
23	Direct Expense
41	Indirect Material
42	Indirect Labour
43	Indirect Expense

Costs can be allocated to the appropriate location, section and type of cost by use of cost codes, for example:

Direct material required for production at Hull would be coded 900121

The cost of administration wages at Sheffield would be coded 300342

The cost of lubricants for the production machinery at Manchester would be coded 500141

It is usual for codes to be built up from left to right.

Alphabetic codes

Alphabetic codes use a system of letters.

Although similar in nature to numeric codes the use of alphabetic systems is sometimes easier because the letters can represent the item more easily that just a set of numbers.

Using the above example coding letters could be used to represent locations:

Code Letters	Location
SD	Sheffield
MR	Manchester
HL	Hull

The next letter represents the section the cost belongs to:

Code Letter	Section
P	Production
S	Sales
A	Administration

And the final two letters represent the type of cost:

Code Letters	Type of cost
DM	Direct Material
DL	Direct Labour
DE	Direct Expense
IM	Indirect Material
IL	Indirect Labour
IE	Indirect Expense

Costs can be allocated to the appropriate location, section and type of cost by use of alphabetic cost codes, for example:

Direct material required for production at Hull would be coded HLPDM

The cost of administration wages at Sheffield would be coded SDAIL

The cost of lubricants for the production machinery at Manchester would be coded MRPIM

Alpha-numeric codes

Alpha-numeric codes are codes that use a mixture of numbers and letters.

This type of coding uses the same principles as the previous methods but can often provide a more detailed system of codes should this be required by the organisation.

Using the above example coding letters could be used to represent locations:

Code Letters	Location
SD	Sheffield
MR	Manchester
HL	Hull

The next letter represents the section the cost belongs to:

Code Letter	Section
P	Production
S	Sales
A	Administration

And the final two numbers represent the type of cost:

Code Numbers	Type of cost
21	Direct Material
22	Direct Labour
23	Direct Expense
41	Indirect Material
42	Indirect Labour
43	Indirect Expense

Costs can be allocated to the appropriate location, section and type of cost by use of alphabetic cost codes, for example:

Direct material required for production at Hull would be coded HLP21

The cost of administration wages at Sheffield would be coded SDA42

The cost of lubricants for the production machinery at Manchester would be coded MRP41

A mix of numbers and letters can be used to represent the codes required and the order in which numbers and letters are used will be different for each organisation.

Coding manual

Each organisation will determine how it will use codes but once the coding system has been devised then in order to ensure consistency throughout the organisation some form of **coding manual** should be prepared.

In some small organisations the coding manual may be a sheet containing the codes used and what each code means. Large organisations may have a person with specific responsibility for issuing codes and maintaining a code list. This role whether in small or large organisations is important because the information provided from the system is only as good as the information which is input into the system. If information is coded incorrectly then the information provided by the system will not be accurate.

A major advantage of using a coding system is that it can provide detailed information about the costs and revenues that an organisation has. This will assist in preparing appropriate reports possibly about individual usage of materials, cost of materials, cost of labour, costs of producing products and revenues earned by a product.

The person responsible for issuing codes will use a variety of sources of information to ensure codes are accurate and of use to the organisation. Such sources of information include:

Labour costs	Time sheets, Salaries and payroll analysis sheets, PAYE and NI records
Material costs	Purchase orders, purchase invoices, inventory records, job sheets
Overhead costs	Purchase invoices, expenses claim forms, bank statements
Revenue	Sales invoices, cash receipts, bank statements

In order to assist the coding of documents some form of grid may be printed or stamped on to the source document. Such a grid would have space for a code to be entered, some form of checking signature or initials and the signature or initials of the person inputting the details on the system.

A good coding system should be capable of meeting the following requirements:

- Simple to understand so that users can easily follow the coding requirements
- Be logical so that items of a similar nature are grouped together
- Be flexible but also comprehensive so that new codes can be issued when required but detailed enough to ensure that costs and revenues are coded to provide appropriate analysis.
- Include a procedure for checking that correct codes are entered and incorrect codes are rejected.

Lesson 12 Practice Questions

Question 12.1

Mango Fruit, a producer of various tinned fruit products, has a coding system for its production.

The coding system identifies costs by distinguishing between material, labour and overheads; and then by whether they are direct or indirect expenses using an alpha-numeric coding method.

The coding system used is as follows:

	Code		Code
Materials	MAT	Direct	110
		Indirect	120
Labour	LAB	Direct	210
		Indirect	220
Overheads	OHD	Direct	310
		Indirect	320

Refer to the above coding table above and correctly code each of the following costs:

Cost	Code
Maintenance workers wages	
Raw Materials of Fruit	
Advertising costs for all products	
Production workers wages	
Cleaning materials for the machinery line	

Question 12.2

Which **one** of the following descriptions matches to the term 'numeric code'?

Description	✓
Codes that use a mixture of numbers and letters to identify the coding requirements	
Codes that require the use of numbers only	
Codes that use a system of letters only	

Question 12.3

Business Publishers, a publisher of various business books, has a coding system for its sales and costs.

The coding system uses a six-letter system firstly identifying the type of business area and then by whether they are costs or revenues.

The coding system used is as follows:

	Code		Code
Accountancy	ACC	Sales in UK	UKM
Human Resources	HRS	Sales in Europe	EUR
Management	MAN	Sales in USA	USA
Marketing	MKG	Author Royalties	AUT
Legal Studies	LGS	Printing Costs	PRC
Strategy	STY	Advertising Costs	ADC

Refer to the coding table above and correctly code each of the following transactions:

Transaction	Code
Sales of Accountancy books in the UK	
Cost of printing Marketing books	
Advertising costs for Strategy books	
Royalty payments for Human Resources authors	
Sales of Legal Studies books in Europe	

Lesson 13

Valuing Stock

Valuing Stock

Objectives:

By the end of this lesson you should be able to:

- *Identify sources of income and expenditure information for historic, current and forecast period*

- *Identify the following different types of stock:*

  Raw materials
  Part-finished goods (work in progress)
  Finished goods

- *Recognise the following methods of stock valuation:*

  FIFO
  LIFO
  AVCO

Lesson 13 – Valuing Stock

Introduction

Materials is a term used previously and can refer in costing to various items purchased by an organisation. These include:

- Raw materials held for use in the production of products e.g. timber and fabrics for use in making furniture, plastic for use in making plumbing products etc.

- Components that will be used within the manufacturing process e.g. hard drives, mother boards etc. used in the manufacture of computers

- Finished goods held for resale e.g. confectionery bought by a local retailer to be sold to its customers

- Items which will be used in the general operation of the organisation and held for consumption rather than resale e.g. stationery such as paper used by a photo-copier, printer cartridges, lubricants for machinery, welding rods, cleaning rags etc.

For a business to run smoothly it will need to hold different types of the above materials in stock.

Stock is the term used to indicate those items held by the organisation that are ready to be used as and when required within the organisation. **Inventory** is the international accounting term which describes the UK term 'stock'.

Types of stock

Three main types of stock may be held by an organisation, these are:

- Raw materials
- Work in progress (goods not yet fully complete)
- Finished goods

Raw materials are goods that will be used in the production process. These goods will be incorporated into the finished product.

Work in progress are those goods that have had some materials added and are only partly completed. Goods that are in a semi-finished state may include cars that have the engine and axle complete but still requires other assembly materials, like seats and bodywork, added to finish the product.

Finished goods are those goods fully complete and ready for sale by the organisation. Some items may be bought fully complete and resold by the organisation.

Stock valuation

Materials held in stock by an organisation will usually have significant value. At the end of the financial year it is essential to determine the value of stock for use in the calculation of profit in the final accounts. The physical checking of stock during the stock take and comparison to stock records allows a value to be calculated for items held in stock. This is done as follows:

Number of items held x cost per item = inventory value at cost

The cost per item is determined by reviewing the cost per unit indicated in the costing system of the organisation.

The general rule is that stock can be valued at either:

- **Cost** - the cost to the business of buying the item(s) of stock (including any costs in bringing the product or service to its present location or condition), or

- **Net realisable value (NRV)** – which is the actual or estimated selling price **less** any extra costs required to complete the item(s) and other costs which may be incurred in selling and distributing the item(s)

It is prudent not to over value stock so the lower of the two costs should be used as the inventory valuation within the financial statements.

Stock valuation methods

In practice a business is faced with the problem of costing-out the items of stock it issues and putting a value on the stock it holds. Three methods are commonly used for the purpose of costing-out stock and valuing stock, these are:

FIFO (First in, First out) - in this method of stock valuation the first cost prices are used first when goods are issued from stores. This means that the stock remaining at a period end is valued at the most recent cost prices.

LIFO (Last In, First Out) - using this method of stock valuation the latest, most recent, cost prices are used first when goods are issued from stores. This means that the stock remaining at the period end is valued at the oldest cost prices.

AVCO (Average Cost Out - Weighted Average Cost) - in this method of stock valuation a weighted average cost is calculated for the goods in stock at a given time by dividing the total cost of all items held in stock by the total number of items held in stock to give an average price for each of the items held in stock.

The weighted average cost is then used when issuing goods from stock. A new weighted average must be calculated each time that goods are received into stock at a price higher or lower than the prevailing average price.

It must be remembered that the above are methods of **valuing stock** and that stock may not be issued/used using the same method.

Stock records

Organisations will tend to operate some form of stock recording system that allows them to identify the level (quantity) and value (cost) of the stock currently held. The system may be computer based or manual using records such as 'bin cards'. Each line of stock will have an individual stock record associated with it. When supplies of goods are received they are entered on the stock record, and when items are sold (or issued to production) they are deducted from the stock record. Using such a recording system an organisation can easily identify the amount of stock it holds at any point in time and its value at cost. The organisation may use stores ledger cards to maintain details within its accounting system.

Stock valuation using the FIFO method

Using the FIFO method assumes that issues will be made from the oldest stock available, leaving the latest purchases in stock.

For example:

In the month of March, Arthur Ltd makes the following purchases of component V. There was no stock of component V held by Arthur Ltd at the beginning of March.

Date	Quantity	Unit cost price	Total cost
		£	£
10-Mar	60	1.00	60.00
20-Mar	40	1.10	44.00
28-Mar	30	1.25	37.50
			141.50

On the 31 March, Arthur Ltd issued 70 units of component V for use in production.

The following stores ledger record was prepared for Arthur Ltd to calculate the cost of stock issued in the month and the quantity and value of stock held at the month end:

FIFO

STORES LEDGER RECORD								
	Receipts			Issues			Balance	
Date	**Quantity (Units)**	**Cost per Unit £**	**Total Cost £**	**Quantity (Unit)**	**Cost per Unit £**	**Total Cost £**	**Quantity (Units)**	**Total Cost £**
10-Mar	60	1.00	60.00				60.00	60.00
20-Mar	40	1.10	44.00				100.00	104.00
28-Mar	30	1.25	37.50				130.00	141.50
31-Mar				70	60 x 1.00 10 x 1.10	71.00	60.00	70.50

The issue on the 31 March is costed-out using the oldest stock first (60 units from 10 March) and, when that is all issued, the next oldest stock (10 units from 20 March) is issued and so on. This means that the closing stock of 60 units is valued using the most recent prices i.e. the cost of the 30 units remaining from those purchased on 20 March, plus the cost of the 30 units purchased on 28 March).

Stock valuation using the LIFO method

Using the LIFO method assumes that issues will be made from the stock received most recently first and issues are costed-out on that basis.

For example:

Arthur Ltd makes the following purchases of component V. There was no stock of component V held by Arthur Ltd at the beginning of March.

Date	Quantity	Unit cost price	Total cost
		£	£
10-Mar	60	1.00	60.00
20-Mar	40	1.10	44.00
28-Mar	30	1.25	37.50
			141.50

On the 31 March Arthur Ltd issued 70 units of component V for use in production.

The following is an example of the stores ledger card completed for Arthur Ltd for the month of March, showing the cost of stock issued in the month and the quantity and value (at cost) of stock held at the end of the month using the LIFO method:

LIFO

STORES LEDGER RECORD								
	Receipts			Issues			Balance	
Date	Quantity (Units)	Cost per Unit £	Total Cost £	Quantity (Unit)	Cost per Unit £	Total Cost £	Quantity (Units)	Total Cost £
10-Mar	60	1.00	60.00				60.00	60.00
20-Mar	40	1.10	44.00				100.00	104.00
28-Mar	30	1.25	37.50				130.00	141.50
31-Mar				70	30 x 1.25 40 x 1.10	81.50	60.00	60.00

The issue on the 31 March is costed-out using the most recently purchased stock first (30 units from 28 March) and, when that is all issued, the next most recent stock (40 units from 20 March) is issued and so on. This means that the closing stock of 60 units is valued using the oldest prices i.e. the cost of the 60 units purchased on 10 March.

Stock valuation using the AVCO method

A weighted average cost takes an average of the relative quantities purchased at different prices in the cost per unit. The weighted average cost is the total cost of the items in stock divided by the number of items in stock.

For example:

An organisation made the following purchases of stock AK during the month of March:

Date	Quantity	Unit price
		£
05-Mar	100	2.40
12-Mar	120	2.63
28-Mar	80	2.80

There were 50 units of AK stock at the beginning of March valued at a cost of £1.80 per unit. Two issues of AK stock were made during the month of March as follows:

Date	Quantity
10-Mar	100
20-Mar	110

The following is the stores ledger record completed for the month of March and shows the cost of stock issued in the month and the quantity and value of stock held (at cost) at the month end:

AVCO

STORES LEDGER RECORD								
	Receipts In			Issues Out			Balance	
Date	Quantity (Units)	Cost per Unit £	Total Cost £	Quantity (Unit)	Cost per Unit £	Total Cost £	Quantity (Units)	Total Cost £
Bal B/Fwd							50.00	90.00
05-Mar	100	2.40	240.00				150.00	330.00
10-Mar				100	2.20	220.00	50.00	110.00
12-Mar	120	2.63	315.60				170.00	425.60
20-Mar				110	2.50	275.00	60.00	150.60
28-Mar	80	2.80	224.00				140.00	374.60

As you can see from the above example different averages were calculated each time stock was received, Differences in the average stock valuations may occur but would be minor depending on whether the valuations were rounded up or down. Closing stock would be valued at £374.60 ÷ 140 units = £2.68 per unit.

Advantages and disadvantages of the three stock valuation methods

Advantages of FIFO

- Easy to understand and simple to calculate
- Follows the concept of most organisation issues in that oldest stock is issued first.

Disadvantages of FIFO

- In times of rapidly increasing prices, materials may be charged out at an early and unrealistic price, resulting in the particular job showing an unusually large profit.
- Due to this method giving a higher stock valuation the organisation will record higher profits and may have more tax to pay.

Advantages of LIFO

- Easy to understand and simple to calculate
- The justification claimed for the LIFO method is that, by using the latest price for costing materials for jobs, the figure obtained is more likely to be in line with other costs and with selling prices.

Disadvantages of LIFO

- Closing stocks will be shown at the earliest prices which means that in times of rapidly increasing or decreasing prices, the stock figure bears little resemblance to the current cost of replacement
- Unacceptable method of valuation for tax purposes because this stock valuation method generally reduces the profits of the organisation.

Advantages of AVCO

- Fluctuations in prices are smoothed out, making it easier to use the data for decision making
- It is easier to administer than FIFO and LIFO, because there is no need to identify each batch separately.

Disadvantages of AVCO

- The resulting price is rarely an actual price that has been paid, and can run to several decimal places
- Prices tend to lag a little behind current market values when there is rapid inflation.

Lesson 13 Practice Questions

Question 13.1

Which **one** of the following descriptions matches to the term work-in-progress?

Description	Work-in-Progress ✓
Goods that have had some materials added but are only partly completed and not yet finished	
Goods fully complete and ready for sale by the organisation	
Goods that will be used in the production process	

Question 13.2

Identify the correct stock valuation method (FIFO, AVCO or LIFO) for each of the following statements by placing the correct stock valuation method in the column by the side of each statement:

Statement	Stock Valuation Method
Stock issues are valued using the oldest purchase price	
Closing Stock is valued at the most recent purchase cost	
Closing stock is valued at the oldest purchase price	
Stock is valued using the weighted average cost of purchases	
Stock issues are valued using the most recent purchase price	

Question 13.3

Identify one advantage and one disadvantage of using the following stock valuation methods:

LIFO: Advantage	
LIFO: Disadvantage	
AVCO: Advantage	
AVCO: Disadvantage	
FIFO: Advantage	
FIFO: Disadvantage	

Question 13.4

A manufacturer uses raw material code BC/120 in the production process. At 1 May 201Y the business held a stock of 50 units of BC/120 valued at £40 per unit.

You are provided with the following information regarding the receipts and issues of raw material code BC/120 in the month of May 201Y:

Receipts			Issues	
Date	**Quantity Received**	**Cost Price £**	**Date**	**Quantity Issued**
3/5/201Y	200	42	6/5/201Y	100
21/5/201Y	250	43	25/5/201Y	300

Given the information provided above, and assuming the business uses the LIFO method of stock valuation, which **one** of the following statements is correct?

	✓
The value of the stock of BC/120 at 31/5/201Y is £4,100 i.e. 50 units at £40 each and 50 Units at £42 each	
The value of the stock of BC/120 at 31/5/1Y is £4,300 i.e. 100 units at £43 each	
The value of the stock of BC/120 at 31/5/1Y is £4,250 i.e. 20 units at £43 each and 50 units at £42 each	

Lesson 14

Labour Costing

Labour Costing

Objectives:

By the end of this lesson you should be able to:

- *Identify sources of income and expenditure information for historic, current and forecast periods*

- *Recognise methods for calculating payments for labour*

Introduction

Labour in an organisation is any person employed by the organisation. The cost of labour is the wages and salaries incurred by employing people.

In practice labour cost may be calculated using several methods depending on how the contract of the employee stipulates they should be paid.

The main methods are:

- Basic pay
- Overtime pay
- Piecework
- Bonus payments

Basic rate of pay

An organisation will need to assess a number of different factors to determine the basic rate at which an employee's pay should be set. These factors will need to include consideration of local and national issues as well as any statutory requirements (such as the national minimum wage rate).

Some examples of the considerations to be made before setting a wage rate will include:

- National wage rates for a similar type of work
- Geographical wage rate issues such as a London weighting allowance
- Local employment issues such as having appropriately skilled labour available
- The local rate of unemployment may lead to a lower pay rate if unemployment is high
- General economic factors such as the level of demand for the products and if this will increase or decline.

Other issues such as inflation may affect decisions about pay rates because once the pay rate is set then employees usually expect annual increases in the pay rate.

The setting of pay rates by an organisation needs to consider the factors but also allow staff to be motivated to work efficiently. The organisation also needs to consider the costs of labour in order to ensure the profits of the organisation are not adversely affected.

Direct labour

Labour costs are the costs associated with employees that include wages and salaries. The direct labour cost is those labour costs that are specific to the product or service being produced. It is necessary for an organisation to distinguish between direct and indirect labour. A number of labour recording devices are available:

Clock cards

This is a mechanical device in to which an employee places his individual card which is then punched with the time of arrival and leaving from work. Any non-working activities will also be recorded thus allowing the correct calculation of hours spent actually working.

Time sheets

Here the employee records time spent working in a week with a precise description of the work undertaken. Time sheets are more common in service industries.

Electronic swipe cards

These are the modern day equivalent of the clock card where an employee simply swipes a card through an electronic machine rather than a mechanical clock card device. The card resembles a normal credit card.

Job cards or job sheets

These are used mainly in manufacturing organisations which produce large individual products such as vehicles, caravans, boats, aircrafts etc. The job card records time spent by each employee on these individual products.

Calculation of gross pay

The calculation of gross pay is of importance to an organisation and its employees. The organisation can understand how much it has paid employees and analyse how the cost of pay is associated with the work done. The employee will be paid based on the gross pay.

Methods of gross pay calculation include:

- Time rate
- Piecework rate
- Bonus payments

Time rate

Many production and manual workers are paid per hour they work. They normally have a set number of hours to work each week. Using the time rate method the hours worked are multiplied by the pay rate to calculate the gross pay.

For example:

An employee works for a standard week of 37 hours at an hourly rate of £8.00. The employee works for 37 hours in week 1.

His gross pay for week 1 would be calculated as follows:

	£
Basic hours (37 x £8.00)	296.00
Gross pay	**296.00**

The above was a simple example because the employee has worked only their basic contracted hours. With a time rate system if an employee works more time than their basic contracted hours then an additional payment may be made. This additional payment is known as an **overtime payment,** overtime may be paid at a premium rate in excess of the normal basic hourly rate.

For example:

An employee works for a standard week of 37 hours at an hourly rate of £8.00. Any overtime is paid at time and a half. In week 2 the employee works for 48 hours:

His gross pay consisting of his basic pay and the overtime element of his pay would be calculated as follows

	£
Basic Hours (37 x £8.00)	296.00
Overtime payment 11 x (£8.00 x 1.5)	132.00
Gross pay	**428.00**

Overtime payment: 11 hours x £12.00 (£8 x 1.5 times)= £132.00

The overtime hours worked was 48 hours less the 37 basic hours giving 11 hours and the payment is based on time and a half so the pay rate is multiplied by 1.5. Thus 11 hours at £12 per hour gives £132.

Different organisations will set their overtime premium rate at different levels. In the above example the overtime premium rate was the extra half paid for doing overtime. The premium rate may be equal to the basic rate (double time) or a quarter (time and a quarter).

Organisations may wish to analyse the extra paid for overtime because the overtime may be caused by factors such as machine breakdown. In this case the **overtime premium** would be calculated instead of the overtime payment.

For example:

An employee works for a standard week of 37 hours at an hourly rate of £8.00. Any overtime is paid at time and a half but the organisation requires the overtime premium to be analysed separately. In week 3 the employee works for 48 hours

His gross pay and his overtime premium would be calculated as follows:

	£
Hours at basic rate (48 x £8.00)	384.00
Overtime premium 11 x (£8.00 x 0.5)	44.00
Gross pay	**428.00**

Overtime premium: 11 hours x £4.00 (£8 x 0.5 times) = £44.00

The overtime hours worked was 11 hours because only the premium is required. The full 48 hours are paid at basic rate but the 11 hours are now calculated based on the premium (a half). Thus 11 hours at £4 per hour gives £44.

Notice that the gross pay remains at £428.00 under both methods but the cost of £44 paid for the overtime worked can be more easily analysed using method two.

Piecework rate

Piecework rates occur where a set fixed amount is paid per unit of output or for each task performed. The fixed rate will often be based upon the standard expected time per unit. This method is an example of "payment by results".

For example:

Martin Tyler works in a handmade specialist burger shop. He is paid a rate of 25p per burger for each burger he produces from materials supplied. In week 10 he produced:

	Number of burgers produced
Monday	200
Tuesday	250
Wednesday	250
Thursday	200
Friday	200

His earnings for week 10 would be calculated as follows:

Total number of burgers produced in week = 1100 x 25p = £275

Some piecework schemes may involve the agreement of a minimum wage payment, particularly where, through no fault of his own, the employee cannot meet the output targets set.

The following is an example of piecework with guaranteed minimum payment:

Martin Tyler works in a handmade specialist burger shop. His employer pays a rate of 25p per burger for each burger he produces from the materials supplied, but guarantees that if production is below 150 on any day, due to circumstances outside of his control, Martin will be paid £37.50 for that day.

In week 12 Martin produced the following number of burgers, however on Thursday due to a shortage of material he was unable to produce any burgers:

	Number of burgers produced
Monday	200
Tuesday	250
Wednesday	250
Thursday	0
Friday	200

His earnings for the week would be calculated as follows:

Piecework earnings -total number of burgers produced in week = 900 x 25p = £225, plus Thursday guaranteed wage of £37.50 = **Gross pay for week 12 = <u>£262.50</u>**

Martin gets £37.50 for Thursday even though he was unable to produce any burgers. The guarantee would also be payable on any day where less than 150 burgers were produced.

For example:

In week 13 Martin produced the following number of burgers.

	Number of burgers produced
Monday	170
Tuesday	125
Wednesday	250
Thursday	200
Friday	160

His earnings for week 13 would be:

	Number of burgers produced	Pay £
Monday	170	42.50 (170 x 25p per unit)
Tuesday	125	37.50 (guaranteed pay)
Wednesday	250	62.50 (250 x 25p per unit)
Thursday	200	50.00 (200 x 25p per unit)
Friday	160	40.00 (160 x 25p per unit)
Gross pay for week 13		**232.50**

The guaranteed wage ensures that staff will earn a minimum amount of pay even if production is interrupted due to circumstances which are outside of their control.

Bonus payments

Bonus schemes are often a combination of a day rate and a piecework system. Earnings will normally comprise:

- A day rate amount based on hours worked and:
- A bonus based on quantity produced (usually above a certain standard) or on time saved in relation to standard time allowance for the output achieved.

For example:

On a particular day David worked for 8.5 hours, producing 15 units. The standard time allowance for each unit is 40 minutes. David's basic hourly rate is £12.50 and he is paid a bonus for time saved from standard at 60% of his basic hourly rate.

David's pay for the day would be calculated as follows:

Basic pay = 8.5 x £12.50 = **£106.25**

Bonus pay
Standard time – 15 units x (40÷60) = 10.00 hours
Actual time = 8.50 hours
Time saved 1.50 hours
Bonus = 1.5 hours x (£12.50 x 60%) = **£11.25**

Total gross pay = **£117.50** (basic pay £106.25 + bonus £11.250)

Further example:

Geoff Druett works in a factory which produces a product called the 'Hammond'. The basic pay rate is £16 per hour. The standard hourly production of the 'Hammond' should be 12 units but a bonus of 10% of the basic pay rate is paid for every unit produced over the standard. In week 20 Geoff worked 38 hours and produced 500 'Hammond's.
Geoff's gross pay and bonus for week 20 would be calculated as follows:

Basic pay 38 hours x £16 per hour = **£608.00**

Bonus pay
Bonus rate is £16 x 10% = 1.60

Standard units 12 x 38 hours = 456
Actual units = 500
Bonus units = 44
Bonus units at Bonus rate 44 units x £1.60 = **£70.40**

Gross pay = £678.40 (basic pay £608.00 + bonus pay £70.40)

In the above examples we have dealt mainly with gross pay calculations associated with production workers. These gross pay calculations would be considered a direct labour cost because these workers are involved directly in the production of goods.

Other workers such as administrative staff, sales staff and supervisors would be paid on a weekly or monthly basis. These staff would be considered an indirect labour cost because they are not directly involved in the production of goods. It is however possible that these staff may also have to work overtime or receive bonuses.

Advantages and disadvantages of methods of calculating gross pay

Time rate

Advantages

- This method is fairly easy to understand and calculate
- It is flexible in nature so can be used for all direct labour staff
- Gives a basic wage based on hours worked but with the option of overtime
- Output should be of a consistent quality
- Organisations do not have to work out a standard level of output thus saving some cost
- Makes the calculation of budgeted direct labour costs easier

Disadvantages

- No motivation for staff to work at increasing output for the organisation
- May lead employees working at a slower pace so that overtime is required
- More supervision of staff may be required
- Difficult to distinguish between good staff and poor staff as output is not a measure of payment

Piecework rate

Advantages

- It produces constant labour cost per unit
- It encourages efficient work – an employee taking more than the standard time per unit will only be paid for the standard time. In order for this to be motivational the standard time must be accepted as fair by the employee.
- Employees can be motivated to produce more to earn more
- Payments are made based on the output

Disadvantages

- Lack of a secure income due to no basic guaranteed wage, which may become de-motivating
- The employee can be penalised for low levels of production, due to factors that are outside their control (i.e. breakdown of machines, faulty materials etc.)
- Quality of output may be variable due to employees attempting to meet wage expectations
- More cost of quality control to ensure output meets required standard

Bonus payments

Advantages

- Employees get the bonus on top of their basic wage
- The efficiency of workers should be improved due to opportunity to earn more
- A group scheme where whole departments are on a bonus provides an incentive to cooperate
- Less supervision should be required and thus a supervision cost should result

Disadvantages

- Bonuses may not be paid due to low levels of production because of factors that are outside their control
- Quality of output may be variable due to employees attempting to meet the bonus requirements
- Inefficient workers may cause friction and distraction amongst efficient workers
- A group scheme may not be workable unless skills and work allocated are similar within the group
- Pay calculations are more complicated which can make the preparation of direct labour budgets more difficult

Lesson 14 Practice Questions

Question 14.1

A company pays an employee a fixed rate per unit based on the amount of production that the employee achieves each day.

Which **one** of the following methods of gross pay calculation does the description above refer to:

Methods	✓
Time rate	
Bonus payment	
Piecework rate	✓

Question 14.2

Identify the method of Gross pay calculation each of the following statements refers to by placing the correct method (time rate, piecework, or bonus) in the column by the side of each statement:

	Gross pay Method
Employees are paid on units of output but have a minimum pay level	Piecework rate
Employees are paid on the basis of hours worked	Time rate
Employees are paid a guaranteed hourly wage but earn extra for production over a certain level	Bonus payment

Question 14.3

In the boxes below give two advantages and two disadvantages of each of the following Gross Pay calculation methods:

Time rate: Advantages	
Time rate: Disadvantages	
Piecework: Advantages	
Piecework: Disadvantages	
Bonus payments: Advantages	
Bonus payments: Disadvantages	

Question 14.4

Tina works for a standard week of 40 hours at an hourly rate of £12.00. Any overtime is paid at time and a quarter. Last week the Tina worked for 45 hours.

Which **one** of the following amounts represents Tina's gross pay for the week?

	✓
£ 540	
£ 555	✓
£ 675	

Question 14.5

Sam is paid on a piecework rate basis. He is paid £1.50 per unit for each unit he produces. If in a week the number of units Sam produces means he fails to earn his minimum pay level on a units produced basis, the company he works for guarantees him a minimum gross pay amount of £300.

Last week Sam produced the following units:

	Units produced
Monday	50
Tuesday	60
Wednesday	12 (machine break down)
Thursday	44
Friday	52

Given the information provided above, which **one** of the following represents Sam's gross pay for last week?

	✓
£ 309	
£ 300	
£ 327	✓